Winning in Business With Enterprise Project Management

Winning in Business With Enterprise Project Management

Paul C. Dinsmore

AMACOM
American Management Association
New York • Atlanta • Boston • Chicago • Kansas City • San Francisco • Washington, D.C.
Brussels • Mexico City • Tokyo • Toronto

This publication is designed to provide accurate and au-
thoritative information in regard to the subject matter
covered. It is sold with the understanding that the pub-
lisher is not engaged in rendering legal, accounting, or
other professional service. If legal advice or other expert
assistance is required, the services of a competent professional person should be sought.

Library of Congress Cataloging-in-Publication Data

Dinsmore, Paul C.
    Winning in business with enterprise project management / Paul C.
Dinsmore.
        p.   cm.
    Includes index.
    ISBN 0-8144-0420-0
    1. Industrial project management.   2. Business enterprises.
3. Success in business.   I. Title.
HD69.P75D573   1999
658.4′04—dc21   98–41020
                                        CIP

Printing number

10 9 8 7 6 5 4 3 2

Contents

What's Going On?

This book is primarily for businesspeople who want to make their businesses prosper. It is based on the principle that prosperity depends on adding value to business, and that value is added by systematically implementing new projects—projects of all types, across the organization. The better those projects are managed, the better—and more prosperous—will be the business.

The book also targets the project enthusiast who wants to make a greater contribution to the organization, as it shows how project management can be fine-tuned and integrated across the company so that the management of all projects is facilitated and that companies reap the benefit of the resulting added value.

The topic is particularly opportune because of the turbulent, chaotic, and uncertain nature of the times. Alvin Toffler flagged this trend in his classic book *Future Shock* in the 1970s. His warning was heeded by a few avant-garde business leaders and ignored by the rest, who now scramble to keep pace with the ever-accelerating changes. To meet the challenges, companies are transforming themselves from the static and staid to the dynamic and mutant. They are becoming less like organizations boxed into a hierarchy and more like a Dixieland band, in which musicians each "do their own thing," yet the aggregate result is lively, exciting, and harmonious.

Project management has long been the pragmatic way to get the right things done on time and within budget. When the lunar module *Eagle* landed on the moon in 1969, it was project management that put it there. Ironically, that was a success of such brilliance that, for another twenty-five years, it kept project management largely identified with the technology-intensive, massive-scale, hard-deliverables world of mega-construction, aerospace, and defense. But all that is changing. In a world where all business endeavors need to be as focused and results-oriented as a moon shot, organizations are applying project management to target strategic corporate needs, rather than merely accomplishing specific, isolated projects. This updated version of project management allows organizations to perceive themselves as dynamic organisms composed of countless projects simultaneously being managed to completion. As some projects are laid to rest, others are kicked off, so that a constant nucleus of projects generates the changes needed for the company to keep itself current and competitive.

Enterprise project management is an idea whose time has come. Because of accelerating change in the business world, corporations are faced with managing a portfolio of projects as opposed to simply operating a corporate hierarchy. Enterprise project management shows how to attain goals by applying project management not only to single projects but also at the enterprise level. It shows how to incorporate the art and science of project management into a new, exciting way to do business. It focuses on consolidating project principles across the organization.

This book is about managing an enterprise, as opposed to managing a project. It differs, therefore, from project management literature in that it is not solely aimed at showing how a specific project should be managed. It focuses instead on how an organization can be run by using project management as an organizational creed. It also offers a unique twist to the standard management literature, since it outlines how to transform a company by putting into place an enterprise project management mind-set and thus sharply boosting organizational productivity.

Companies are proposing project management as a broad-brush approach for formulating plans and taking care of daily business. In other words, project management is becoming a piece of organization managerial philosophy, like total quality or customer satisfaction or lean management. It is becoming inbred, part of the fiber of the company, an accepted way for accomplishing goals. Throughout this book you will find organizations like American Express, EDS, ABB, Citibank, and IBM showcased as examples of businesses that have taken substantial steps toward applying project management principles on an enterprise level.

Enterprise project management is compatible with ongoing management philosophies such as client-focused management, quality movements, revamping of business processes, or even process management. Applying project management on a broader basis within the organization adds speed and productivity to ongoing processes. The objectives of enterprise project management, which are based on the sacred triad of project principles (time-cost-quality) are also coherent with overall company objectives.

As leading companies stay at the forefront in terms of managerial innovation, other organizations strive to boost their competitive positions and accelerate delivery of both strategic and operational projects. The key principles for achieving such objectives through enterprise project management are summarized here. They are divided into two parts—one including the enterprise concepts and the other summarizing what it takes to make enterprise project management actually work.

There are fourteen principles put forth this book. The first six, covered in Part I, are nature-of-the-game principles that encompass the concepts and basic rules of the enterprise project management game. They represent the core principles for managing organizations by projects. Each principle corresponds to a chapter that elaborates on that theme. The eight playing-the-game principles covered in Part II target the practicalities of getting in shape, staying in shape, and ensuring game-winning performance. They focus on the actions necessary to ensure that enterprise project management is more than a passing fad, that it becomes an integral part of a philosophy based on solid managerial principles.

HOW TO READ THIS BOOK

Since Part I covers the basics of managing organizations by projects, it is appropriate for those who want an overview of the topic. Part I tells why there's a trend toward applying project management on an organizational level, explains what enterprise project management is all about and why the portfolio-of-projects view is critical to success, tells how to fill the gap between company strategies and the implementation of projects, lays out the steps for making the structural and organizational changes required for bringing enterprise project management up to speed, explains how the organization needs to be supported through one or more forms of a project office, and finally tells about the importance of stakeholder management in putting enterprise project management into place and keep it running.

Part II features what it takes to get in shape for enterprise project management and for the organization to stay that way. The reader who is more interested in the nitty-gritty of enterprise project management should look at these chapters in detail. Part II takes on topics like the basics of project management, education, competence, organizational maturity, reward system, communication, and preparing for the future. It starts off with a chapter that gives tips to executives, shows how to ask the right questions, and tells how to survive in these projectized times.

FOR THE SEASONED CHAPTER SKIPPER

Aside from the conventional cover-to-cover approach, which follows a theory-to-practice logic, there are ways for the busy person looking for specific information to read this book. This means skipping back to the Contents and honing in on those topics. Here are two four-chapter options for the time-pressured reader:

1. For the uninformed on the basics of project management, the recommended sequence is Chapters 8, 2, 4, and 9.
2. For those already initiated in project management but unfamiliar with the principles of enterprise project management, the suggested sequence is Chapters 2, 3, 4, and 5.

The book is designed to be used in different ways by different people within the organization. Although everybody can read the material to get current on an important management trend, it can be used as a framework for change in companies moving toward a more project-based organization. Here are some of the ways the book can help bring about change:

• *By the CEO.* If the CEO wants to move the organization toward enterprise project management and the rest of the organization hasn't yet signed on, the tactics given in Chapter 4 need to be brought into play. The book itself should also be put into the hands of key influencers within the company.

• *By High-Level Executives.* For executives who find themselves in the flight path between corporate strategies and the implementation of multiple projects, the book can be used as suggested reading, and the concepts given in Chapters 2, 4, 7, and 8 might be used in workshops aimed at helping executives deal with the multitude of projects that make up their daily fare.

• *By Mid-Level Change Agents.* Change agents charged with making more dynamic, powerful, and effective organizations can use as a planning tool the blueprint for a work breakdown structure furnished in Chapter 5. The educational programs given in

Chapter 9 also serve as an outline for designing training programs aimed at change.

- *By Managers and Project Professionals.* Managers and other project players often face the challenge of managing projects in an organization that is not prepared to provide adequate support. Here, the book can be used as a guide for middle management and professionals, and concepts from the book can be channeled to upper management.

- *By Academics and Consultants.* Academics can tap the book both as a research source and as recommended reading in business schools as a new twist on management, based on solid technical principles. Consultants who are trying to convince clients to gear up for a more project-oriented world can draw from the sources cited to support proposals and recommendations.

Since the pressure is on to do things both well and quickly, project management techniques are the way to get the right things done on time, and within budget.

This book shows you that way.

PART

1

THE NATURE OF THE GAME

Principle
No. 1

Developing and delivering faster, cheaper, and better products and services depend on an organization's ability to cultivate the chicken-and-egg relationship between project management and process management.

1 CHAPTER

Everything Is a Project

*E*verything in business is a project or is project-related. Making an organization flat and lean is a project. Putting in a quality-improvement or productivity program is a project. Meeting annual targets and setting up a home office are projects. So is a new marketing campaign, or a technology upgrade to a paperless procedure, or a let's-go-global business initiative, or organizing for a mega-convention for Rotary International. That doesn't even mention the obvious stuff, like building a new outlet store, implementing an integrated database computer system, or managing a *Pathfinder* journey to Mars. Hundreds of the activities tackled daily in organizations are project-related.

Projects are *nonrepetitive initiatives*—one-of-a-kind undertakings with a beginning and an end. Because of the relentless and accelerating crunch of change, industry is taking on a new face, a project look, although repetitive-motion activities persist. While bolt tightening at an auto plant is not a project, the design and prototyping of a new four-wheel–drive roadster is, as are continuous improvement activities, maintenance upgrades, production-line revamps, and the development of "integrated project teams" to improve productivity. So while production lines are processes by nature, it is projects that give them life and that keep them competitive by shortening the product cycle.

"If you have short product cycles," says Stephen Sprinkle of consulting giant Deloitte & Touche in a *Wall Street Journal* article on project management (August 19, 1996), "you do everything fast, by assembling teams of people." Deloitte & Touche is one example of a company that rode the crest of the project wave; after implementing an enterprise-wide project approach, the organization saw its revenues increase by 44 percent in just one year (1995–1996).

Since organizations are up to their earlobes in projects, the way these multiple endeavors are managed determines whether companies prosper or founder. If the projects—both strategic and specific—are well managed, then the company tends to meet its goals. If these projects are poorly conducted, the winds of fate will blow harshly on the organization. So there is a strong justification for beefing up the organization's ability to manage projects.

Here are more reasons organizations are developing project management capability:

- More managerial energy is expended on projects than in maintaining ongoing operations.
- An organization's success depends on new projects, as opposed to excessive concentration on "business as usual."
- The time-to-market squeeze companies experience demands that projects be completed on time, within budget, and meet the required quality standards and customer requirements.
- Quantum leaps in bottom-line effectiveness come from new initiatives, and that calls for project management.
- With project management in place, companies tend to improve customer satisfaction, market penetration, and financial results.

Project management's classic theme of performing tasks on time, under budget, and to quality standards directly targets the modern-day concern for making things "faster, cheaper, and better." Results begin to materialize as the projects are carried out. Organizations that successfully implement a project approach find savings through reduced rework and through revenue gains from timely completion. The project management thrust of time-cost-quality provokes a positive response provided the projects are aligned with company strategies and focus remains on the following items: results, methodology, indicators of product and process improvement, and customer needs.

Some of the most illustrious management thinkers and writers of our time have come out in strong support of the *projectized* organization—that is, an organization that views its entire operation as a portfolio of project management endeavors. Warren Bennis of the University of Southern California, author of eighteen books on leadership and management (two of which earned the coveted McKinsey Award for the Best Book on Management), believes that organizations will become highly project-oriented. He affirms, "Organizational charts will consist of project groups rather than stratified functional groups." The authors of *Harvard Business Review*'s article "Make Projects the School for Leaders" say, "Over time, the ranks of the senior executives will be filled by people capable of integrative leadership with a rich background of getting things done through projects."

On the other hand, some believe that the secret to increased productivity and competitive advantage is to increase emphasis on *process* management, not project management. In *Beyond Reengineering*, author Michael Hammer talks of process-centered management as the paradigm of the future. And there is strong justification for the process line of reasoning. For instance, process-oriented organizations such as petrochemical plants or electronics manufacturers might seem unlikely candidates for applying a management-by-projects approach. After all, the key to success for those industries is high productivity through replicated activities based on standardized processes. Yet projects are essential for process improvement and for developing and implementing quantum-leaping new processes. So, are projects subordinated to processes, or vice versa?

PROJECT AND PROCESS: THE CHICKEN AND THE EGG

Figuring out the importance of a project versus a process is akin to answering the chicken-and-egg question. It is an interesting mental exercise, but which came first, or which is more important, is irrelevant. Both the chicken-egg and project-process issues are reflective of integrated relationships, part of interdependent systems. For one part to exist, the other must also exist, as shown in Exhibit 1-1. Projects are dependent on processes; processes depend on projects. Because of this inbred dependence between process and project management, as processes proliferate, so does the need to manage projects related to those processes.

For those who look at the world through process eyeglasses, it is easy to dovetail the project concept into the process world. After all, projects can be portrayed as "enabling processes" or "transition processes": a sequence of activities carried out to get the target process up and running. Projects deal with the nonrepetitive part of processes, smoothing the transition from process conception to operation. Projects also come into play for nonroutine maintenance and major upgrades.

Exhibit 1-1. Projects and processes.

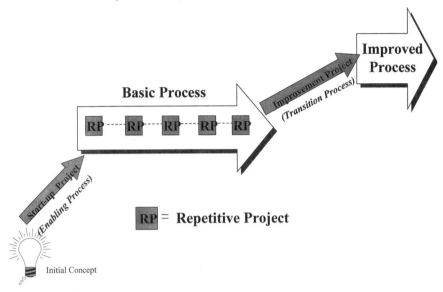

Hammer takes yet a different tack regarding the project-process relationship. In an interview with *PM Network* magazine, he stated, "There are very strong correlations between process and project: in a process, you do each project not once but repeatedly." Thus in the process school of thought, a project is seen either as an individual task that is optimally repeated in a process (Hammer's view) or as an "enabler" that helps design and implement a process. Continuous improvement projects can also be seen as a process, reflecting Deming's classic PDCA (Plan-Do-Control-Act) circle in which the circle eternally repeats itself in an effort to keep pace with the winds of change.

Although the word *project* is a notable rarity in Hammer's writings, he uses terms such as *process design, modify process,* and *replace process* (*Beyond Reengineering,* pp. 77–81), which are clearly projects when seen through project-tinted glasses. So the entire process view can be perceived through a different prism.

For those who view the world with a project bias, operating processes might be seen as the pauses that take place while the next project is geared up. Since all operating processes are doomed to obsolescence, anything that is operating today is the target of a new project that will either bring about incremental improvement or revolutionize what was being done before. New projects—which bring better processes on-line—are therefore responsible for advancement in terms of effectiveness and general improvement, while operational processes are the faithful gatekeepers of on-

going efficiency. So no matter what the conceptual bias and se-
mantic differences may be, it brings us full circle.

Because of this inbred interdependence between process and
project management, as processes proliferate, so does the need to
manage projects related to those processes. Therefore, powerhouse
corporations continue to move quickly toward the management-by-
projects paradigm. It is not by chance that project management has
been picked up in the business literature as a way of getting things
done. That trend will continue as the business scene grows increasingly demanding and resources become scarcer. The tendency
toward management techniques that get quality things done on
time, within budget, and to the satisfaction of client-users will stay
on the rise. That's why companies like AT&T, for example, have
been moving increasingly toward project management since the
early 1990s. The company encourages managers to receive certification by the Project Management Institute (PMI). AT&T has professionals at vice presidential level certified by PMI.

ABB, the European electrical equipment manufacturing conglomerate, believes strongly in project management. The company
contracted a program through George Washington University, in
Washington, D.C., designed to spread the project management
techniques throughout the organization. ABB's director for Latin
America, Roberto Muller, affirms the need for "global project management" since the company's ability to coordinate its commercial
actions greatly affects its international competitiveness. Cedric
Lewis, president of ABB's Brazilian operation, also believes in
"closely coordinated training programs, following ABB's global
policies," toward developing project management competencies
throughout his organization.

Citibank has also hopped on to the project management bandwagon, as have EDS, Allied Signal, Federal National Mortgage Association (Fannie Mae), PECO Energy, Chrysler, Andersen Consulting, and hundreds of other organizations.

As awareness among executives increases, corporations are
starting to promote project management as a method of formulating plans and taking care of daily business. Bruce Miller, senior
vice president of Corporate Planning at Northwestern Mutual Life,
says, "Project management is an important management tool, with
emphasis on the management word as opposed to tool. What major
functional organizations like ours need is more project management to knit together the activities across the organization." Project management thus presents itself as a solution to daily corporate challenges. On one hand, this appears to be good news, yet at
the same time this solution can raise concerns.

Since the early 1990s, organizations have been subjected to so many quick fixes that many have overdosed. Companies have been right-sized into "flat, flexible structures." They have been urged to become "learning organizations" composed of "empowered" employees. "Self-directed teams" have been formed to fill the management gap, since managers have largely been reengineered out of the company. Organizations have even been urged to "self-destruct" in hopes of rising, Phoenix-like, from their ashes. This organizational revolution has resulted in workers having to do "more with less"—and managing those organizations using a project slant makes that possible.

How Is It Happening?

As formal structures are knocked down, management personnel are thrust aside, and companies are increasingly projectized; those left are obliged to search for ways to get work done in a new setting. New angles are required to increase productivity. These new angles may involve revising the work scope, using new systems, or applying different work methodologies.

The search for new methods has made more people take a closer look at project management. It has set off a rush to sources of project management education and information, such as available through the Project Management Institute, by both companies and individual professionals who crave information on the subject. Membership in the Project Management Institute has grown from 15,000 to 45,000 people, from 1994 to 1998.

The availability of user-friendly scheduling software has also boosted the movement toward project management. Hundreds of such programs are being actively marketed. Aside from classic project-tracking software, project-related products such as risk management, maturity models, and competency evaluation are also appearing on the marketplace. This software boom has obliged practitioners to brush up not only on the software programs but also on the project management basics.

Max Feierstein, a director with Canadian IT (information technology) consulting firm LGS Group, stresses that buying software is not the same as implementing project management. "Organizations frequently say, 'Okay, we're going to do project management. Go out and buy software.' They ignore the importance of training," says Feierstein. "But if I may use an analogy, if somebody doesn't know how to drive, it doesn't matter if they have a Chevy or a Lexus sitting in the garage." He advises looking at the organization's infrastructure very critically before thinking about software.

As more individuals are exposed to project management training and software tools, the concept of management by projects begins to grow organically within organizations. This process gets a jump-start when organizations create spots to care for and nurture the art and science of managing projects. McDonald's Corporation, IBM, and Johnson Controls are companies with active centers of excellence in project management. Israel Electric in Haifa has in its organization a position of Head of Corporate Project Management.

The growth in project management in some companies is exponential. At 3M, the company's special-interest group for project management, Project Management SIG, has over 4,000 members and publishes a monthly *PMPost* to keep members up to date. In 3M alone, there are more people involved in project management than there were members of the international Project Management Institute in 1987.

Bob Storeygard of IT Education & Performance Services is one of the professionals who earned the role of growing competent, productive project leaders for 3M. One approach used at 3M was to lay a foundation for the development of project management expertise through a project management competency model and curriculum. Then, to complement the company-wide project management SIG and fine-tune communications between project leaders, the IT group formed the Project Management Professional Development Center (PM PDC), which performs tasks like consulting, applying, researching, educating, and supplying support services. The PM PDC features a quarterly Project Leader Forum and a Practitioner Advisory Board that coordinates project management development in the forums. An Electronic Project Office meets the needs of professionals who can't make it to the forums. The EPO offers such services as providing general reference information, supporting project initiation, updating current project management techniques, and supplying an interactive meeting place.

GLOBAL PROJECT MANAGEMENT

Global interest in project management is also reflected in the issuance of international quality standards (ISO Guide 10006: "Quality Management: Guidelines to Quality in Project Management"), which, while not entirely consistent with PMI's *Guide to the Project Management Body of Knowledge*, is a recognized international document that covers the major areas. At the first Global Project Management Forum, initiated by Dallas-based consultant David Pells and held during the Project Management Institute Seminars and Symposium in October 1996 at New Orleans, a discussion group included Wayne Abba of the U.S. Department of Defense (who has won awards for his project-related initiatives at the DOD); Anders Österlin, now-retired vice president of ABB in Sweden; Merritt Ranstead, director of Project Management Programs at AT&T Global Information Systems; and Klaus Pannenbacker, then-president of the International Project Management Association. The discussion group reinforced the need to coordinate efforts among the growing number of project management organizations in the world. Representatives from twenty-six countries were registered for that first global forum, and the number of representatives at such forums has increased with each year. Interest in the broader view of project management has been expressed at numerous global forums, held in such diverse locations as Paris, Bali, India, and Australia.

PROJECT-DRIVEN VS. FUNCTIONAL ORGANIZATIONS

The big change in how things are being done is in the functional, operational-type organizations—those companies that traditionally run repetitive operations, such as manufacturing and distribution. Since most of the repetitive functions have been taken over by robots and computers, management effort is largely aimed at conducting continuous improvement or change projects. The old managerial skills needed for supervision of repetitive activities have had to make way for skills in developing and managing projects. Since most managers were not schooled in managing projects, a major education program is required to bring the management core up to speed.

There's a big difference between using a widespread project management approach in a project-driven organization and applying project management in a functional setting. In project-driven scenarios (construction, architecture and engineering, systems designers, build-to-order job shops), people naturally tend to do things in a project-like way. They think in project terms and are familiar with project concepts and techniques. Paradoxically, there is often not much going on in terms of formal project management training, since on-the-job learning happens all the time. Also, the application of project management within project-driven companies doesn't mean they are applying the concepts across the board to areas such as marketing, human resources, and organization change. So even project-driven organizations are underutilizing the power of project management.

Traditional functional organizations (e.g., public utilities, manufacturing facilities, and operations-type companies) need training in the specifics of project management to apply these tools to the management of their sundry projects. In the functional setting, enterprise project management represents a breakthrough that requires a substantial investment in time and resources to get the organization into a projectized mind-set.

Whether functional or project-oriented, organizations that pick up on the "everything is a project" trend and accept this new reality will leap ahead of the competition. This leg up comes from taking advantage of the countless applications inherent in this powerful set of concepts. In times when *faster, cheaper, better* are the bywords of the marketplace, an organization that adopts the project management creed is bound to come out ahead.

Principle
No. 2

Enterprise project management is based on the concept that most managerial energy is expended on the development, planning, and implementation of an organization's portfolio of projects, as opposed to the running of repetitive operations.

2

CHAPTER

Making an Enterprise Work

As market pressures jolt organizations into the world of projects, company executives are obliged to adopt a new organizational mind-set—to think about business differently. As opposed to a "business as usual" tack, top management is required to target and achieve corporate goals in a new way. Rather than falling back on old-time "silo thinking," executives must perceive themselves as managers of a web of simultaneous projects—projects that include operational improvement and organizational turn-around programs, as well as traditional capital expansion and information technology undertakings.

In this setting, players see their work as that of managing and successfully completing projects, as opposed to occupying a slot on a static corporate structure. The question, "What do you do in your company?" no longer sets off responses like, "I am manager of the finance department," or "I head up the parts warehouse." The answers now tend to be: "I'm part of the quality team charged with increasing productivity by year's end," or "I work on three projects now and start coordinating a fourth one in June."

I initially called this trend MOBP, or managing organizations by projects, because it is a holistic way of applying classic project management methodology on an organizational scale. As the concept has evolved, however, I merged the system-based concept of enterprise management with the organizational MOBP view, so in this book I use the term *enterprise project management* to refer to the management of organizations by projects. Simply put, enterprise project management is an organization-wide managerial philosophy based on the principle that company goals are achievable through a web of simultaneous projects.

The enterprise project management trend points to a way of doing business sharply different from the practices of the not-so-distant past. Enterprise project management is a distinct twist on management, brought about by the changing times. Organizations are applying project management to meet overall strategic corporate needs by managing projects from an *enterprise* perspective, as opposed to merely accomplishing specific, isolated projects. This updated version of project management allows organizations to perceive themselves as dynamic organisms composed of countless projects simultaneously being managed to completion. As projects are laid to rest, others are kicked off, so that a constant nucleus of projects generates the change needed for companies to keep themselves current and competitive. Enterprise project management thus offers big-time advantages to companies that aim to beef up their bottom lines.

PUTTING PROJECT MANAGEMENT INTO PERSPECTIVE

Traditionally, project management literature targeted how to deal with a specific project. This focus prevails in most project-related writings and educational programs, reflecting the cravings of practitioners and corporate executives to boost the knowledge and competence of project team members in implementing projects. This first view of project management includes an array of theory and methodologies aimed at single projects and is usually referred to simply as *project management*.

The second major view encompasses the management of multiple projects in all areas of the company, the related organizational issues, and the alignment of projects with business strategies. Enterprise project management is part of this second group, with broad project concerns such as standardization, methodologies, strategic alignment of projects, support systems, and integrated project systems. This is project management in an organization context and includes several sometimes complementary, sometimes overlapping concepts.

Here are some of the forms project management takes when looked at from an organizational viewpoint:

• *Modern Project Management (MPM)*. A term coined in the early 1990s suggesting that project management is broadly applicable outside traditional technical fields, in areas such as marketing, human resources, organizational change, and total quality programs.

- *Management of Projects.* The pluralist view of project management, with emphasis on applications to multiple projects. Corporate interface and the management of project managers are key issues in the management of projects.

- *Enterprise Management.* Covering the entire organization, this is a bottom-line focus on multiple projects under a common umbrella, with emphasis on the integrated systems, information processing, and control side of management.

- *Program Management.* A series of related projects, or an ongoing ever-renewing effort, such as the "space program," commonly used in the U.S. Department of Defense and aerospace and electronics industries.

- *Managing Organizations by Projects* (MOBP). A holistic way of putting classic project management methodology into practice on an organizational scale.

- *Enterprise Project Management.* An organization-wide managerial philosophy based on the principle that company goals are achievable through a web of simultaneous projects, which calls for a systemic approach and includes corporate strategy projects, operational improvement, and organizational transformation, as well as traditional development projects.

Other industry-specific terms are out there, such as construction management, preferred in capital construction projects, and product management, used in consumer product industries.

What's Different About Enterprise Project Management?

In essence, enterprise project management isn't t all that different from basic project management. It varies sharply, however, in the way it is applied and the emphasis that is given to each area of expertise. Whereas basic project management is aimed largely at answering "How can we get this project done effectively and efficiently?" enterprise project management poses the question, "How can we make this business more adaptive, responsive, and thus more profitable in a rapidly changing, multiproject environment?" The two concepts are highly complementary, and work together to boost company productivity and effectiveness.

To manage projects effectively, a combination of three sets of knowledge and practice is required: (1) general management principles, (2) project management principles, and (3) application area principles. General management abilities, such as negotiating and decision making, are needed in all business settings. Project management skills such as scope management, planning, and tracking are required for all projects. And specific applications such as systems engineering and construction value analysis are needed in given applications. In fast-paced organizations, the overlap of general management and project management is steadily growing. As this intersection of general management and project management increases, enterprise project management will emerge as the new form of management. This interface area, shown in Exhibit 2-1, graphically represents the enterprise project management concept. As mentioned earlier, enterprise project management contains the basic components of traditional, technically oriented project management, but with variations. A summary of some of the distinc-

Exhibit 2-1. Relationship of enterprise project management to other management disciplines.

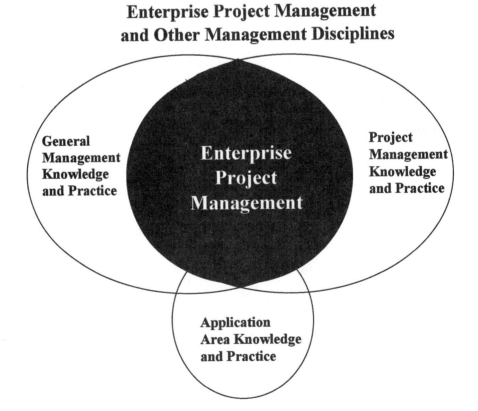

Enterprise Project Management and Other Management Disciplines

General Management Knowledge and Practice

Enterprise Project Management

Project Management Knowledge and Practice

Application Area Knowledge and Practice

tions is shown in Exhibit 2-2. As general management and project management intersect, enterprise project management emerges as the new projectized form of management.

While major corporations may be awakening to the organizational applications of project management and perceive them as new, it can be argued that related concepts have been around for a long time. For instance, "Management by Projects" was the theme of the 10th World Congress on Project Management, held in Vienna in 1990. In that congress, topics such as "Flat Flexible Organization Structures" and "Top Management and Project Management" were dealt with. Tom Peters touted the glories of project management applications within certain "projectized" organizations. Peters may have been oversimplifying, of course, when he pointed to companies like Bechtel and EDS as examples of project management. Naturally, they are good at managing projects—projects are their products and that's what they do. The challenge is surely greater for companies that are not project-driven. Yet whether project-driven or not, all companies with projects require strategic alignment of those projects with overriding company strategies.

A PORTFOLIO OF PROJECTS

Organizations are, then, "portfolios of projects." The aggregate results of an organization's projects become the company's bottom line. Missions, visions, strategies, objectives, and goals are transformed into company-wide programs that translate corporate intentions into actions. Those programs are, in turn, broken down into projects that are managed by corporate staff or professional project management personnel. The portfolio-of-projects concept is shown graphically in Exhibit 2-3. How the organization breaks down into its component projects is demonstrated by the example of an organizational portfolio in Exhibit 2-4.

ABOUT ENTERPRISE MANAGEMENT SYSTEMS

As companies become projectized, and functional middle management gives way to project management, new means of controlling and consolidating results need to be examined. The move away from hierarchy—a trend that's been happening for years—means that corporate results can be viewed from an aggregate project perspective, as opposed to the conventional departmental template. This summation of project results converges in an overview called *enterprise*. Enterprise management suggests a bottom-line focus

(text continues on page 24)

Exhibit 2-2. Differences between traditional project management and enterprise project management.

Project Management Area	Traditional Project Management	Enterprise Project Management
Overall context	Project-oriented, specific scope, start-to-finish	Organization-oriented, company view, ongoing
Management processes	Project methodologies coordinated within corporate processes	Continuum of overlapping life cycles integrated with corporate processes
Integration	Ad hoc interface management with other areas	Overall interface management built into the organization
Scope	Project interface management, work breakdown structure	Organization interface management
Time	Project schedule, dates, finite time span	Program schedules, multiple projects, continuing time frame
Cost	Project estimates, budgets, actuals	Corporate and program estimates, budgets, actuals
Quality	Specific project quality assurance and control	Overall quality compliance
Communications	Project-based communications	Company-wide, interproject communications
Human resources	Resources for the project at hand	Project-experienced personnel for entire organization
Supply, contracts	Project-based contracts and suppliers	Company policy for integrated suppliers
Risk	Specific project risk	Overall risk for company programs

Exhibit 2-3. Modern organizations can be seen as portfolios of projects.

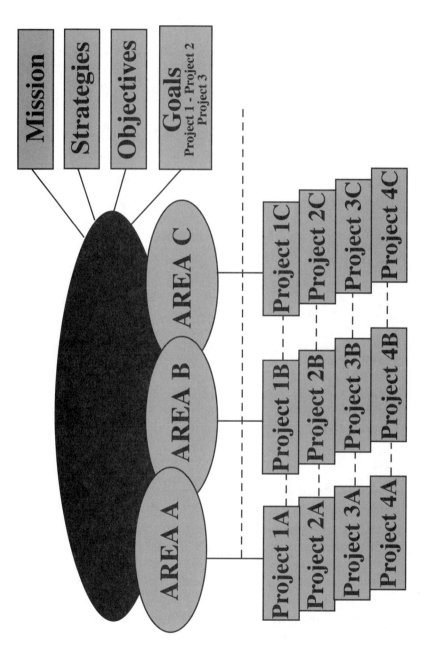

Exhibit 2-4. Sample portfolio of projects.

Major Project Categories	Sample Projects
Strategic undertakings	Develop learning organization and instill employability concepts. Obtain ISO 9000 certification. Develop participative leadership style. Outsource all activities that aren't part of the core business. Prepare organization to enter global marketplace. Introduce customer-based marketing approach.
Product–market	Product strategy and mix. Market surveys for major new project. Product design and launch.
Operational	Continuous improvement initiatives. Maintenance projects. Meet annual operational targets. New workplace layout. Software development. Training and development programs. Standardize working criteria worldwide.
Capital expansion	New factory. Major process equipment upgrade in plant. Telecommunications upgrade. New integrated database installation.

for multiple projects under a common umbrella, with emphasis on the information consolidation and control side of management.

Ultimately, all an organization's projects can be expressed in monetary terms by summing the costs of equipment, materials, labor, services, real estate, and financing. Even time can be presented in monetary terms. Organizations perform both financial and economic balancing acts as they walk the tightrope between budgeted funds and required expenditures for their multiple projects. Through enterprise project management, with systems linked to the company's databases, integrated information about the status of individual and multiple projects can be obtained immediately for use by operational or managerial personnel.

There's bad news and good news in managing companies as enterprises of projects. The bad news is that many corporate-wide integrated database systems are not project savvy, since they use a process-based logic. More bad news is the fact that big systems tend to create information overload.

But the good news is that both the integrated database software fabricators and the project management software developers are moving in a common direction. Versions of project management software are available for corporate-wide database systems, while large systems are becoming more project sensitive.

The challenges involve both the enterprise-wide systems and the people who have to deal with them. Communications across the enterprise become a particularly relevant issue. These problems are frequently considered at meetings of the Fortune 500 Project Management Benchmarking Forum, an ad hoc benchmarking group that receives support from the Project Management Institute. Here are some of the situations that have been discussed by participants of the Forum:

- Intranet-based communications systems may not carry the detail and high-level roll-up capability, as was once the case at Morgan Stanley.

- The opposite situation may be true, as at Dow, where project data are accessible through the Internet, but there's so much of it that people have suffered from information overload.

- Many companies operate from different platforms and use different communications systems, a situation that was experienced at Kelly Services.

- Enterprise-wide, consistent document management for projects is difficult to achieve. That situation is being rectified at Alcoa, where managers are implementing a software-based document management system.

- Hybrid systems involving paper, voice, and electronic data communications sometimes joust for priority. EDS has solved this in the project-approval phases by implementing a paperless approval process.

ENTERPRISE PROJECT MANAGEMENT AS AN UMBRELLA FOR ENTERPRISE MANAGEMENT

Enterprise management, from an information technology view, is largely focused on the task of aligning project management–related systems so that they are coherent across the organization. The objective—an extremely noble one—is to eliminate the *project archipelago* syndrome, in which projects are islands of information, process, and functionality. The thrust of this information-based enterprise management is to promote the commonality of project methodology, procedures, software, platforms, language, and culture across the organization. This information-based view is part of a broader *enterprise project management* panorama.

The enterprise project management solution is based on three principles. First, a consistent project management methodology must be understood and practiced throughout the organization. Second, some form of "project office" is needed to provide support. And third, the right tools have to be elected to guarantee functionality and the interests of top management from an enterprise perspective. To have timely and accurate visibility of projects and related resources in their organizations, executives must embrace the three principles.

Implementation of these principles results from basic common sense—an analysis of what isn't quite right and a logical solution to the apparent problem. In a global multiple-project setting, where the project archipelago syndrome is likely, conventional logic leads one to conclude that there *must* be a commonality of methodology, some sort of project support office, and an intelligent choice of tools involving the functions of scheduling, integration with corporate accounting, and resource planning and administration.

While this approach covers the basics for planning and tracking projects using a common framework, it does not include other project-related enterprise issues of importance to the executive, such as the strategic alignment of projects in accordance with the organization's business needs. A broader view takes into account the need for prioritizing projects, battling for resources, having the information necessary to abort projects, and ensuring that all projects are continually in harmony with ongoing business objectives.

This view calls for a quantum leap in productivity when dealing with an enterprise of projects. Simply improving the way things are done is not enough. Such extensive change means going beyond the obvious, reaching out to a second level of logic, and looking at the situation through a different set of glasses. In enterprise management, that means adjusting managerial philosophy from the top down, to ensure that proposed improvements in efficiency are matched by a strategic approach for managing projects across the organization.

Company executives are thus obliged to assume a new organizational mind-set—to think about business in a new way. In the case of enterprise project management, it means putting a far-reaching, executive-level enterprise mentality into place. To obtain significant gains in productivity, for example, executives must perceive themselves as managers of a web of simultaneous ongoing, ever-changing projects that constitute the lifeblood of the organization. Enterprise project management fits this need, as it points to a distinct way of doing business and reflects a holistic, systematic approach for applying project management techniques to the enterprise.

Principle
No. 3

Successful enterprise project management requires bridging the gap between the company vision and the projects underway, which in turn calls for coordination among corporate strategies, general project alignment, specific project alignment, and project implementation.

3
CHAPTER

Bridging the Gap Between Company Strategy and Projects

A well-oiled multiple-project enterprise is like a flock of geese flying south: they both comprise individuals moving energetically toward a common goal. When wild geese take off or shift formations in flight, they juggle about for quick transition so they can align themselves to take advantage of the aerodynamics of the V formation, and minimize excess wear on the feathers of the lead duck. The birds in secondary positions thus meet less wind resistance and are able to take the lead in turn. By working together and "drafting" off of each other, they create a group synergy that brings them efficiently to their destination.

Projects in an organization are like geese in flight. The projects require similar alignment to make sure company goals are met; the transitions have to be quick and smooth to eliminate unnecessary loss of energy. Unfortunately, keeping projects moving along the trajectory of company strategies is often more akin to a cattle-herding exercise than the in-flight pattern of geese.

For example, as the projects proliferate, the task of bridging any gaps between company strategy and project implementation becomes monumental. This is partially due to the nature of projects: they strive for survival and independence, even at the expense of other projects and overriding company interests. The challenge of dealing with these rebellious projects rests with top management. The British Standard (BS 6079: 1996) on project management underlines this theme, with an entire section on the corporate responsibility for project management. It points out that "senior management is responsible for establishing the objectives and constraints within which the project has to be delivered."

At the quarterly meetings of the Fortune 500 Project Management Benchmarking Forum, the topic of strategic alignment of projects spurs lively discussion. And that's no wonder. As representatives of powerhouse companies that are shifting toward management by projects, the forum participants know firsthand how important projects are to maintaining a competitive edge. Frank Toney, a consultant who provides the scientific support for the forum surveys and conclusions, observed, "There is a clear consensus among Forum members that stronger interface is needed between business planning and the strategic management of projects."

Other Forum participants share that view. Carl Isenberg, director of project management at EDS, observed that "project management involvement needs to be quicker." In fact, Isenberg's group, which performs project management for third parties, believes that project management should begin with the contract sales process. NCR's Patricia S. Peters agrees. As director of program management for her company's Worldwide Services, she cited NCR's Foundation Statement that "Projects begin with the decision to make a proposal" as an example of the tie between NCR business offices and project offices.

For a company's new projects to hit the ground running, with project management methodology already in place, it takes a corporate commitment to making project management part of business planning. "Project management disciplines should be integrated with all core competencies in companies," stated Forum participant Martin O'Sullivan, vice president and director of business process management for Motorola. "This includes strategic planning and project concept stages." Jeff Koriknay, while director of program services, IT, at Honeywell, stated, "Everything has to be linked to the business strategy." Still, it is one thing to recognize project management as an important partner to strategic planning, but how do you get this to take place?

FROM BUSINESS PLANNING TO PROJECT IMPLEMENTATION

To align projects there must be a coherent pathway from the strategies determined by the company to the actions taken by project teams. The steps for making sure projects are lined up strategically are shown in Exhibit 3-1.

• *Company Strategies.* Company strategies are arrived at through conventional strategic planning, which may include creation or ratification of mission and vision statements and company values, review of economic scenarios, analysis of competitors, an overview of strengths and weaknesses, a survey of risks and opportunities, and articulation of the organization's strategic objectives. These strategic objectives are the starting point for all projects, whether they be specific strategic undertakings or projects related to a product launch, capital expenditures, or operations.

• *General Project Alignment.* Once the strategic objectives are identified, successful strategic project alignment depends on establishing a fundamental interface between those objectives and each project's specific setting. Activities that bridge the gap between strategic objectives and specific project planning are stakeholder management, prioritization, risk management, enterprisewide management systems, and strategic project planning.

• *Project-Specific Alignment.* Each major group of projects has its peculiarities. Strategic projects, for instance, are tightly tied to the company mission, vision, values, and objectives, and they depend heavily on high-level coordination and influence management to achieve their goals. Product- and market-related projects depend on establishing product targets, creating product portfolios, and monitoring market opportunities. Capital expansion projects, on the other hand, involve issues such as logistics, team mobilization, and major procurement. Operational projects depend on operational goals, scarce resources, and multidisciplinary teams.

• *Project Implementation.* Based on the project-specific alignment, a detailed set of project plans are outlined and the projects are managed to completion using the principles outlined in Chapter 8. During a project's life, periodic audits ensure that, in its current form, the work conforms to the organization's strategic goals.

FILLING THE GAP

Traditionally, company projects have been divided into two phases, or worlds. The first is the "idea-to-kick-off world." Here, the project is composed of a concept, some studies, lots of discussion, and a decision to start. This part of a project's life coincides with the company's strategic planning. Once the decision is made, the project is pushed along to the functional areas or operating units, which are

Exhibit 3-1. From corporate strategy to project implementation.

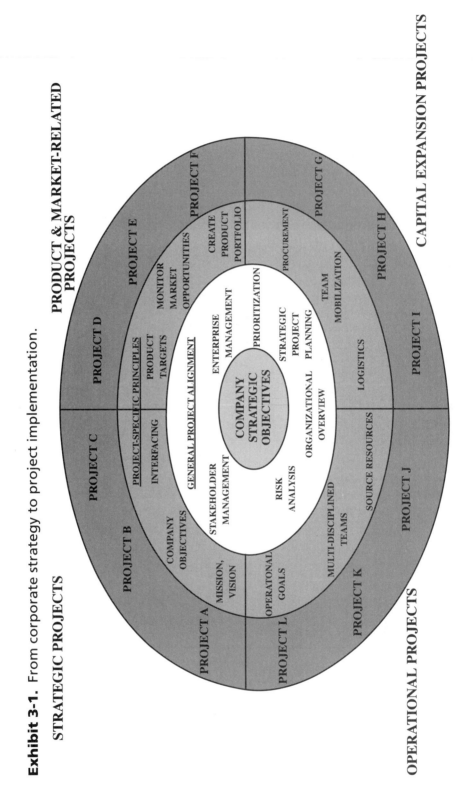

then supposed to "get the job done." This pragmatic part is the project's second world, where formal project management starts to take place. The major challenge in managing an organization by projects is to bridge the gap between the two worlds and ensure that projects receive enough attention and support from upper management.

The Guardian Angel Approach

The traditional gap-filler between the parent organization and projects underway in the company is the *project sponsor*. The sponsor is charged with caring for and nurturing a project so it receives resources and gets political coverage within the organization. Project sponsors act as "guardian angels," both to the project and for the project manager, in that they oversee and protect both of them from risk and potential negative impact.

Some organizations formally assign project sponsors as part of their project management methodology. Others operate on an ad hoc basis, using sponsors in some situations and not in others. Yet others ignore the project sponsor concept altogether, laying the burden of nurturing on their project managers, who, it is hoped, have the talent and fortitude to carry out both the implementation tasks and the upper-level political hobnobbing.

To meet this challenge, the project sponsor needs to have the following characteristics:

- A vested interest in the project
- Knowledge and ability in strategic and project management
- Capability to influence other executives and important groups
- Basic understanding of the project technology
- Rapport with the project manager and team

These requirements for project sponsor vary from company to company. For instance, criteria for choosing a project sponsor at American Express include demonstrated leadership capacity (vision, energy, influence as a change agent, communication skills), a stake in the outcome of the project, demonstrated cross-cultural perspective, and authority for underwriting success.

Likewise, project sponsorship can take on a number of forms. The sponsor is usually not the hierarchical boss of the project manager, although in an exception this could be the case. Traditionally, the project sponsor is someone positioned "diagonally upward" from the project manager. Here are some of the classic ways projects are sponsored:

- *Single Sponsorship*. An approach that involves an individual who has all or most of the characteristics given above and who takes on the sole task of sponsoring a given project.
- *Double Sponsorship*. Where two sponsors are often used, particularly when there is a strong need for a technological as well as a conventional management person.
- *Collective Sponsorship*. A group approach that makes sense in some situations and may take the form of a steering committee, a project council, or an advisory board charged with fulfilling the sponsorship duties.

The role of project sponsor varies depending on company tradition, the nature of the project, and the management styles of the sponsor and project manager. A strong, politically savvy project manager may need little support from the sponsor. On the other hand, a less seasoned project manager with a newly formed team on a nontypical project may call on the sponsor to do some major mentoring. Here's what project sponsors need to do for their projects:

Early On

- Ensure that project strategies, plans, and controls are in place.
- Provide support for mobilizing the project team.
- Make sure the project is properly kicked off and that team-building initiatives are taken.
- Provide political coverage for the project in the executive suite.
- Coach the project manager as needed.

As the Project Evolves

- Participate in periodic formal project reviews.
- Be available for support and consultation.
- Follow project progress reports.
- Get involved if the project veers off course.

When the Project Is Winding Down

- Monitor the project-to-operations transition.
- Stimulate a rapid project closeout.
- Ensure the documentation of lessons learned.

The guardian angel approach of project sponsorship has proved to be an effective way to fill the gap between organizational strategies and project implementation. The concept evolved out of necessity and has been responsible for keeping many projects on course. Yet what started as a helping hand for troubled projects and evolved into a formal strategy still falls short of reaching its goal unless the company is structured specifically toward managing organizations by projects.

General Project Alignment

For project sponsorship to be effective, an organization's projects need to be supported by enterprise-wide techniques, methodologies, and systems that make the job easier. After all, project sponsorship is a part-time activity, taken on in addition to the sponsor's regular activities. So here are some of the tools and techniques that help smooth the transition from the first world of corporate strategy to the second one of implementation. Using these tools and techniques will guarantee that, when appropriate, *intelligent backtracking* can be done to rethink, restructure, redirect, or even suspend a project. The cornerstones of general project alignment are stakeholder management, project prioritizing, risk management, a balanced "scorecard," enterprise-wide management systems, and strategic project planning.

Managing Those Stakes

Dealing with stakeholders in an organization is such an important part of managing projectized companies that Chapter 6 is dedicated to this subject. Stakeholder management is the glue that holds together the pieces of an organization managed by projects. Pro-active stakeholder management means that more projects will get done right the first time and that less time will be wasted dealing with unnecessary conflicts.

Getting Ready, Taking Aim, and Prioritizing

To provide maximum impact to the organization, projects need to be ranked in a systemic way showing the high priorities. One such customer-related approach is based on a technique used in product development, called *quality function deployment,* or QFD. This technique is used to identify which product characteristics are important to the customer; once those characteristics are determined, the technique helps identify design factors that the product development team can monitor to ensure that the product has those attributes. This means that the project team can work with firm design metrics that ensure the product meets customer desires.

This same process is applicable to a product development project as a way to rank those goals that best meet customer and company needs. Since QFD aims to match customers' requirements with maximum quality, using fewer resources and in a shortened cycle time, the technique is compatible with the time-cost-quality triad of managing projects. Thus QFD can help companies focus and prioritize their projects.

The background for this approach is the classic strategic planning strengths-weaknesses-opportunities-threats (SWOT) categories. Based on these strategic factors, the projects that should rank high on a company's list of priorities can be readily determined. For instance, the SWOT factors might show that a company should prefer projects that:

- Help open new markets.
- Enhance the image of the company.
- Develop know-how to be used on future projects.
- Will create a strong competitive advantage.

Based on the company's strategic criteria, projects are then prioritized, pointing to which projects require immediate attention and which should be put on the back burner.

For QFD to be effective, organizational objectives have to be translated into workable selection criteria. This isn't an easy task, as the selection criteria must allow for estimates of when the project should begin, be applicable to all projects, and point the way for corrective action when necessary. The selection criteria also need to be prioritized, since some criteria should carry more weight than others. Once the criteria are prioritized, a matrix is formed displaying the projects along one axis and the selection criteria along the other. The cells in the matrix are then evaluated in terms of their potential to improve the organization's performance. The result is a classification of projects likely to have a positive impact on the company's objectives. Decisions regarding prioritization are generally made by a project priority board—a group of executives and other qualified professionals who review the information and classify the projects as green for go, yellow for maybe, and red for those that should be axed.

The project priority board needs to convene from time to time to reassess the rankings. As time goes by, situations may change. Markets heat up or cool down, an organization's overall priorities shift, schedules may slip, and money gets scarce. Strategic alignment of projects means reevaluating these situations and juggling project priorities such that the organization goals are still met. In some cases this may involve killing a project, either before it really gets going or as it develops. This is where risk management techniques come into play.

Assessing the Risk

Projects are risky business. General project alignment includes the oversight of the accumulated risks of an organization's projects. This means that processes must be in place for identifying, quantifying, developing responses, and controlling risk. And those processes are applied across the board on all company projects, in a language that everyone will understand.

The focus has to be on establishing and communicating a risk management methodology, and for rolling up and monitoring portfolio project risk data regularly. The risk management approach needs to take into account both business risks and risks associated purely with each project. Determining a business risk means calculating the probability of a favorable market in two years' time for, say, iron ore pellets to be produced in a yet-to-be-completed ore-pelletizing plant. A pure project-related risk involves force majeure, or acts of nature, accidents, delivery delays, and resource limitations that directly impact project implementation. Both types of risk need to be looked at and managed.

Risk has three components: (1) the event or fact that characterizes the risk; (2) the probability of the event actually happening; and (3) the impact, measured in financial terms, if the event happens. Risk management involves identifying those possible events, calculating the probabilities and impacts, developing responses to deal with the events should they occur, and controlling the overall process. Since risk management is not something that's done intuitively by most project managers, there must be a methodology to cover risks from inception through project completion. Here is a summary of some tools and techniques of risk management:

1. *Identification.* Tools for identifying risk include expert interviews, brainstorming, Delphi technique, nominal group technique, Crawford slip, and affinity diagramming, all of which are aimed at pinpointing probable events that might result in risk for a project.

2. *Quantification.* Classic tools for quantifying risk include impact analysis using probability, path convergence, cost risk factors, economic and financial factors such as those used for fixing project priorities (profitability, return on sales, return on investment, economic value added, cost of capital, net present value, internal rate of return, expected value), and decision trees (risk analysis forms).

3. *Risk Response.* When a risk-related event happens, the response needs to be "on call." This requires choosing among risk strategies and then developing possible responses. The classic risk

management strategies are acceptance (accepting the consequences), avoidance (eliminating potential threats by eliminating the causes), and mitigation (reducing the risk). If the strategy is not to accept the consequences of the risk, nor is it to avoid risks altogether by pulling the plug on the project, then the alternative is to mitigate. The options for mitigation include minimizing the probability, minimizing the value of the impact, and deflecting by passing the impact on to others (insurance, etc.) or doing workarounds to minimize the effect.

4. *Risk Control*. Since both projects and risk are dynamic creatures, periodic reassessment is part of the program. This means using the risk response criteria developed earlier to establish control. These reassessments can be tied to calendar dates (weekly, monthly, quarterly) or to specific indicators that influence the project (for instance, during a gold-mining project, the price of gold plummets below two dollars an ounce). Risk control encompasses reviewing new risks and the probabilities and impacts of other ongoing projects, as well as revising mitigation strategies and plans.

Scoring a Project's Contribution

A management evaluation technique called the *balanced scorecard* (*Harvard Business Review*, January 1993) suggests that the health of a business can be sized up from four different angles: (1) financial, (2) client, (3) internal processes, and (4) learning and growth. Assuming that all projects are designed to improve the company's health, then these areas need to be examined in terms of the contribution each project makes to the company. Here's a view of these company-wide factors from a project perspective:

1. The financial contribution of a project is easy to size up, since this involves the application of one or more of an array of conventional financial indicators. Business concepts such as projected return on sales, return on investment, economic value added, cost of capital, economic value added, net present value, and internal rate of return are standard ways of sizing up and prioritizing projects.

2. The client perspective on a new project can be looked at through surveys to evaluate such items as service, value, and quality. Face-to-face interviews, questionnaires, and third-party surveys are all valid ways for assessing the client perspective. The QFD approach is another systemic way of ensuring that what is truly important to the client is included in the project.

3. The impact a project has on critical internal processes is a factor to be reviewed. On the one hand, the project might be di-

rectly aimed at improving a process by implementing a new system, such as an on-line banking system. On the other hand, the project may require putting new systems into place—say, for remote communications or an integrated tracking of progress.

4. What does the project contribute to the company? This question bears pondering in these times of turbulence, as does the need for unlearning, relearning, and new learning. Since projects by nature are based on the premise of change, all projects—not only those with a clean learning thrust like education projects—can be used to leverage learning and individual growth.

Since executives are responsible for the destiny of the organization, they need to evaluate and monitor ongoing projects to ensure that they are contributing to the four critical areas. If the contributions of a given project are concentrated, say, on the financial side, then a reevaluation is called for to see how the project can be leveraged so that it has a broader impact on the organization, bringing greater benefit to the client, improving internal processes, and contributing to the organization's learning process. This reevaluation can be done subjectively, based on a major-item checklist for project evaluation and approval, or via a formal, detailed scorecard that can be developed specifically for the project.

Engaging an Enterprise-Wide Data Bank

For an organization's strategies and products to meld, the matter of money has to be dealt with. This means managing the initial estimates, the detailed project budgets, the actual expenditures versus the estimates, and the cash flow. Ideally, this task is handled through an integrated enterprise-wide data bank, such that information flows freely from the project level to the enterprise level and vice versa.

The strategic alignment of projects also involves a global review of available versus required resources—not only personnel but also financial and material resources. An enterprise-wide resource data bank is needed for projects to consult and draw upon, yet the existence of a "project-friendly" system depends partly on how the organization is structured to support projects. If the organization has strong project office support, then the upper management task of aligning and providing support to projects becomes an easier one. Chapter 5 covers the various kinds of project offices and presents the characteristics of each type.

Planning Strategic Projects

The strategic planning of projects aims to ensure that each project develops and implements the necessary strategies to guarantee that its objectives are met. This calls for developing a project charter that includes business objectives, project objectives, schedule timeline, budget baseline, and the constraints and assumptions that affect the project.

SURPRISE MANAGEMENT

The road that links company strategies to completed projects should be straight and sure if the practices outlined in this chapter are followed. Once a company's overall strategies are clear, then the general project strategies and specific strategies outlined are the map and highway signs needed to ensure that projects are aligned with company goals. Smooth cruising along the highway to completion is guaranteed, providing there are no accidents, bad weather, new construction, or detours along the way! But that's what *surprise management* is all about. The pathway from the strategies determined by the company to the actions taken by the project teams is shown here. Corporate strategic objectives are the starting point for all projects that use enterprise project management principles. Once these objectives are identified, successful strategic project alignment depends on carrying out fundamental interfaces between those objectives and the specific setting for each project.

On a long trip, such as a cross-country vacation or a journey toward corporate growth, it would be both naive and reckless to assume a roadway ahead free of roadblocks and "road construction" signs. These undesirable yet real obstacles need to be handled quickly and effectively, otherwise the final destination won't be reached on time. There are a couple of ways to mitigate the effects of surprises that pop up along a journey.

The first way is to build into the strategic planning process a "crystal-ball" step to preview surprises that might destroy otherwise well-thought-out plans. This previewing attenuates the effect of surprise and allows for previously determined alternatives to be put into place—hence, the need for contingency planning and "Plan B" steps.

The second way to deal with surprises—especially strategic surprises that weren't "crystal-balled" ahead of time—is to immediately identify the crux of the problem, and use a structured project approach to resolve the matter. This means deciding who is to do what, when, and how. It involves establishing timelines and a responsibilities and communications plan to make sure the solution works. The strategic issue that has been affected by a surprise situation owing to its importance requires a foolproof approach, and that approach is to treat it like a project, with a beginning, middle, and end, using all the tricks and tools project management has to offer.

Some strategic surprises are simple in nature but not always that easy to resolve. For example, Promon, a primary project management company in Latin America, encountered such a surprise. Promon's principal client, a state-owned telecommunications company in Brazil, began delaying its payments, adding up to $500 million on services already rendered. The cause of the problem was ultimately traced to a governmental austerity program put in place in reaction to an Asian economic crisis. Yet in practice, there were numerous technical and administrative details that had to be straightened out to make sure there were no justifiable bureaucratic reasons for further delaying payments. Promon appointed a multidisciplinary team to take on this complex challenge, involving not only cash flow matters but also politics, international economics, and major jockeying and stalling moves on the part of the client. According to Promon president Carlos Siffert, "It was the no-stone-unturned project approach that ultimately jarred loose the waylaid payments."

STRATEGIC ALIGNMENT OF PROJECTS

Aligning the company's portfolio of projects so that their contributions to the organization's objectives are maximized calls for formal coordination to ensure that each project's actions move in arrow-like fashion toward corporate targets. It requires more than the old "grenade over the wall" approach, in which the business planning staff identifies and characterizes the project and then tosses it to an uninformed and uninvolved project management group that is supposed to complete the project. As any primer on modern management says, folks have to "buy in"— everyone must be onboard before charging ahead.

The concurrent engineering approach to managing projects is based on this theory of buy-in. Yet the corporate-strategy-to-project transition is sometimes overlooked, perhaps because of fine past performance by both business planning people and project management people. Normally both groups do sterling jobs in their respective areas. Just think what these talents could do if they interfaced effectively at transition time! Here's a checklist of questions for senior executives and sponsors to help make sure the corporate projects are aligned:

Is the corporation committed to using project management strategically? In most companies, hundreds of projects are underway at any given time—transformation projects, continuous improvement programs, plant expansions, maintenance fix-ups, worker empowerment, resizing, outsourcing, and quality-of-life projects. Managers, who in the old days supervised people or acted as information brokers between lower and upper corporate levels, now serve as project managers, or as managers of project managers. Since the nature of a manager's work has changed, there must be corresponding corporate commitment to the art and science of managing projects. Things have changed and corporate policy statements must reflect those changes. The project policy statement might address timing (as in the case of NCR) or the use of principles and techniques.

Is there a policy of formally preparing project charters? Since projects are the way corporate strategies are put into effect, it is fundamental they be done in accordance with the original corporate philosophy, strategy, and intent. Project charters are the instrument for doing this. The charter, with the participation and approval of upper management, should answer the basic question: "In what ways will the project enhance overall corporate objectives?" The charter should also cover such topics as objectives, relationships of stakeholders, methodologies, project management philosophy, scope statement, principal interfaces, and a brief project management plan.

Is synergy created between the business group and those responsible for project implementation? To avoid the grenade-over-the-wall syndrome, there needs to be early involvement by project implementation people. While this principle may seem sound, the practice of it presents a challenge. First, business planning people may prefer to plan without the help of perceived "outsiders." Then, there's a good likelihood that the right project people might not be sitting about just waiting to brainstorm and analyze the early stages of a business proposal. Finally, there's the effort required by senior management and sponsors to articulate the relationship between the business planning people and the project management office.

How can senior management make sure that projects don't veer away from the chartered objectives? Maintenance events, programmed into the lives of a project, are a way to keep the project aligned with corporate interests. One classic method is the two-day project management audit. This audit typically compares on-site practice against the project management plan, which is the road map for project implementation. If the audit is expanded to include the project charter and senior management sponsorship issues, this will ensure that questions of strategic project alignment are addressed. The audit can also be used to pinpoint the need for strategic adjustment, if some of the original premises have changed as the project evolved.

For people looking to achieve a quantum leap in company performance, or who just want to tweak an already effective management machine, keeping an eye on the sky during bird migration is a good reminder of how results can be boosted. After all, strategic projects within an organization are like geese in flight; we return to our analogy of the effectiveness of the V formation in considering the strategic alignment of projects. By working together and "drafting" off of each other, both geese and strategic projects create the synergy that carries them effectively to their destinations.

Principle
No. 4

Changes are required in organizational structure and culture, managerial style, and information flow for enterprise project management to be effective.

CHAPTER

Cookbooks, Restaurants, and Enterprise Project Management

How does a company make itself more project-oriented? How does it shift to enterprise project management? And what is the recipe for making such a transition?

Companies make the functional-to-project transition in different ways, based on their cultures and on what is going on in the outside world. In some cases, the market demands a project approach; in others, the pressure comes from within the company. In any case, for the transition to be effective, an *organization change project* needs to be designed and implemented. Since organizations range from large to small, high-tech to low-tech, and formal to informal, there is no one-size-fits-all formula for making the move.

For instance, in organizations that were not originally project-driven, the traditional operations-oriented management was sufficient to do the job. Now, these companies require a substantial cultural swing to start thinking project-wise. Some notable multinational companies provide examples.

Citibank, under John Reed's leadership since 1984, changed from its traditional structure to that of a fast-tracking, project-based organization aimed at meeting emerging needs. Unilever's chairman, Morris Tabaksblat, emphasized the need for organizational restructuring projects as an ongoing effort to mold the company for the changing times. This Anglo-Dutch consumer product giant also uses project management in technology, marketing, and product development. Procter & Gamble's president John Pepper saw a constant array of projects underway in his organization, including "constant reengineering," launching new and better products as well as upgrading technology.

In other companies, the transition to enterprise project management is a question of fine-tuning; not much change is needed to make the shift, since these companies are already "project literate" in given areas. The steps for implementing enterprise project management are still required, yet the speed of implementation is enhanced by an existing project-based culture. A classic example is ABB, the manufacturing conglomerate that makes robots, energy-generation equipment, and high-speed trains. The two staid European-based companies that merged to form ABB (Asea of Sweden and Brown Boveri of Switzerland) already had traditional structures oriented toward manufacturing projects. When Percy Barnevik revolutionized the companies back in 1988, he engineered a decentralizing program that would later earn him international notoriety (the cover of *Fortune* in 1992). Through decentralization and big-time delegation to smaller units, Barnevik laid the groundwork for a "multidomestic" federation of companies that manage projects both globally and locally. ABB moved naturally and smoothly toward an enterprise project management mentality as a consequence of external market pressures and major organizational adjustments.

So it is easy to see how a cookbook approach to moving projectward would never work. Marge Combe, a pioneer in spreading the project gospel at Northwestern Mutual Life, originated the culinary analogy when she pointed out, "A great cookbook doesn't make a great cook. Anyway, what we are trying to do is run a great restaurant!" Just as it takes more than great recipes to make a great restaurant, so too it takes more than some simple formulas to create the ambiance for superior project management. To make an organization more aware and competent in the art and science of managing multiple projects, broad guidelines and models are needed as a reference to piece together a workable plan. These concepts follow in the form of key success factors, a project breakdown structure, and a phased approach for implementing enterprise project management.

KEY SUCCESS FACTORS

Attention to organization design criteria facilitates a smooth and effective transition to a full-fledged company that manages by projects. These criteria are drawn from findings by the Fortune 500 Project Management Benchmarking Forum, which outlined the key success factors for best-in-class project management organizations in multifunctional enterprises:

1. High qualification standards for professionals
   - Professional degrees, either application-specific such as aeronautical engineering or in project management
   - Training in the project management body of knowledge, as detailed in Chapter 8
   - Formal certification as a project management professional, by an accredited institution, as described in Chapter 10
   - Appropriate people-related attributes and skills
   - Experience in similar or equivalent projects
2. Strong executive management support for the project management approach, which can be enhanced with demonstration of the value added to the organization by using that approach
3. High level of authority and control of projects from concept through completion (the premise for the Fortune 500 group is that the projects surveyed justify a full-time project manager)
4. High level of prestige and influence of the project management function, with personnel who are well compensated based on the required qualifications, job responsibility, and performance

So these key success factors must be taken into account during the design and implementation of change projects aimed at implementing enterprise project management. Selection and training need to play a big part in the development of the organization. Top-level support ensuring necessary authority, prestige, and influence also ranks high on the list of design criteria. Once the awareness level of the key decision makers has been raised and the green light has been given for enterprise project management, the success factors are wired into the organizational transformation project.

A PROJECT BREAKDOWN STRUCTURE APPROACH

For major organizational change to take place, all of the activities outlined in the work breakdown structure shown in Exhibit 4-1 may be required. For a less radical change project, some items need not be performed. Yet for all situations involving change in an organization, this project breakdown structure provides a comprehensive checklist of activities. For more about the role of the proj-

Exhibit 4-1. Breakdown structure of organizational transformation project.

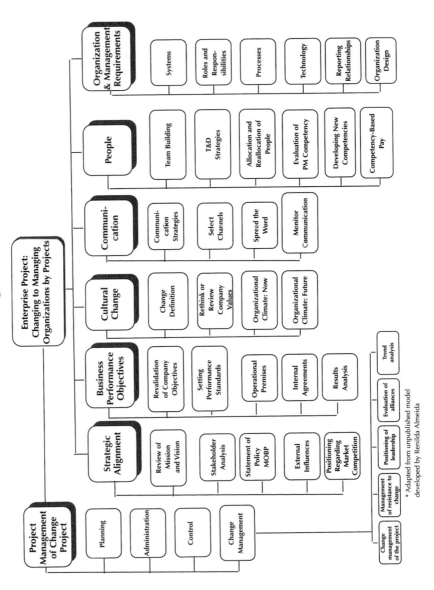

* Adapted from unpublished model developed by Renilda Almeida

ect breakdown structure in successful project management, see Chapter 8.

The major headings and their contents for a structured approach to implementing enterprise project management are as follows:

- *Project Management of the Enterprise Project.* Encompasses the planning, administration, control, and change management of the enterprise project. Change management includes dealing with changes in the project itself, management of resistance to change, positioning of leadership, evaluation of alliances, and trend analysis.

- *Strategic Alignment.* Includes review of mission and vision, stakeholder analysis, statement of enterprise project management policy, external influences, and positioning regarding market competition.

- *Business Performance Objectives.* Takes in revalidation of company objectives, setting of performance standards, operational premises, internal agreements, and results analysis.

- *Cultural Change.* Involves change definition, rethinking or reviewing company values, and comparison of the organizational climate now in relation to the desired future climate.

- *Communication.* Encompasses communication strategies, channel selection, spreading the word, and monitoring communication.

- *People.* Means team building, training and development strategies, allocation and reallocation of people, evaluation of project management competency, development of new competencies, and competency-based pay.

- *Organization and Management Requirements.* Includes systems, roles and responsibilities, processes, technology, reporting relationships, and organization design.

This universal project breakdown structure is applicable to enterprise project management projects, or any other form of organizational change project. It lends itself particularly to situations where a major transformation is called for and where resistance tends to be strong. The classic approach of breaking down the transformation project into its components and then managing those parts amounts to practicing the preachings of project management!

IMPLEMENTING ENTERPRISE PROJECT MANAGEMENT IN PHASES

Like any other project, the implementation of an enterprise project management approach takes time. It evolves through the phases of a conventional project life cycle and eventually transforms into a steady state in which the organization behaves as a project-oriented organization. There are five stages an organization must pass through to get from initiation of the concept to being a full-fledged, purring organization that is dynamically and productively managed by projects.

1. *Achieving Buy-In.* The primary organizational stakeholders must be exposed to the enterprise project management concept and agree to pursue it. This may involve influencing upward, laterally, and downward in the organization. Here are some of the steps required for achieving buy-in to initiate the project:
    * Create awareness by distributing literature, promoting benchmarking meetings with companies having similar interests, and offering presentations by internal and guest speakers.
    * Develop and distribute literature evaluating the benefits of the change and other pertinent project issues.
    * Conduct executive briefing sessions to spread the word and obtain valuable input from key stakeholders, as outlined later in this chapter.
    * Develop a project charter for implementation of enterprise project management in the organization.
2. *Planning.* The processes for managing the organization by projects and the roles of the various stakeholders must be defined. This involves making both policy and procedural decisions such as these:
    * Develop and refine a work breakdown structure for the enterprise project similar to that shown in Exhibit 4-2.
    * Define the project implementation team and sponsor.
    * Name the form of project office most suitable for the organization: Project Support Office (PSO), Project Management Center of Excellence (PMCOE), and Program Management Office (PMO), or some combination thereof, as described in Chapter 5.
    * Reevaluate or define policies and procedures for strategic alignment of projects, standard methodologies, competency standards, organizational maturity in project management, reward systems, integrated databases, selection of project sponsors and project teams, communications, project assessments, global reporting, and process improvement.

Exhibit 4-2. The phases for implementing enterprise project management.

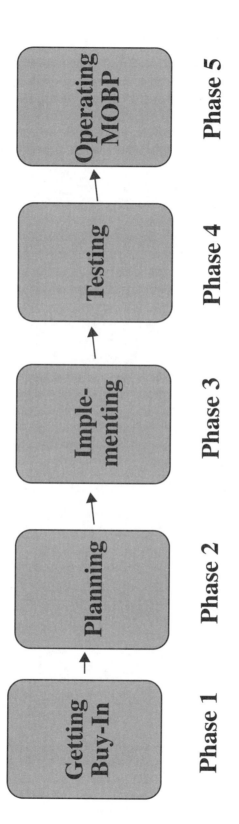

Phase 1 — Getting Buy-In

Phase 2 — Planning

Phase 3 — Implementing

Phase 4 — Testing

Phase 5 — Operating MOBP

3. *Implementing.* The necessary education programs must be carried out at all levels in the organization and the necessary processes and procedures put into place. Fundamental change is taking place in the organization and involves these activities:
   - Educate across the organization on project concepts and methodology, team building, interpersonal skills, facilitation, and coaching.
   - Initiate use of a project priority board that has go-no go powers over company projects and approves resource allocation to projects.
   - Put policies and procedures into place; project sponsors and teams operate in accordance with these processes.
   - Have internal coaches to support project teams.
4. *Testing.* The wrap-up phase of the implementation project, this stage revolves around the key question, "Is everything working the way it is supposed to for the organization to manage itself by projects?" Here is what needs to take place:
   - Make organizational adjustments as necessary, including final definition of project office concept.
   - Carry out a formal assessment of the new approach: highlight the benefits achieved and pinpoint areas that need improvement.
   - Make sure all the enterprise-wide project management systems are working to the content of all stakeholders.
5. *Operating Enterprise Project Management.* All organizations are dynamic, so operating adjustments are inevitable. New communication or tracking technology calls for periodic changes. Organizational maintenance, involving continued education programs and management audits, is also needed, along with these action items:
   - Carry out periodic project management maturity assessments to evaluate how far the company has evolved toward a fully projectized organization (see Chapter 11 on maturity models).
   - Institute a continuous improvement program to guarantee that the process is kept up-to-date.
   - Maintain benchmarking relationships with other organizations.

THE EXECUTIVE SESSION

Whether the organization is new to the project management concept or simply underutilizing the tools and techniques available, a specific initiative will get things moving toward a project management culture. Getting the attention of potential converts or enthusiasts may require subtle methods and involves finding allies, spreading the word, and working out some plans. But it also requires staging an event—a happening of sorts—to shine the light on the topic and let the idea sink in. That is where the *executive session* comes in. The executive session is a half-day meeting of interested parties and decision makers.

Getting the Ball Rolling

When carefully articulated, the executive session answers the challenge of garnering people's support for a project management culture. To get things moving by way of an executive session:

1. *Identify allies.* See who else believes that boosting project management within the organization is a worthy cause. Pinpoint the key stakeholders who need to be on your bandwagon. Initiate informal chats and gather ideas as to how to get others to sign on.

2. *Spread the word.* Use house organs and internal forums to talk up the topic. Use every opportunity to raise the subject. Distribute articles and literature that will raise the awareness level of key stakeholders, as described earlier.

3. *Plan an executive session.* Set an objective for an initial half-day executive session—something like: "To promote stakeholder support for creating a project management culture within the organization." Write up two to three pages of summary information aimed at promoting the executive session; include topics such as background information, goals, scope, participants, and form of facilitation. Include pre-work, facilitation of the session itself, and postsession debriefings.

4. *Select a person to articulate the executive session.* Someone needs to orchestrate the executive session—an internal facilitator, an experienced change agent from another area of the company, a local university professor, or an outside person you have worked with and trust. The facilitator should be involved not only in conducting the session itself but also in designing the invitational documentation, developing the event, and holding the postsession debriefings.

Step by Step Through the Executive Session

Once you've rounded up some allies and have spread the word by distributing literature on the topic, there are concrete steps you need to take to get the program moving:

1. *A Presession Questionnaire.* Prepare two pages of questions along these lines:
   - "On a scale of 1 to 10, how do you rate your business unit's capabilities in the following areas of project management: project time management, project cost management, project quality management, project scope management, project communications management, project procurement management, project human resources management, project risk management, project integration management?
   - List the three major difficulties encountered in managing projects in your business unit.
   - What are three strong points of the present way of managing the business unit's projects?
   - Why bother improving the organization's project management culture? What do you believe would be the benefits? What could be the downside of encouraging a project management culture?
   - Additional comments.

2. *A Presession Interview Script.* Interviews consist of five individual fifty-minute chats between the facilitator and selected key executives slated to participate in the session. Although the interviews should follow an open format and be free-flowing, there are basic questions that will help the facilitator customize the session. The interviews should touch on the following topics:
   - Interviewee's background and knowledge of project management.
   - Interviewee's perception of the business unit's capability in project management.
   - What the interviewee thinks the problems are. What he or she sees as solutions.
   - Who the major stakeholders are in making a change to a project management culture.
   - Advice and suggestions.

3. *The Executive Session Plan.* The session itself needs to be outlined so as to fit the content into the four-hour time span. Here is a suggested approach:
   - Opening (Why are we here? What are we going to do? How are we going to do it?). This is a joint review of consolidated questionnaire results, comments on readings, and group discussion aimed at creating consensus on the need for improved project management. There is a brief presentation on the concept of managing by projects.
   - Brainstorming and discussion of the enablers and inhibitors for establishing project management as part of the

organization's culture. The session wraps up with a discussion of ideas, suggestions, and possible next steps.
- The debriefing outline (written and oral) for postsession follow-up. The debriefing materials should include questionnaire results; relevant points from the interviews; a summary of discussions; the enablers and inhibitors; a summary of the project management concepts presented at the session; a summary of ideas, suggestions, and possible next steps; and the facilitator's comments.

After the session, remember to follow up and keep on pushing. Once the session has been held, keep the ball rolling. Conclusions from the executive session may need to be nurtured and monitored; a follow-up visit by the facilitator may be in order, as well as the need to address the question, "What do we do now?"

A POTENTIALLY ROCKY ROAD AHEAD

The road to enterprise project management is not without bumps and potholes. Here are some of the potential road hazards that face executives responsible for making organizations more project-oriented:

- *Personal Adaptation From Position-Based to Project-Based Management.* Not everyone readily makes the shift from a position-based management to a project approach. For those linked to hierarchical status and power, the adjustment tends to be, at the least, painful. Some don't adjust at all, and either opt out or are ushered out of the organization.

- *Looser, Less Structured Organization.* Multiproject settings are challenging for those accustomed to clear lines of function. When organizations take on a matrix form, the ambiguities and "fuzziness" of the situation create insecurity in professionals new to the setting. Those who don't adapt readily to the scene need to be trained or transferred to other spots.

- *Challenge of Stakeholder Management.* A project approach requires taking on full responsibility for the success of one's projects. This means that all factors affecting the projects must be managed by the project team, including the project stakeholders. Specific training in stakeholder management may be a need for some projects.

- *Task of Developing Competent Project Personnel.* Project management requires a special mind-set from team members, one that differs sharply from a traditional operating mentality. The effort to make this shift may be underestimated by optimistic change agents, resulting in either slow or ineffective change.

• *Overall Integration of Projects.* Managing a portfolio of projects calls for strong interface management to ensure coherence and direction for the multitude of ongoing undertakings. This task requires high-level attention and a project interfacing culture throughout the organization for enterprise project management to be effective.

KEEP ON COOKING

As mentioned at the outset of this chapter, there is no cookbook process for moving an organization into a projectized posture. Some companies lean in that direction because "the word" has been spread by project champions in the organization. Other organizations require a wake-up call in the form of an executive session, followed by a campaign and a structured implementation program. But no matter what approach you use, there are two key success factors that must be part of the transformation design criteria: (1) training and education in project management; and (2) addressing top management's issues regarding authority, prestige, and influence. As the increasingly competitive times spotlight techniques that boost an organization's bottom line, and top management tunes into the power of managing organizations by projects, the guidelines and models presented here will gain increased attention and application.

Principle
No. 5

The project office is key to ensuring that project management is effectively applied across the organization.

5

CHAPTER

"Oh, Give Me a Home": Roaming Buffalo, Project Offices, and CPOs

You'd think it would be easy, but tracking down where project management should live within an organization is not always a simple task. Like the buffalo that roam, project management is found at specific spots within an organization, as well as on alternative grazing grounds depending on the season and the times. Here are some of the places project management resides within a company:

- Within an engineering group
- In the information technology area
- In a centralized group where all projects report
- In a group that concentrates management of high-priority projects
- On a specific project
- In a support area that provides scheduling and control assistance
- In a staff group charged with spreading the word on project management

Ideally, project management should permeate the organization; that's the premise behind enterprise project management. This view calls for across-the-board buy-in of the concept as a management philosophy, implying that project management should be just about everywhere—everything should be translated into projects, from classic capital undertakings and information technology (IT) ventures to marketing, continuous improvement, annual operational targets, and organizational change. The enterprise project management approach calls for big-time investment in training and development. And it requires a home for project management, a source from which project management flows out to all the parts of the organization.

Enterprise project management is not a prerequisite, however, for seeing that project management has a home. Any organization with a project backlog needs to support its projects from some coherent base. A project management home is just such a vantage point from which to support, influence, and direct project management endeavors. That need for a home is one of the design criteria included in the organizational change project outlined in Chapter 4.

IN SEARCH OF THE PROJECT OFFICE

There are some classic "homes" for project management; they are sometimes referred to by the catchall term "project office," even though they vary considerably in concept.

The Autonomous Project Team

Some projects are autonomous. In these situations, the project management function rests within the project. Project management practices are derived from the previous experience and practice of the project leaders; there is no support provided by the organization. The leadership nucleus for the autonomous project team (APT), which includes the project manager and administrative and technical support personnel, is sometimes referred to as the project office. All costs for the project leadership team accrue directly to the project. The function of this type of project office is to manage and run the project in its entirety. Therefore all of the project management functions are carried out by the assigned project team, and full accountability for the success of the project resides with the project leadership as shown in Exhibit 5-1.

• *What APTs Are Supposed to Do.* APTs perform all the tasks of managing projects: time management, scope management, cost management, quality management, risk management, procurement management, communications management, human resources management, and integration management.

• *How to Make Sure That the APTs Are Successful.* Success rides primarily on the shoulders of the project manager. If the proj-

Exhibit 5-1. APT: autonomous project team.

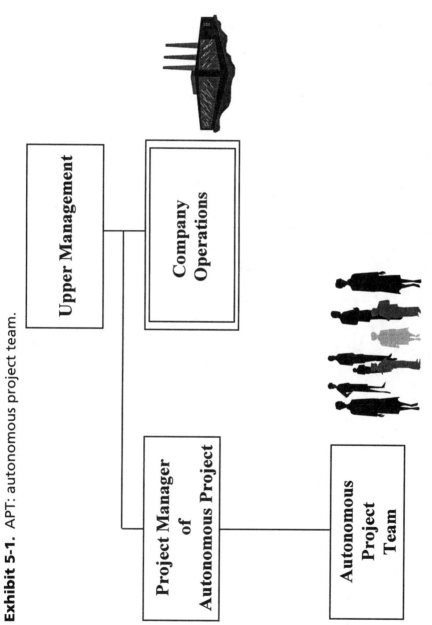

ect manager has the expertise and surrounds himself with the right people and procedures, then the probability for success is high. Another factor for success includes a powerful and supportive project sponsor or steering committee from the company to ensure that factors outside the project context are managed and interfaced.

• *Normal Applications for APTs.* As the name implies, the APT works well when the project has no major need to interface with the rest of the organization and the company has little project expertise to offer. For example, a new factory being built for a company that rarely does a capital expansion.

The Project Support Office

The project support office (PSO) provides services to several project managers simultaneously, as shown in Exhibit 5-2, although in some cases it exclusively supports a given project manager. These offices furnish administrative and technical support, tools, and services for planning, scheduling, scope changes, and cost management. The resources involved (hardware, software, and personnel) are billed to the projects, either internally or externally, depending on the nature and contractual structure of the projects. Sometimes people are loaned out from the project support office for the kickoff phase or even for an extended stint on a project. Accountability for project success does not rest with the PSO, but with project managers who use the services. The PSO is also known by other names such as *project office, project management office, administrative support office,* and *technical support office.*

• *What PSOs Are Supposed to Do.* According to a consensus reached at a meeting of the Fortune 500 Project Management Benchmarking Forum in September 1997, PSOs may provide all or some of the following services: planning and scheduling, tracking, contract preparation and administration, administrative and financial services, scope change administration, project management tools, project metrics, document management, asset tracking, and status audits.

• *How to Make Sure the PSO Is Successful.* There are four keys for ensuring a high-performing PSO:

1. Technical resources: up-to-snuff hardware, processes, and tools. Quality equipment and the latest software are a must for a project office to be effective.
2. Methodology: coherent procedures spelling out how to do projects. This methodology needs to be tied to a project

Exhibit 5-2. PSO: project support office.

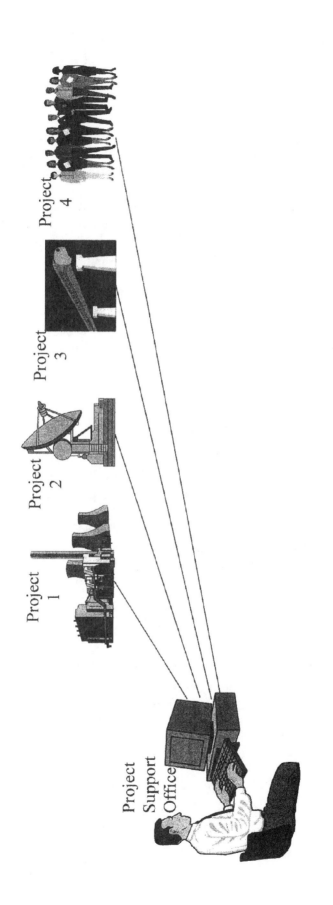

management competency model that is understood and respected by all project players.

3. Interface: organizational premises and across-the-lines communication. Since the project support office often operates in matrix settings, interfacing becomes a highly relevant issue.

4. Competence: people versed in doing and managing technical support. The essence of the PSO lies in developing support people who supply the tools and information needed to get projects done on time and within budget.

• *Normal Applications for PSOs.* Project support offices are particularly applicable for settings where projects are led by strong project managers, where project management awareness exists within the organization, where there is a heavy requirement for support documentation and formalized tracking, and where there are lots of projects going on.

Project Management Center of Excellence

The project management center of excellence (PMCOE) is the gathering point for expertise but does not assume responsibility for project results. It is a general overhead expense and not billable to projects. Sue Guthrie, who initiated IBM's center of excellence, sees the challenge as "raising organizational competence and changing the maturity level of the entity." The PMCOE's task is largely of a missionary nature: getting out the word, converting the nonbelievers, and transforming believers into practitioners. The PMCOE is charged as the caretaker of methodologies. It keeps communication channels open between projects and with the outside project management community, as indicated in Exhibit 5-3. Alternative names might include project management center of competency, project management professional development center, project management organizational development center, project management process center, project management competency center, project management leadership center, corporate project center, and enterprise project center.

• *What PMCOEs Are Supposed to Do.* The Fortune 500 Project Management Benchmarking Forum came up with this listing of responsibilities for the PMCOE, recognizing that the center of excellence concept varies considerably from company to company: training, process standardization, internal consulting, competency

Exhibit 5-3. PMCOE: project management center of excellence.

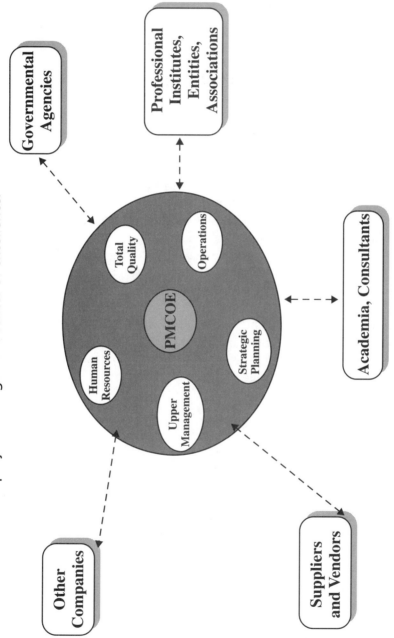

enhancement, identification of best practices, project prioritization, tool definition and standardization, enterprise or portfolio reporting, advocacy of the project management cause, and state-of-the-art benchmarking.

- *For the PMCOE to Work.* Here are the main requirements:

1. Sponsorship: big-time support from upstairs. PMCOEs are most effective when there is resonance from upper management.
2. Leadership: politically articulate. PMCOE leadership is not based on power, but rather on knowledge and the ability to manage and influence affected stakeholders.
3. Added value: what's in it for the practitioners? PMCOEs must be able to demonstrate the benefit of buying into the project management practices they are proposing.
4. Professional development: outside training, on-the-job programs, benchmarking. Only to the extent that it develops competent project managers, leaders, and team members will a PMCOE make its mark on an organization.
5. State-of-the-art: expertise, information sources, resources, techniques. To maintain credibility, the PMCOE must be on the leading edge of project management practice and knowledge.

The PMCOE approach is particularly suitable for corporations with global responsibilities, companies with projects of differing natures (such as information systems, marketing, engineering, and organization change), and organizations that prefer the soft approach to influencing internal culture.

The Program Management Office

Shown in Exhibit 5-4, the program management office (PMO) manages the project managers and is ultimately accountable for project results. In major corporations, the PMO concentrates its efforts on prioritized projects. Other projects are managed by departments or units and are given support by the PMO as needed. The PMO, by nature, comprises the functions of the PMCOE and, in some cases, of the PSO. Alternative names are the project management program office, program office, project portfolio office, and project portfolio management.

- *What PMOs Are Supposed to Do.* Here's the Fortune 500 Project Management Benchmarking Forum's view on the type of

Exhibit 5-4. PMO: program management office.

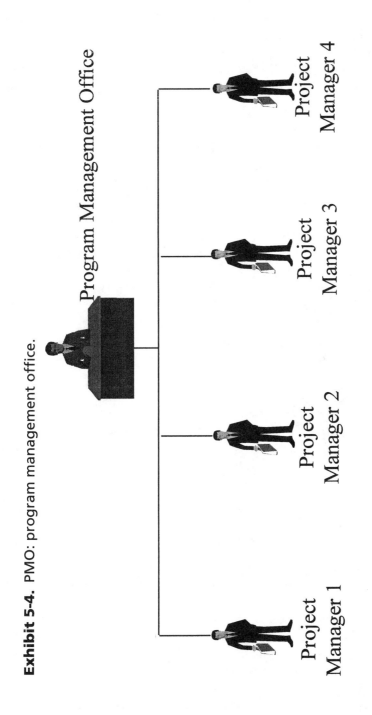

activities performed by the PMO: resource assignment and management, recruiting and developing project managers, project selection and prioritization, alignment with business strategies, portfolio reporting, methodology and project management processes, accountability for programs or projects, human process change management, and coordination of the project managers.

• *For the PMO to Work.* Here are additional requirements for a successful program management office:

1. Power: authority within the company power structure. PMOs have to be a part of the organization's power structure if they are going to be effective.
2. Corporate priority: from corporate strategy to project implementation. Part of the PMO function is to determine which projects will be handled by the PMO directly, which will be farmed out to third parties, and which will be handled at a unit level.
3. Enterprise-wide control: reporting of pertinent project information on a multiple-project basis. The PMO is expected to have an overview of aggregate project results as well as trends in individual projects. This double focus may call for sophisticated tracking systems.

PMOs are normally applicable when corporate management has committed to managing priority ventures by projects, when there is adequate organizational maturity for a program management office to operate effectively, and when not managing by projects will have strong negative consequences.

Now Presenting . . . the CPO

In some organizations, the challenge of coordinating hundreds, or even thousands, of complex projects—many of which are cross-functional in nature—may prove too large for the project office variations described above. As the trend continues, more companies are likely to call on top executives for high-level oversight of multiple projects and major programs. At the moment, overarching responsibility for projects in most organizations is fuzzy at best. But enterprise-oriented companies need a politically savvy, project-wise, system-literate executive facilitator to do the caring and nurturing of projects throughout the organization. New titles may even evolve for these upper-echelon project facilitators.

Enter the chief project officer (CPO), as shown in Exhibit 5-5. What would the CPO do? How would he or she operate? What would the responsibilities be? The questions are numerous and the sweeping response is obvious: "It depends!" It depends on the degree of maturity of the organization with respect to project management (methodologies, experience, and support already in place), the size and complexity of the projects, the conviction of upper management with regard to using an enterprise approach to managing projects, and the nature of the organization—whether it is project-driven, like an engineering company, or functionally based, like a manufacturer of consumer products that uses project management as a means to an end.

The CPO job makes sense in special circumstances: in organizations that are global, enterprise-oriented, multidisciplined, and that require timely delivery of multiple, complex projects. A CPO's responsibility is the care and nurturing of the organization's portfolio of projects, from the business-decision stage to final implementation. This includes the following:

- Involvement in the business decisions that result in new projects
- Strategic project planning
- Setting priorities and negotiating resources for projects
- Oversight of strategic project implementation
- Responsibility for an enterprise-wide project management system
- Development of project management awareness and capability throughout the organization
- Periodic project review, including decision to discontinue projects
- Top-level stakeholder management, facilitation, and mentoring

How might the CPO concept work in an organization? Here are two examples where a CPO could add value to a company's strategic targets.

Scenario 1. A worldwide company provides services and products, involving thousands of complex projects. Its PMCOE embraces the organization on a global basis, while numerous PSOs operate based on geographic criteria. The CPO oversees the PMCOE and works through a council of executives to implement enterprise-wide planning and control systems that concentrate on the project side of the corporation, as opposed to repetitive activity-based operations.

Exhibit 5-5. CPO: chief project officer.

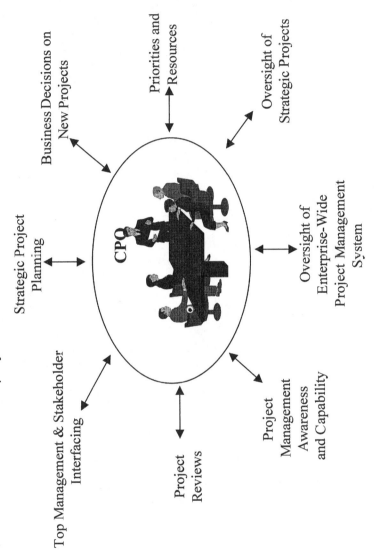

Strategic Project
Planning

Business Decisions on
New Projects

Priorities and
Resources

Oversight of
Strategic Projects

Top Management & Stakeholder
Interfacing

Oversight of
Enterprise-Wide
Project Management
System

Project
Reviews

Project
Management
Awareness
and Capability

CPO

Scenario 2. A traditional functional organization needs to shift to an enterprise approach to speed up its information technology and new product development projects. The CPO sets up new channels of communication through a matrix-based program management office, which includes the project support function made available to project managers in various areas. The CPO also establishes a virtual PMCOE that involves professionals working on various projects.

There's Gotta Be Another Way

Yet, in the here and now, while the CPO concept is an option, it is not a position that's needed in all companies. It doesn't make sense for an organization to swing to something drastically different until both the situation and the times are right. All organizations do not need CPOs. If the organization has survived and prospered for years without a CPO, obviously there are other ways of dealing with strategic project management issues. Who else within the organization can take on the functions earmarked for the CPO?

• *The Chief Operating Officer.* The COO could well divide time between process-related activities and projects. Although operations (keeping things running) and projects (doing new things) theoretically require different mind-sets, a capable COO with experience in project work can blend the two functions.

• *The Vice President of Planning.* This high-echelon performer might extend his or her mandate and take on the oversight of project implementation and enterprise tracking, as well as the up-front strategic side of projects. The vice president of planning would have to be well versed in the art and science of managing projects.

• *The Program Management Office.* The head of the PMO can take on the CPO's function, provided resource allocation, supervision, and tracking of projects are sufficiently delegated to the project managers and the PMO is placed high enough in the corporate order of things.

• *The Executive Team.* If the executive team is sufficiently conversant in strategic project management, then the CPO's duties can be distributed among the members. For example, to deal with the needs of strategically aligned work being performed by cross-functional teams, an automobile manufacturer might assign a "vehicle line executive," who reports back to a corporate strategy board to these platforms.

So alternative approaches abound for dealing with the issues outlined for the CPO. If there is a cultural resistance to establishing such a position, then the alternatives should be looked at closely (nominating a CPO may not be a good political or practical solution in some companies). Other titles might be used for the same function—names like executive project office or corporate project office. Exhibit 5-6 compares the characteristics of the five project office options presented in this chapter. Rarely will all five forms exist within a given company, but rather variations and hybrid combinations are usually present.

HYBRID STUFF

In real life, the roads to enterprise project management wander outside the boxes described here. There are complementary initiatives that enhance the performance of these standard approaches. For instance, at Allied Signal, Tom Booth, who supports management for major projects, involved a panel of higher executives and outside experts to size up the quality of Allied's project management practices. American Airlines' Susan Garcia reports that priority projects undergo a detailed review by upper management when they show signs of criticality. At EDS, Carl Isenberg helps boost corporate performance by giving a list of pointers for upper managers to ask while conducting project performance reviews. Warren Marquis and Lou Rivera from Citibank, who participated in the Fortune 500 Project Management Benchmarking Forum in September 1997, are part of a group that provides such a combination of PSO and PMCOE functions. Don Colvin, director of corporate project management for FedEx, has commented, tongue in cheek, about the ubiquitous project office, "I'm not sure we have one; we may have several."

These project office concepts materialize in various forms depending on the company's culture and previous practice, and on the characteristics of the projects at hand. The exception is the autonomous project team (APT), which stands alone, since APT-run projects are independent of a company's organization. Here are some of the hybrid forms:

- The PMO incorporates the functions of the PSO, PMCOE, and CPO.
- The PSO and PMCOE are one unit.
- The CPO and PMCOE are combined into one function.

Exhibit 5-6. Five options for managing project management in an organization.

Project Management Functions	Autonomous Project Team (APT)	Project Support Office (PSO)	Project Management Center of Excellence (PMCOE)	Program Management Office (PMO)	Chief Project Officer (CPO)
Time	perform	support	educate	supervise	oversee
Scope	perform	support	educate	supervise	oversee
Cost	perform	support	educate	supervise	oversee
Quality	perform	support	educate	supervise	oversee
Risk	perform	support	educate	supervise	oversee
Procurement	perform	support	educate	supervise	oversee
Communication	perform	support	educate	supervise	oversee
Human resources	perform	support	educate	supervise	oversee
Integration	perform	support	educate	supervise	oversee
Multiple project responsibility		support	articulate	coordinate	
PM consistency across organization			articulate		oversee
Develop PM competence		support	promote	coordinate	oversee
Alignment of business strategies with projects					articulate
Track projects on enterprise-wide basis					perform

SO HOW DO YOU PUT A PROJECT OFFICE INTO PLACE?

Obviously it depends on what project office you are talking about. Requirements for an autonomous project and those for a chief project officer are at opposite ends of a long spectrum. The support function, center of excellence, and program office also vary substantially in responsibilities and needs. Yet there are commonalities when it comes to the implementation of these differing forms of the project office. Let's take a look at the building blocks for each type of office.

Planning

Surprise, surprise! Planning is the foundation for making any of these concepts work. Yes, it is back to basics. The first step is to draft a project charter that includes background information, the objective for establishing the project office, the assumptions and constraints associated with the project, and the expected results. Then there is the need for a walk-through of questions based on the areas of project knowledge expertise (see Chapter 8). What is the scope of the proposed project office and the scope of work required to put the office in place? What about the time frame and cost of the project office project? What quality standards are to be adhered to: the best of the best or a standard less costly? The human resources required also need to be looked at, as must the procurement of vendors or outside consultants. A communications plan should be set up for project implementation and also for the postimplementation phase. Risks involved in implementing a project office also need to be considered. Once these ABCs for managing a project have been accomplished, theoretically, the project office project is ready to roll. Yet there are specifics that call for special attention when planning the project office.

Hardware, Software, and Interconnectivity

Computers and related equipment need to be specified to meet foreseen data-crunching, text, reporting, and presentation needs. The number of workstations is also a factor, as well as compatibility with other company gear. Remote data access and interconnectivity within the company and with the client are also relevant issues. All of these decisions need to be coordinated with the company's information technology people. The only exception for a stand-alone situation regarding hardware, software, and interconnectivity would be the APT working on a completely independent project. Yet even in that case, an up-front look at compatibility is advised to save headaches down the road. The PSO supporting several projects, as well as the PMO that has formal accountability for a group of projects, needs to be designed for multiple project tracking and reporting capabilities. The PMCOE and the CPO have company-wide concerns, so information technology that is sensitive to enterprise-wide project management needs is the key thrust for both the center of excellence and the chief project officer.

Methodology and Procedures

To accomplish any kind of project work, there has to be convergence on how things will get done. This means developing a common road map for getting to project completion. A project management methodology spells out the steps to be followed for the development and implementation of a project. A sample sequence of a project methodology starting after project approval is: develop project charter, gather initial information and benchmark other projects, develop project management plan, define activities in the work breakdown structure, establish activity relationships in precedence network, estimate time and resources, perform activities, track progress, take corrective action, and perform evaluation and wrap-up functions.

Methodologies vary widely from industry to industry and from company to company. For example, Japanese product development methodologies are sharply different from U.S. software development methodologies. Global companies like IBM that do a wide range of projects, like product development, network services, manufacturing, and information technology systems integration, face the challenge of creating a common methodology that meets the needs of all project users. Once a methodology is in place, it has to be documented in the form of procedures. Procedures are the detailed "how to" instructions describing the steps in the methodology. With the exception of the APT, where an ad hoc methodology will do, the other project office variations call for a standardized project methodology, so that people and systems can speak a common language across a multiple-project enterprise setting.

People, Power, and Politics

The technical aspects described in the previous two sections represent only part of the challenge in building a project office. The other side of the task involves people and the methods needed to get them to perform in convergence—to get them to fly in formation, like migrating geese. This calls for artful and diligent stakeholder management as outlined in Chapter 6. It means developing a detailed stakeholder plan to ensure that the interests and opinions of all project-related players are cared for and nurtured. The APT and PSO are reasonably immune to major organization pressures. The PMO, PMCOE, and CPO are right in the midst of enterprise politics. So the people issues, which involve power and politics, both within projects and across the enterprise, are likely to determine the success or failure of the project office.

HOME, SWEET HOME

This kaleidoscope of approaches for running projects within organizations has been presented for a reason. Project management originally appeared in companies as an ad hoc discipline; rarely was it an across-the-board kind of thing. As change brings projects into virtually every area of a company, pressure grows to establish a backdrop, or a home, for project management.

"Home" for project management is akin to "Home, home on the range" from the lyrics of the old cowboy tune. Project management's home, too, needs to be all-encompassing, spacious, and "roamable," as in the buffalo days. The ideas outlined here portray contrasting yet complementary pathways for dealing with that challenge. The APT, PSO, PMO, PMCOE, and CPO are all neat solutions, yet they're not built-to-order fixes; issues of organizational culture, project management maturity, and project mix need to be taken into account before a final design can be approved. It is hoped that, once designed and built, the chosen project management dwelling will prove a solid, productive, and harmonious home.

Principle
No. 6

In an enterprise project management setting, stakeholder management is a must in order to generate synergy and minimize conflict among key players.

CHAPTER

The Guys Who Hold the Beef: A Model for Dealing With Key Players

A foreign-born student of mine once tried to translate the term "stakeholder" literally and came amazingly close when he guessed, "The guy who holds the beef?" All those who somehow hold a stake in a project (and who sometimes end up with a "beef") are stakeholders. They are people or parties who are positively or negatively affected by the activities or final results of a project or program; they stand to win or lose. They have a claim or vested interest. These parties include project champions, project participants, and external parties. They include people working on projects, those who influence them, and others who will ultimately be affected by them. In an enterprise setting, the stakeholders are those people who gain or lose by supporting the management-by-projects approach.

MANAGING STAKEHOLDERS ACROSS THE ORGANIZATION

Stakeholder management is the cornerstone of enterprise project management. It is the oil for the wheels of enterprise project management to turn. It deals with the so-called soft interfacing issues, which involve questions of power, politics, and influence. Special interests, hidden agendas, and interpersonal conflicts also come into play in stakeholder management.

There are two principal stakeholder management scenarios that arise in organizations that undertake enterprise project management. The first involves the implementation of enterprise project management itself, when a change in organizational mind-set takes place. This calls for a *start-up* stakeholder approach, one that focuses on the unique issues of implementing the organizational change project. The second is a *maintenance* setting, where an enterprise philosophy already reigns and stakeholders have to be managed to keep the organization lively and productive. In both situations, these so-called soft issues (which often involve some hard-knuckled action) are present.

Power

"Power is the greatest of aphrodisiacs," Henry Kissinger reportedly said when he was U.S. Secretary of State. This suggests that power has an almost sensual attraction; people are drawn to power by a magnetic, quasi-erotic force. Whether this is true or not, the fact is that power is necessary for executives and other important project players to get their jobs done. Without power, it is hard to get things done. Power provides the energy to take initiative, lay out plans, and follow up on results. From a company standpoint, the attraction people feel to power is a healthy influence, since, when power is properly used, it moves the enterprise in the right direction. For enterprise project management, here are the prevalent forms of power.

- *Formal.* Stemming from position power, formal power indicates that the player has received some charter to do a job. A scope of work is associated with that job, which is to be carried out within the culture and values of the company. Formal power is the easiest kind to see and understand. It is usually expressed in an up-front manner.
- *Relationship.* "It's not what you know but who you know" goes the old expression. Access is a form of power, whether that access be through blood relationships, an old-boy network, or church or community acquaintances. Relationship power opens doors.
- *Knowledge-Based.* Power and authority go hand in hand. While authority can be of a formal nature, it can also be couched in knowledge. Nobel Prize winners, for instance, are not always steeped in formal power, but their recognized knowledge makes them leading authorities, which in turn becomes power.
- *Competence.* Competence power transcends that of knowledge, in that the person is recognized as someone who gets things

done. Power derived from competence stems from both technical knowledge and behavioral and political skills.

Cultivating one or a combination of these power factors considerably boosts the potential power of executives and other significant players in an enterprise. From a stakeholder management viewpoint, it makes good sense to establish a firm power base and even to brandish power when necessary, provided that ethics and people's feelings are respected. It takes power to get things done, particularly in a wide-reaching web of power brokers exercising their influence across the enterprise. Here are tips on how executives and other players can move up the power ladder:

1. *Understand your organization.* All organizations have a fundamental culture. They have traditions and a history. Even though major surgery may be needed, understanding the essence of an organization is fundamental to putting together a project-oriented enterprise.

2. *Polish up on your interpersonal skills.* For enterprise project management to work, both senior executives and project team members must have high levels of the emotional quotient (EQ) of behavioral and political skills needed to deal intelligently with the power factors present.

3. *Build up your image.* Just as products need to be marketed to convey an image, you and other key players in a projectized setting need to keep your images polished. Call it self-marketing, blowing your own horn, or whatever, your personal image as a competent and articulate project-based player deserves constant nurturing.

4. *Develop and cultivate allies.* Enterprise project management is like a team sport. Individual actions become significant only within the context of a series of actions. As in volleyball, where one player receives the ball, a second sets it up for the third player to spike, players in projectized organizations require support from teammates.

Politics

Politics has been described in government circles as the "art of the possible." The possible in companies depends on politics and the art of conciliating differing interests and opinions among the people who make up the network of power within the organization. Executives, therefore, need to act politically to influence the company's decision-making process in order to bring about decisions consistent with their interests and opinions—and that at the same time are possible. The key to politics lies in understanding that facts are not the important factor in making political decisions. Much more important are the interests at stake, such as departmental or sectorial interests, power-based interests, economic and financial interests, and personal agendas. And most important, the opinions of individuals, formed for whatever historical, cultural, or psychological reasons, are the essence of everything political. When managing stakeholders in an enterprise setting, here are some recommended techniques for successful politicking in favor of a given cause:

1. Plant seeds of action by casually remarking on issues, circulating articles, or citing third parties.
2. Don't press the issue; give people time to absorb and process new ideas and issues.
3. Involve others, since politics by nature includes and affects groups of people.
4. Give details in support of your cause as discussions evolve.
5. Include the suggestions of others and negotiate any details involving the interests of all.

Influence

In an enterprise setting, influence is closely related to competence. The greater the level of technical and behavioral competence, the greater the level of influence. Because of the large number of network and matrix relationships in an enterprise setting, power and politics have to be wielded in a subtle fashion, using different forms of influence. Here are the assumptions for effective influence management:

1. Most executives possess the basic experience and knowledge necessary to exercise influence management, yet they do not fully utilize that potential.

2. One of the easiest ways to influence others is to give them positive feedback, provided the feedback is timely, relevant, and sincere.

3. The art of listening, although an apparently passive stance, is a powerful technique for influencing others. It creates a bond that inevitably pays dividends in terms of relationships and goodwill.

4. The classic approach of "different strokes for different folks" continues to be valid when it comes to influencing other people.

This means customizing your behavior for individuals with differing characteristics so that each person gets a made-to-order treatment.

5. Interface management, or the building of bridges for communication and conciliating interests between company stakeholders, is a key activity in projectized organizations.

6. Multidirectional relationships between executives and key project players, involving vertical, horizontal, and diagonal communications, are the norm in organizations that are managed via projects.

7. Conflict management is part of the executive's job in any organization; in organizations managed by projects, the propensity for conflict is even greater because of the multiple relationships.

STRUCTURED STAKEHOLDER MANAGEMENT

The power, politics, and influence issues involved in managing multiple projects can be looked at using a structured format. A stakeholder management plan maps out a structured way to influence each player. The key word is *structured*, as opposed to using a purely intuitive approach. Although stakeholders have always been managed in some form, structured stakeholder management allows for comprehensive planning and staging of what needs to be done to influence the doers and opinion makers.

Dealing with stakeholders in a customized, needs-based manner boosts chances for smooth sailing in a project environment. Conversely, lack of a systematic slant on handling both the obvious decision makers and the behind-the-scenes opinion makers is an open invitation to disaster: sooner or later a disgruntled stakeholder will toss a curveball. At minimum, the fix for this situation is backtracking, rework, and the management of grief.

Who Are the Stakeholders, Anyhow?

The first manned moonshot in 1969 had lots of stakeholders, including the President of the U.S., Congress, the Soviets, the media, and of course NASA.

Certainly Neil Armstrong felt himself a major stakeholder in the *Apollo* project. Some people carry higher stakes than others, just as the pig's stake in a dish of ham and eggs is unquestionably greater than that of the chicken. Folklore has it that NASA astronauts added the words "and bring him safely back to Earth," to the original purported *Apollo* project objective: "Before the end of this decade, we will land a man on the moon." Here are some stakeholders who carry different stakes.

• *Project Champions.* The champions are responsible for the project's existence. They are those who initiate the movement and are ultimately interested in seeing the project get to its operational stage. They shape the way an organization perceives and manages its projects. These champions determine to what extent the company is prepared to manage multiple projects. Examples of those who champion the cause are investors, project sponsors, upper management overseers, clients (external or internal), and politicians (local, state, federal).

• *Project Participants.* This group performs the project work. From an enterprise project management standpoint, these stakeholders merit special care, since they are the ones who bring home the bacon. The role of the project team members is related to the project itself; they are usually not involved in the conceptual phases and likely will not follow into the operational phases. Some of these key players are project managers, team members, suppliers, contractors, specialists, regulatory agencies, and consultants.

• *External Stakeholders.* These parties, while theoretically uninvolved, may suffer from "project fallout." In other words, they are affected by the project as it unfolds, or by the final results of the project once it has been implemented. They also may influence the course of a project. Some of these external influences may not be manageable by the team assigned to a project; in such cases, support is required from elsewhere in the organization. Examples of external stakeholders are environmentalists, community leaders, social groups, the media (press, TV, etc.), and project team family members.

What Are the Steps to Stakeholder Management?

While intuition is important when dealing with stakeholders, a step-by-step overview is recommended to ensure that all issues are taken into consideration, as shown in Exhibit 6-1. The exhibit shows the suggested sequence of activities, as described below, aimed at ensuring stakeholders are properly dealt with.

1. *Identify and gather preliminary information about stakeholders.* Make a list of all who lay claim, in any form, to a share of the project's outcome. In the case of the project to implement enterprise project management, who are the champions, the project

Exhibit 6-1. Four-step approach to managing stakeholders.

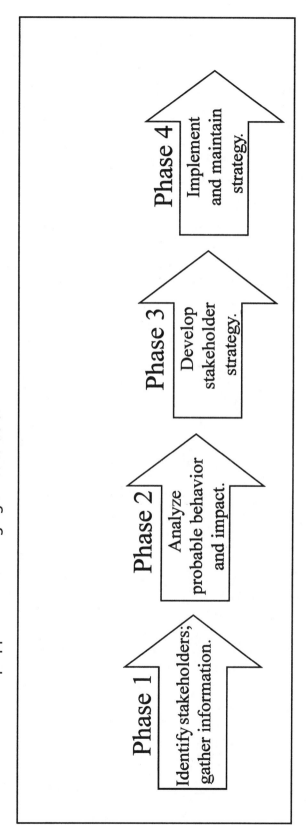

participants, and the external stakeholders? Remember that stakeholders must be identified as individuals—with names and faces—as opposed to departments or groups. Be sure to include the following information:

Names
Background
Role of the individual
Special circumstances
Past experiences

2. *Analyze each stakeholder's probable behavior and potential impact*. To what extent can stakeholders have an impact on a project? And to what extent can their behavior be influenced? Here is a simple way for classifying the stakeholders:

A = stakeholders who can be influenced strongly.
B = stakeholders who can be influenced moderately.
C = stakeholders who can be influenced very little.

Stakeholders can also be classified by their degree of impact on the project. For instance:

D = stakeholders who have a strong impact on the project.
E = stakeholders who have a medium impact on the project.
F = stakeholders who have a weak impact on the project.

3. *Develop stakeholder strategies*. Stakeholders are the way they are—except when they are different! Just as in team sports, it takes people with unique characteristics, each carrying out a differing role, to manage a project-oriented organization. Professional teams, whether football, basketball, soccer, or cricket, all have on-field and off-field players. The off-field players include owners, managers, promoters, coaches, athletes, and support groups. Organizations that manage by project have a similar cast, and all parties have to do their part for the organization's goals to be met. A plan needs to be developed to spell out how each stakeholder should be managed.

To understand how to handle stakeholders, ask yourself these questions:

1. What is the stakeholder's stated objectives or position regarding the project?
2. What is the likely hidden agenda?
3. What influences are exerted on the stakeholder?
4. Who is the best person to approach this stakeholder?

5. What tactics should be used?
6. What is the best timing?

The answers to these questions provide the input for developing a tailor-made approach for each project stakeholder.

4. *Implement and maintain the strategies.* This phase calls for carrying out activities planned in the previous stage, via a stakeholder management *implementation* plan. This plan pinpoints the specific actions, responsible parties, and the completion dates for the actions. Then that plan will be adjusted and reworked as needed. But to begin, the stakeholder strategies are implemented in accordance with the relative importance of the stakeholders. For instance, there would be major emphasis on a small number of stakeholders who have a strong impact, normal efforts toward an intermediate group, and moderate attention to stakeholders reckoned to have a lesser impact.

Influencing Stakeholders to Buy In: Not an Easy Task

A bank owned by a European automaker faced a stakeholder alignment challenge when several project management thrusts were taking place within the enterprise at the same time. The bank's Achilles' heel was a centralized credit approval project that was intended to speed up processing and eliminate bureaucracy at car dealerships, where credit applications were traditionally dealt with. The project was a source of major conflict between the information technology (IT) people, who were managing the effort, and upper management, who was exerting heavy-handed pressure to put the far-behind-schedule system in place. The head of training perceived a need for improved project performance and arranged for courses on the basics of project management. These courses did not take place, however, because the bank's quality group became convinced that the time was right to introduce a management-by-projects slant for running the organization—but they needed a go-ahead from upstairs to proceed. Upper management did not give the nod, as the executives were not attuned to the need for a strategic approach to handling projects. The IT people, who were competent technically, had little or no training in how to run projects. No one, at any level, had taken into account the fact that the new structure would substantially shrink the functions of dozens of people and would play topsy-turvy with the power balance within the bank. This situation is a classic portrait of unaligned stakeholders. Each had a different perception of what the problems were and what needed to be done.

Since the responsibility for stakeholder management lies with the party who has the greatest awareness of the need for enterprise project management, in the example of the bank, the quality group carried the burden of influencing stakeholders to rally around the management-by-projects philosophy. Once that commitment was received—and after an in-house "awareness talk" by a guest expert—the quality group began making headway toward changing the organization to a manage-by-projects format. This example illustrates the two principles given earlier: first, analyze who the stakeholders are and what their stakes are; and second, introduce your new approach to management in a way that is sensitive to the interests and concerns of all involved.

Promoting Project Management Among Company Stakeholders

Creating awareness is the first hurdle in developing any project to transform an organization. You have to get people's attention. They have to hear opportunity pounding at the door—an opportunity to spread the faster-cheaper-better logo across the organization, along with the tools to make it happen. Those persons could be upper management, middle management, or organizational change agents or internal facilitators. No matter, the procedure for getting people to sign on is much the same. Since participation is needed for anything to work, several articulated moves can spread the spirit of project management across the company.

Another view is the evolution theory to promote a cause. Tom Peters looks at the issue like this: "How do you 'sell' this concept 'up' to your bosses? Don't!" Instead, he says, the positive results obtained through project management should filter up through the system and do their own marketing. Third-party marketing, then, by way of the customer or internal client, is a way to let bosses know what a great job is being done via the diligent application of project management.

If Peters's approach sounds a bit simplistic, there are more pro-active ways to promote project management among corporate stakeholders. One way is to compare performance with other companies or participate in benchmarking groups to see what practices are prevalent and effective. Numbers are another way to go; showing the potential savings of project management will surely move even the most resistant corporate executive.

No Longer Holding the Beef

Successful stakeholder management calls for a structured approach to deal with the various parties who have vested interests in the project. This means that champions, participants, and external stakeholders need to be managed using steps outlined in an implementation plan. So stakeholder management comes into play in two distinct ways. First, to put an enterprise project management project in place, the stakeholders have to be managed during the implementation phase. Second, once the concept is put into place, company executives must ensure that the stakeholder concept is part of all the company projects.

PART II

PLAYING THE GAME

Principle
No. 7

A key role of executives, sponsors, and managers in enterprise project management is to ask the right questions at the right time during the project cycle.

7

CHAPTER

The Fine Art of Asking Questions: Tips for Executive Survival

Executives, whether they realize it or not, are program managers. Because of their positions, they are accountable for a number of interrelated projects, strategic and otherwise. Ultimately, the responsibility rests with them for herding the sundry projects to a final destination consistent with the organization's strategic goals. This means providing direction for the herd, making sure that maverick projects are roped in, and ensuring that the project cowhands are cared for and supported. To do this, they need to be "project savvy."

Most top executives make it upstairs through a career path other than project management. Production, finance, marketing, and operations are common springboards to the upper echelons. Any project management experience was probably the result of being the right person in the right place. Project management has even been called the accidental profession for that reason: project management career paths were nonexistent in most companies until recently.

Thus the journey to the top leaves some top managers void of project experience. For these otherwise competent executives, the lack of vision and experience with project management is bound to become a serious deficiency at some point. Executives with some experience but no formal training are also at a disadvantage. And even executives whose career path has passed through the trenches and classrooms of project management will find themselves with a liability if they don't keep up with new developments. This chapter provides tips for executive survival in this world of fast-paced project management. It is designed to jump-start the unexposed and to update the experienced on how to herd the project "dogies" along the trail to completion. Chapter 8 is also recommended for a brushup on the basics, as is Chapter 9, on education.

Looking Astute

Executives in the third millennium will face a peculiar challenge: they are ultimately responsible for the success or failure of projects, yet they rarely have the authority to command how those projects are done and in how much time. Although, theoretically, higher executives possess power, in our modern era that power is more closely related to skillful articulation and influence than it is to commands and obedience. Even in military settings, where superior authority is absolute, the laws of nature sometimes refute the power of command. For example, the command of a ship captain to change course is obeyed—not instantaneously, but many minutes later when the forward movement of the vessel is overcome by the power of its engines and steering mechanism. If nature resists authority even in command-and-obey settings, imagine the challenge when power is based on competence, political skills, and communications.

Yet even the uninitiated executive can appear astute by asking timely, intelligent questions. Of course, the partially experienced can also benefit from asking the right questions, as can veteran executives well versed in the practice of managing projects. You can never go wrong by asking the questions reporters use when they prepare stories: who? when? where? why? what? and how? These words are good to ask yourself and also to ask of project managers and project teams. They are effective questions during all phases of project management, yet each phase has issues that call for specific questions, too. The matrix shown in Exhibit 7-1 illustrates the right time for asking and the right slant for questions. This matrix is designed as an executive "crib sheet" to help formulate timely, incisive queries to project managers and teams at each project phase.

It is important that question-and-answer sessions have a "show and tell" format. In other words, all of the answers should be documented in report or graphic form and reviewed jointly. Below are ex-

Exhibit 7-1. Type of questions to ask along the project life cycle about given areas of project management.

Project Management Area	Pre-Project Feasibility, Approval	Phase I Conceptual: Design, Kickoff	Phase II Planning: Detailed Plans	Phase III Implementation Progress Reviews	Phase IV Final: Transition to Operations	Post-Project Assessment
Integration	CP	CP	CP	IP	WR	WR
Scope	CP	CP	CP	IP	WR	WR
Time	CP	CP	CP	IP	WR	WR
Cost	CP	CP	CP	IP	WR	WR
Quality	CP	CP	CP	IP	WR	WR
Communications	CP	CP	CP	IP	WR	WR
Human resources	CP	CP	CP	IP	WR	WR
Supply contracts	CP	CP	CP	IP	WR	WR
Risk	CP	CP	CP	IP	WR	WR

CP: Conceptual and planning questions.
IP: Implementation and progress questions.
WR: Wrapup and review questions.

amples of questions senior executives need to ask the project team during each of the project phases. Additional questions can be drawn from the organization's own project methodology and from the literature on project management and professional organizations.

Pre-Project Phase

1. Does the project meet company standards in terms of profitability or return on investment?
2. Is it congruent with the organization's strategic plans?
3. Are resources available to carry out the project?
4. Are the premises and numbers used in the feasibility study valid?

Concept Phase

1. Is there a project charter that defines the project mission and primary objectives?
2. Is the overall scope of the project clearly defined?
3. Is all information for the project to proceed available and organized?
4. Have the design assumptions been validated?
5. Have the client requirements been formally confirmed?
6. Has a macro risk assessment been carried out?
7. Are key stakeholders involved?
8. How about the project manager? Does he need more support? Or on-the-job training? Or could she use additional guidance during a given phase?
9. Has a formal project kickoff been planned? What format is planned—meeting? workshop?

Planning Phase

1. Has a quality assurance plan been developed?
2. Are project management and implementation strategies and methodologies in place?
3. Have project risks been identified, quantified, and risk responses identified?
4. Are systems for document management, activity scheduling and tracking, procurement management, estimating, budgeting, and cost control in place?
5. Have the systems been debugged and is the staff competent at operating them?
6. Has an overall, technically oriented detailed project plan been developed (what is to be done on the project and how will the work be performed)?

7. Has a project management plan been developed (how will the project be managed)?
8. Is there a stakeholder management plan?
9. Have statements of work (SOWs) been written for the work packages?
10. Has the project communications plan been developed?
11. Have the meeting and reporting criteria been developed?

Implementation Phase

1. Are regular tracking meetings taking place?
2. Is change management being formally managed?
3. Is decision making pro-active and solution-oriented?

Final Phase

1. Have project closeout procedures been developed and are they in place?
2. Has a transition plan (from project completion to operation phase) been prepared and is it being followed?

Post-Project Phase

1. What was done right on the project and what needs improvement on the next one?
2. How did the project size up with comparable projects within or outside the company?
3. What lessons learned need to be shared with others in the company?
4. How can project results be used for marketing and promotional purposes?

QUESTIONS FROM THE PROJECT MANAGEMENT BODY OF KNOWLEDGE

An alternative approach is to ask questions stemming from the body of knowledge. Key questions are selected from each of the areas, for asking at approval time or upon review during the project. The following is a list of sample questions using a body-of-knowledge logic at points during the project when executive involvement is critical: at the beginning at project kickoff (k) and throughout the project during periodic reviews (r).

Integration

1. Do project charter and detailed project plans reflect the work that needs to be performed? (k)
2. Are the project plans being tracked (actuals versus estimated) and are all changes being registered and monitored? (r)

Scope

1. Is there an agreed-to project scope statement, work breakdown structure, and scope change procedure? (k)
2. Have all scope changes been reviewed, and are the lowest-level activities of the project breakdown structure fully detailed? (r)

Time

1. Is there a master schedule that outlines deliverables and milestones for the project? (k)
2. Is the schedule up-to-date, showing actual progress versus scheduled progress, and are appropriate efforts being made to manage the critical-path items? (r)

Cost

1. Are all the assumptions documented for costing and estimating and is the preliminary project budget based on a resource plan? (k)
2. Is there an updated cost report that flags potential overruns and distinguishes between in-scope and out-of-scope work? (r)

Quality

1. Has the project documentation been reviewed by the project team and the customer and has agreement been reached regarding quality standards? (k)
2. Are periodic project reviews being held and are quality issues being dealt with in terms of technical quality and customer satisfaction? (r)

Communications

1. Has a project communications plan been developed outlining how information is to be managed during the project? (k)

2. Is information flowing in accordance with the communications plan? What present project challenges are attributable to communications problems? (r)

Human Resources

1. Have a project mobilization chart and a team-member responsibility matrix been developed, and have provisions been made for building a productive team? (k)
2. How is the team performing with reference to expectations? What is needed to improve performance from a human resources standpoint? (r)

Supply, Contracts

1. Has a contracting plan been developed that defines the scope and basic conditions for all third-party furnished items? (k)
2. Have changes been made to the original scope contracted? Are they documented? What other changes may happen? (r)

Risk

1. Has a risk plan been developed that identifies, quantifies, and foresees a feasible response to probable risks? (r)
2. What changes have come about that affect the risks as originally assessed? How are risks being controlled? (r)

SHORT AND SWEET: A THUMBNAIL GUIDE TO PROJECT MANAGEMENT

Asking questions ensures that executives focus on the critical project issues. Yet questions alone aren't sufficient to ensure that projects are successful. Some basic building blocks have to be in place to ensure a happy ending. For the busy executive, here's a thumbnail guide for making sure projects are done right. If these five executive actions are taken, probability for success is greatly boosted.

1. *Ensure strong executive sponsorship.* Executive sponsorship means the ultimate caring and nurturing of the project from a strategic standpoint: making sure that the foundations for managing the project are in place. It also involves ongoing strategic alignment of the project with the organization's overarching business objectives, as outlined in Chapter 3.

2. *Staff the project with the right manager and team.* If the project is staffed right, most matters will take care of themselves. A seasoned project manager is aware of the broad project issues that need to be dealt with.

3. *Champion the cause for project team alignment.* Team building takes place through inspired leadership, kickoff workshops, planning sessions, team integration programs, and on-the-job training.

4. *Make sure that project management methodology and support are in place.* For the core project team to work effectively, the team members need a methodology coherent with the company culture and with the project's needs, and they require support personnel to look to for help in project scheduling and project administration.

5. *Ask questions.* Ask the right ones, at the right time. EDS, the giant, Texas-based information-technology consulting company, has institutionalized the question-asking process. The company has a listing of suggested questions for executives to ask at project approval time and during project reviews.

PROMOTING ENTERPRISE PROJECT MANAGEMENT

For the executive looking to champion the cause of enterprise project management in the company, following the format of questions and suggestions given above is a good start. After all, setting the right executive example goes a long way toward creating a projectized culture. Executive involvement, through skillful articulation and intelligent questioning, sets the tone for a strong project management culture.

To make the cultural shift to enterprise project management, however, it takes a lot more than articulation and intelligent questioning. Managing an organization by projects calls for a substantial cultural shift, as discussed in Chapter 5. A full-fledged trans-formation project needs to be carried out for a management-by-projects mind-set to develop.

Overall Sponsorship: A Key Responsibility for Executives

Although project sponsors are formally assigned to specific projects, as detailed in Chapter 2, in a broader sense all company executives are project sponsors, no matter what their formal relationship is to given projects. Successful projects are in the interest of the company, and thus all projects deserve support, aid, and guidance. This general sponsorship role is akin to that of executive facilitation, in which the role of executives is to clear away roadblocks and generally facilitate the work of others.

American Express is an organization that takes upper-level project support seriously. "If your project fails, our company fails," is the way American Express executives perceive their accomplice-like relationship with project managers. That relationship is bolstered by a "We will not let you fail" posture, according to Kathy Mayer, vice president for advertising and interactive business development. Roles of senior management at American Express, according to Mayer, include (1) communicate the project need clearly in the context of strategic direction; (2) ensure full alignment across functional lines; (3) ensure access and senior management accountability to the project team; and (4) underwrite success of all strategic initiatives. Strong involvement in project work is clearly a part of the job profile for American Express executives. As Mayer puts it, "Senior managers won't be senior managers much longer if they don't get up to par on managing projects."

Setting the Shining Example

If executives want their project people to upgrade themselves on the practice of project management, then they need to show the way. At AT&T and Lucent Technologies, hundreds of executives and professionals are certified as project management professionals. This program was spearheaded initially by Dan Ono, now of Lucent Technologies, who influenced AT&T management at the time to invest heavily in the program. (Formal certification is a heavily weighted factor for promotion at AT&T, as it is at Lucent Technologies. Project management professionals at both AT&T and Lucent number in the hundreds.) There are fringe benefits for executives who take professional certification exams. The first is the expanding knowledge. And increased managerial productivity comes as a natural outcome of this augmented learning. A final bonus is greater employability, meaning higher worth to the corporation and in the marketplace.

A SELF-EXAMINATION FOR EXECUTIVES

Aside from aiming questions at other project players, executives need to target themselves with a few reflective queries. If you are an executive or are aspiring to be one, here's a checklist that will help you size yourself up with regard to how you stand in terms of supporting, aiding, and guiding the projects under your control.

What You Know and Have Done

1. On a scale of 1 to 10, where would you place your knowledge of basic project management concepts? (See Chapter 8 for a summary.)
2. Have you ever formally managed a project, with title of project manager or equivalent?
3. Have you developed a project charter?
4. Do you know how to develop a work breakdown structure? A precedence diagram?
5. Do you know how to plan a project kickoff meeting?
6. Have you acted formally as a project sponsor?
7. Have you had formal training in project management?
8. Have you been instrumental in articulating team-building programs for a project?

If you place yourself below a 6 in terms of project management knowledge, and if the noes outnumber the yeses on the remaining questions, it is clearly time to bring yourself up-to-date on the theory and practice of project management. To do so, solid commitment is required. Here is a list of questions that will help you evaluate your degree of commitment to improve:

1. What degree of improvement in project management would you like to achieve? Describe.
2. What do you need to do to improve? Make a list.
3. How much time do you wish to take to reach the level of knowledge and competence desired?
4. How will you measure your progress and your level of achievement?
5. Who will be your mentor to support you in carrying out your commitment?

JUMP-STARTING YOUR CONTINUING EDUCATION

If you aren't fully up to speed in the art and science of project management, that should come as no surprise since many managers and executives climbed a "non-project" career ladder. So being below par on the subject is no reason to despair—provided, of course, you make a firm commitment to learn the basics of project management and realize the role of senior executives in making this a powerful tool for attaining company goals.

For an executive, being below optimum speed in the management of projects is akin to not knowing how to use a personal computer. In both cases, it is possible to survive in the business world, but the odds are increasingly against it. For those who are just getting in touch with the subject, a quick read of this book and mastering the art of asking astute questions will provide a jump-start toward achieving a new level of effectiveness through the application of project management.

Principle
No. 8

Making organizations effective in the management and support of multiple, fast-tracking projects requires top executives and managers who know the basics of managing stand-alone projects.

CHAPTER

Project Management, Elephants, and the NBA

The job of project management can be viewed from different angles. The variations are subtle though substantial: if we assume that everything related to projects is part of one great "project management thing," there is an analogy to the story of the elephant and the three blind men. Three blind men were led up to an elephant and asked to name what the object was. The first felt along the flank of the giant beast and said, "This is a wall." The next man grabbed the trunk and proclaimed, "This is a pipe." The third took hold of the tail and cried, "This is a snake." Each conceived a mind-picture of something that was, in fact, much bigger than his individual perception.

The burgeoning field of project management, too, spans a broader spectrum than most people perceive. Applications include anything that starts, develops, and ends. In spite of this broad range of project types, the finite nature of a project is the common thread that binds them. And this finite life is what makes a common project management approach feasible for all types of projects. Although multiple projects are the main thrust of this book, each project must adhere to the basics of stand-alone project management to end successfully.

Managing multiple projects within an organization, under any of the names given in Chapter 2, amounts to eternally competing for the NBA championship, where each game is a battle for the lead. It is a concentrated effort that depends on a combination of small, individual successes to accomplish its goal: each project has to be completed on time, within budget, and to the client's satisfaction. For that to happen, the players need to master the basics; they need to know how to manage projects one by one. Just as dribbling, shooting jump shots, making lay-ups, and playing defense are basketball basics, project management fundamentals such as stakeholder management, general project alignment, and project offices are elements of managing multiple projects.

Managing a single project is akin to playing a basketball game. The action is dynamic, challenging, stressful, and exciting—and the objective is to win. In both cases, winning depends on the team's mastery of the fundamentals. Not even the most brilliant strategy can succeed if the players lack basic skills. What follows here is an overview of what company players need to know to manage a project successfully. If you are well versed in managing projects, skip the rest of this chapter. But if you need to brush up on the basics, or want to confirm your understanding, read on.

PROJECT MANAGEMENT 101

A project is a temporary endeavor undertaken to create a unique product or service, according to the Project Management Institute's *Guide to the Project Management Body of Knowledge*. Project management is the application of knowledge, skills, tools, and techniques to project activities in order to meet or exceed stakeholder needs and expectations. Note that this definition refers to single-project management.

Projects are carried out during a given time frame, known as the project life cycle. Since projects, like people, are finite by definition, they are designed to be born and to be buried. Projects also live a life and go through distinct phases during that lifetime. An example of a life cycle is given in Exhibit 8-1.

A Model for Viewing Project Management

In the early 1990s, *life-cycle project management* was the model used for explaining what managing projects was all about. By the mid-1990s, the body-of-knowledge approach was introduced to workshops and seminars on project management practice, largely owing to the popularity of the *Guide to the Project Management Body of Knowledge* (PMBOK) published by the Project Management Institute.

Exhibit 8-1. Example of a project life cycle.

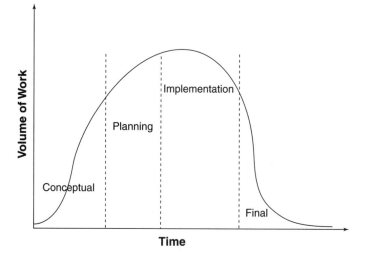

The PMBOK model breaks down into the project management framework, core project management areas, auxiliary areas, and integrative processes. In this summary, the PMBOK *Guide* is the basic reference.

People are both the cause of and are affected by everything that happens on a project. Anyone who is positively or negatively affected by a project is called *a stakeholder*. Stakeholders include external parties such as customers or end users of the project's product and vendors who supply pieces of the project, while internal stakeholders are parties such as project team members and various functional departments whose work may be affected by or linked to the project. (This topic is covered in detail in Chapter 6.)

Developing the right organization for projects depends on company culture, the size and priority of projects, past experience, and stakeholder opinions. The classic organization forms are as follows:

• *Functional Organization or Hierarchy.* These organizations are organized by a geographic, product, or specialty logic and obey formal communications channels that are controlled by functional managers. Project managers are virtually nonexistent or operate as coordinators from a weak power base.

• *Matrix or Cross-Functional Organization.* The matrix structure maximizes the potential for allocating human resources by assigning people to multiple projects, when feasible, and by providing separate managerial and technical oversight for each project. In this setting, functional managers and project managers share the organizational power.

- *Task Force or Project Organization.* This organization is like a separate unit that operates relatively independently of the company. The project manager receives a mandate and is supreme in making the necessary decisions.

Aside from needing project-specific skills, running a project calls for general management attributes such as leadership, problem-solving capability, and influence management. Finance, team-building, production, self-management, strategic, and operational planning and marketing skills are other competencies required. In other words, the more management skills the players have—both project-specific and general—the greater the probability for completing successful projects.

Sociological and economic trends also affect project destiny. These include standards and regulations, globalization, and cultural influences. If a given project is set in a context sensitive to any of these influences, specific attention needs to be focused on the influencing factor; otherwise well-intentioned management efforts may be derailed.

THE BASIC PIECES OF THE PROJECT PUZZLE

The essence of project management used to be represented by a triangle, depicting the need to manage time, cost, and quality, as shown in Exhibit 8-2. These core areas have been expanded into a square, as scope management has taken on a spot of its own because scope is so tightly related to the other three topics. Scope-time-cost-quality are the areas essential to perform the ABCs of project management, as depicted in Exhibit 8-3.

Project Scope Management

Managing *scope* means defining and controlling what is or is not included in the project and in the respective work packages necessary to complete the project. Scope management consists of the following:

- *Initiation.* Define basic assumptions and constraints, assign project manager, establish project charter.
- *Scope Planning.* Develop overall project scope statement and a plan for managing scope throughout the project.
- *Scope Definition.* Develop a project breakdown structure (PBS), identifying the work packages necessary to carry out the project, as shown in Exhibit 8-4.

(text continues on page 120)

Exhibit 8-2. The classic triad of project management.

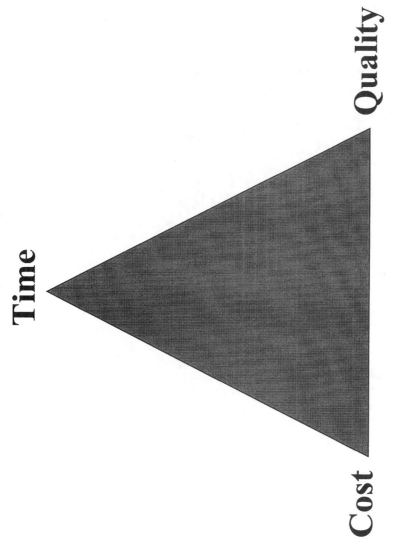

Exhibit 8-3. Scope management is integrally related to time, cost, and quality.

Time **Scope**

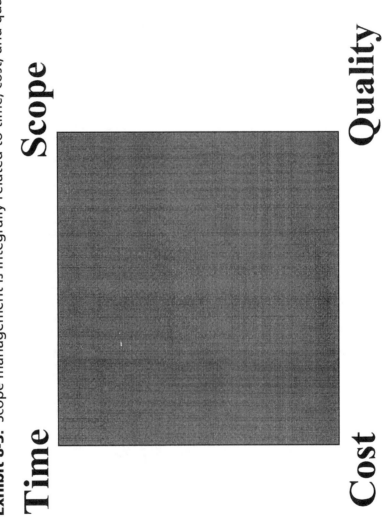

Cost **Quality**

Exhibit 8-4. Sample project breakdown structure.

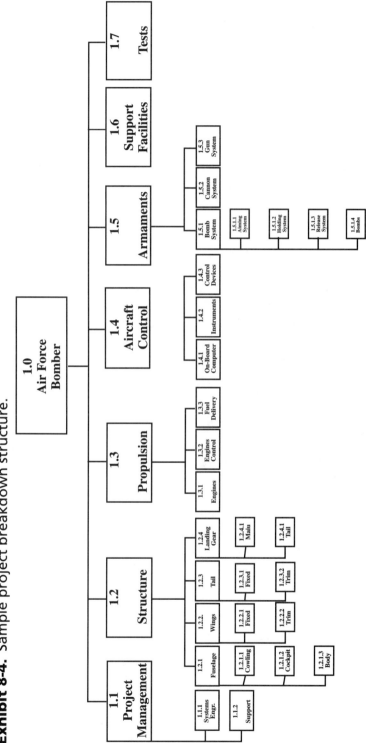

- *Scope Verification*. Formally attest, by client or user, that the work scope has been performed.
- *Scope Change Control*. Documentation of scope changes, corrective actions, and lessons learned for future projects.

Managing scope means defining and controlling what is or is not included in the project and in the respective work packages necessary to complete the project.

Project scope management is the foundation for the other core project management skills. Once the overall project scope is defined and translated into work packages via the work breakdown structure, then time, cost, and quality can be managed from a common, solid base.

Project Time Management

The focus of project time management is to ensure the timely completion of the project. It starts from the data generated in the scope management phase and comprises these activities:

- *Activity Definition*. Refine work breakdown structure and make auxiliary lists of all activities to be performed.
- *Activity Sequencing*. Put activities into a logical sequence using precedence diagramming method (PDM, also sometimes referred to as PERT or CPM). These networks map the logical flow of activities and show parallel paths for simultaneous work. See Exhibits 8-5 and 8-6.
- *Activity Duration Estimating*. Define a time duration for each activity, based on a realistic estimate, preferably using historical data as a reference.
- *Schedule Development*. Establish project schedule (normally in bar chart form, using appropriate project management control software), along with criteria for managing the schedule itself and updates on resource allocation that might affect the schedule.
- *Schedule Control*. Perform periodic updates and take corrective actions.

Exhibit 8-5 shows the precedence diagram method, PDM (also sometimes referred to as PERT or CPM) used to put activities into a logical sequence.

Exhibit 8-6 shows a precedence diagram for a construction project, mapping the logical flow of activities, and shows parallel paths for simultaneous work.

Exhibit 8-5. PDM: precedence diagram method.

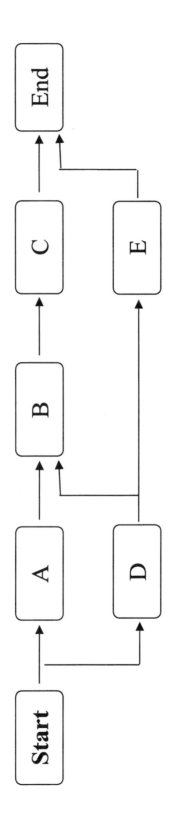

 = **Activity**

Exhibit 8-6. Simplified PDM network for construction project.

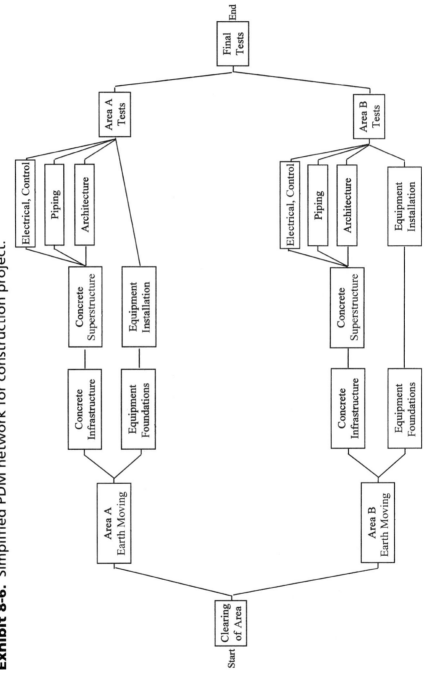

Project time management is so basic to the concept of project management that the terms are sometimes thought to be synonymous, just as schedule control software may be seen as being more than just a piece of the overall management effort. In fact, managing time on a project is one of the most important duties. Yet no area stands alone in project management. There are other areas that interface and influence what goes on in the schedule.

Project Cost Management

The primary focus of cost management on projects is on the cost of resources needed to complete project activities. This includes tasks such as planning, estimating, budgeting, and control. Cost data are reported in the graphic form such as shown in Exhibit 8-7. Here is what the cost-related tasks involve:

- *Resource Planning.* Identify and formalize resource requirements (monetary, human, material, equipment, intellectual) for the project work packages.
- *Cost Estimating.* Translate resource requirements into estimated costs for each work package, and establish a cost management plan.
- *Cost Budgeting.* Establish a baseline budget based on the estimates.
- *Cost Control.* Publish periodic cost variance reports, update estimates and budgets, take corrective action.

Exhibit 8-7. Earned value performance report.

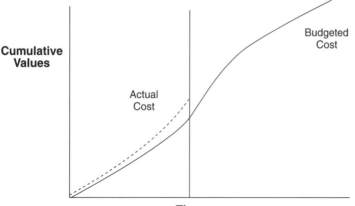

Cost management for projects is sometimes done on an integrated company-wide basis but is also performed on a just-for-project basis. The nature of the project and the degree of maturity of the organization with respect to project management are strong influencing factors.

Project Quality Management

The concept of quality in project management ranges from the conventional "compliance to specifications" to the disconcerting "satisfaction of the stakeholders after project completion." Part of quality management is to define this concept of quality as it applies to the project at hand, and to carry out the activities of planning, quality assurance, and control necessary to make sure the standards of quality are met. Standard techniques such as cause-and-effect diagrams (Exhibit 8-8) and flowcharts (Exhibit 8-9) are used in managing quality on projects.

- *Quality Planning.* Define a quality management plan with appropriate definitions. Elaborate checklists and criteria.
- *Quality Assurance.* Examine and improve processes through quality audits and other initiatives such that quality will be improved.
- *Quality Control.* Inspect results and apply quality tools and techniques, make acceptance decisions, and monitor rework.

The International Standard ISO 10006 *Quality Management: Guidelines to Quality in Project Management* takes the view that everything that has to be managed on a project is quality. Paradoxically, the topic quality is not covered in the ISO guidelines, exactly because of that premise. It does cover, however, the other main topics given in the PMBOK *Guide*.

OTHER STUFF THAT NEEDS MANAGING: AUXILIARY AREAS

In theory, well-managed scope, time, cost, and schedule factors should make for a smashingly successful project. Yet it takes much more to bring a project to a triumphant conclusion. There are auxiliary areas that strongly affect a project, such as human resources management, communications management, risk management, and procurement management, as illustrated in Exhibit 8-10.

(text continues on page 128)

Exhibit 8-8. Cause-and-effect diagram.

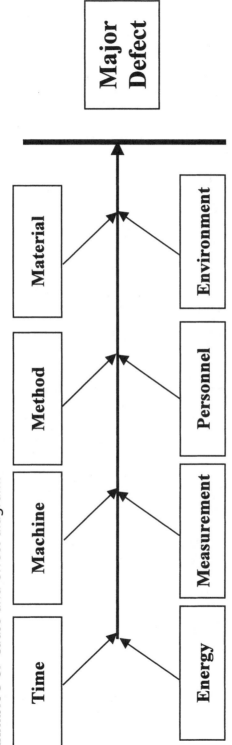

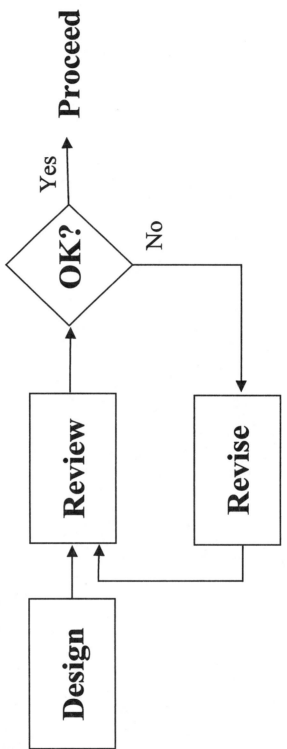

Exhibit 8-9. Sample process flowchart.

Exhibit 8-10. Auxiliary areas of project management.

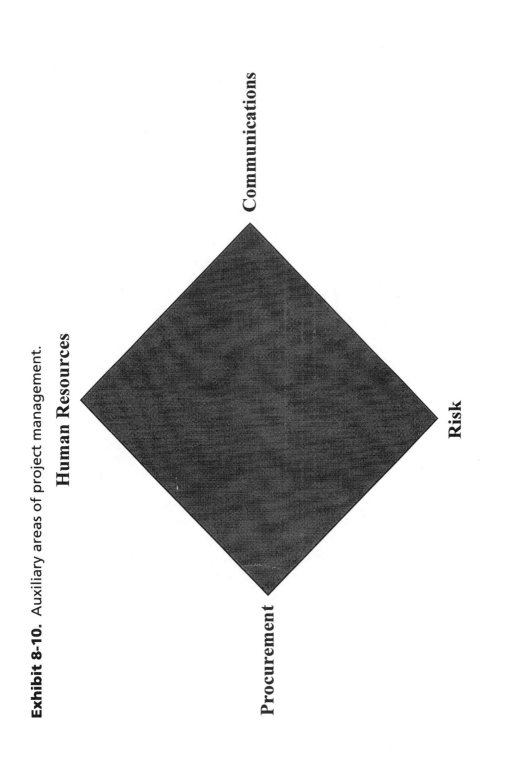

Human Resources

Communications

Risk

Procurement

Project Human Resources Management

Projects happen because people make them happen. So whatever is done right regarding the people side of projects will boost the project itself. The activity-responsibility matrix (Exhibit 8-11) and the resource histogram (Exhibit 8-12) are two techniques used in human resources management. Here are the pieces of the people side of project management:

- *Organizational Planning.* Elaborate staffing plan, fix roles and responsibilities, and define working relationships
- *Staff Acquisition.* Formalize and communicate assignments.
- *Team Development.* Improve performance through team building, training, recognition, and reward systems.

People are the organizers, planners, workers, articulators, and controllers of all project activities. People are the true basic resource that makes everything else happen.

Project Communications Management

Communications on projects involves the timely generation, collection, distribution, storage, and ultimate disposition of project information. *Communication* implies the exchange of information that is of use to people to carry out the work effectively. Here are the processes necessary to manage project communications:

- *Planning.* Develop a communications plan based on a stakeholders' needs analysis—who needs what, for what reason, when, and in what form.
- *Information Distribution.* Dissemination of the planned communications via an appropriate information distribution system.
- *Performance Reporting.* Publish performance reports (time, cost, productivity, etc.) and change requests.
- *Administrative Closure.* Obtain formal acceptance, determine document and data destination, bureaucratic closure.

Other general techniques are also necessary for effective communications to permeate a project. Subjects like communications barriers, transmission effectiveness, listening skills, choice of communications channels, meeting management, form of presentation, writing style, and the like have a major impact on the success of a project. (Communications is presented in more detail in Chapter 13.)

Exhibit 8-11. Activity-responsibility matrix.

Activity \ Responsible Party	A	B	C	D	E	F	...
Requirements	S	R	A	P	P		
Functional Analysis	S		A	P		P	
Design	S		R	A	I		P
Development			S	A		P	P
Testing			S	P	I	A	P

P = Participant   A = Accountable   R = Review   I = Input   S = Approval required

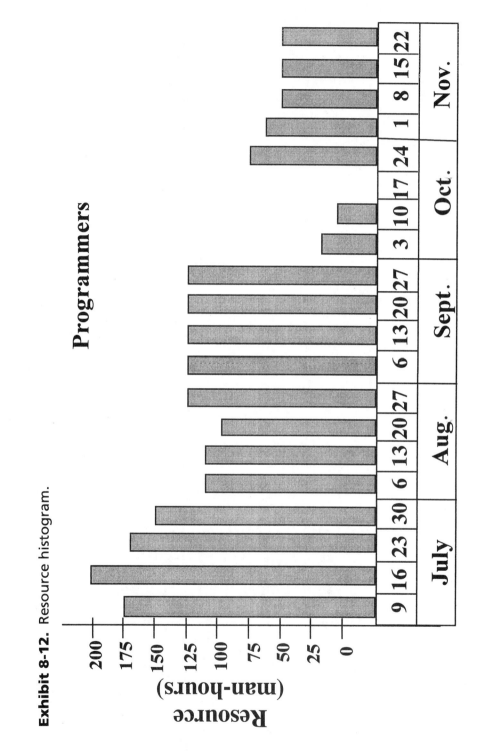

Exhibit 8-12. Resource histogram.

Project Risk Management

Risk management on projects encompasses identifying, analyzing, and responding to risk. Risk permeates the other knowledge areas of project management and tends to repeat itself through the various chronological phases. (This topic was dealt with in Chapter 3.) Here are the risk-related processes for managing projects:

- *Risk Identification.* Identify sources and symptoms of risk, as well as potentially risky events or occurrences.
- *Risk Quantification.* Evaluate opportunities versus threats, using judgment or risk-assessing tools.
- *Risk Response Development.* Prepare a risk management plan, including contingency plans and allowance for reserves.
- *Risk Response Control.* Take corrective action and update the risk management plan.

The type of project strongly affects the need to invest time and energy in risk management. A construction venture may have relatively predictable accident and foul weather probabilities available, whereas a cutting-edge software initiative may face the uncertainties of local competition and the swings of the global economy. Analytical techniques such as the decision tree shown in Exhibit 8-13 are used in managing risk. Risk management on projects encompasses identifying, analyzing, and responding to risk. Risk permeates the other knowledge areas of project management and tends to repeat itself throughout the various chronological phases.

Project Procurement Management

Procurement management involves, initially, identifying which project needs can be best met by buying services or products outside the project organization. It also encompasses issues of how, what, how much, when, from whom, and where to procure. Exhibit 8-14 summarizes procurement management, and here are the processes involved:

- *Procurement Planning.* Prepare a procurement management plan, defining what is to be procured, and define the scope of work for each item to be procured.
- *Solicitation Planning.* Elaborate procurement document, establish evaluation criteria, and update statements of work.

Exhibit 8-13. Decision tree approach to risk management.

Decision Tree: Diagram of Possible Acts, Events, and Outcomes

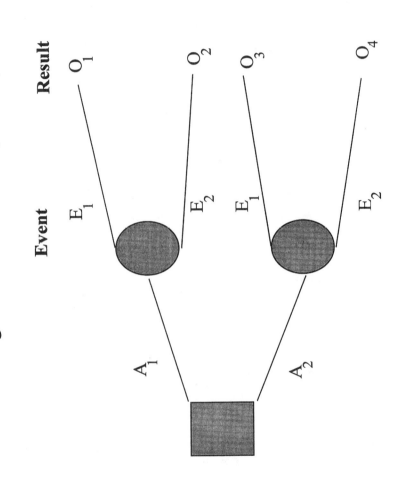

Exhibit 8-14. Procurement management.

Planning	Sourcing	Managing
• Procurement planning (what and when) • Solicitation planning (procurement packages, market survey)	• Solicitation (bids, proposals, offers) • Decision (select supplier)	• Contract kickoff (initial actions, meeting) • Contract administration • Close-out (technical and administrative close-out)

- *Procurement Sourcing.* Obtain proposals for the work scope defined, choose the winning bidder, and enter into contractual agreement.
- *Procurement Managing.* Initiate actions, maintain communications, monitor changes, approve payments, and close out contracts.

On many projects, virtually all the work is performed by third parties. Therefore, the success or failure of a given project is directly proportional to the effectiveness of the project procurement management.

The basics of project management, therefore, consist of eight areas, all of which have to be managed to make things work. A slipup in one area is enough to have a domino effect that can affect other areas. For instance, a communication glitch in the procurement cycle might set off an unscheduled time delay, which then affects quality and results in a cost overrun. This may put the project at risk and have a strong impact on human resources.

PUTTING IT TOGETHER AND KEEPING IT THAT WAY

For all the activities described above to contribute to overall project success, they must be integrated, as symbolized in Exhibit 8-15. Project management integration involves the coordination of the various project elements, including the necessary trade-offs among competing objectives and alternatives in order to meet stakeholder expectations.

Integration efforts are required in three basic areas:

- *Project Plan Development.* Prepare an integrated overall project plan using input from all the other knowledge areas.
- *Project Plan Execution.* Coordinate project activities using general and project management techniques supported by the project management systems applicable to the project in question.

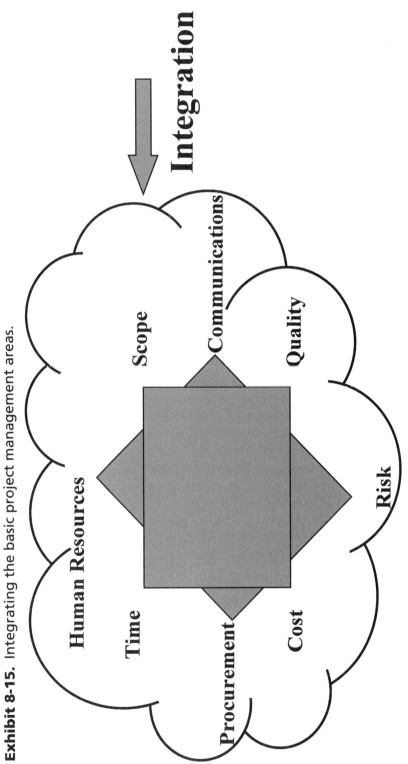

Exhibit 8-15. Integrating the basic project management areas.

- *Overall Change Control.* Document changes, update project plans, and take corrective action, as indicated in Exhibit 8-16. Change control is an important element of managing project scope.

KEEP ON DRIBBLING

The field of project management encompasses a broad spectrum of projects, from the small and plentiful to the highly complex and concentrated. Indeed, the nature of the project may vary from research and development in North Carolina's Research Triangle to the architectural design of New York skyscrapers to World Bank

Exhibit 8-16. Coordinating changes across projects.

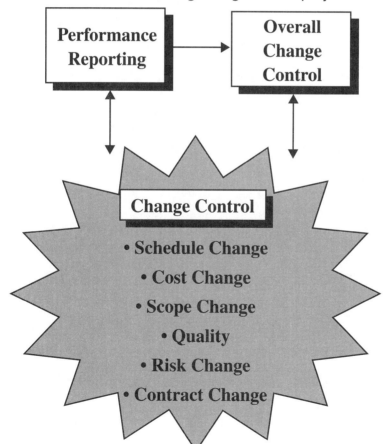

projects in Africa. In spite of this, project theory and practice are generally applicable across this wide range of projects.

For multiple project management to work, company players have to know the basic game: how to manage projects one by one. Just as basketball basics have to be mastered by the players, project management fundamentals are the fundamentals for success in managing projects across the organization. Once the basics are mastered, then the team can accelerate its move toward spreading the project mind-set through the organization.

Principle
No. 9

Extensive education, training, and modeling of proper project practices throughout the organization are needed to make enterprise project management work.

CHAPTER

Project Management, Education, and Quackery

How many practicing engineers haven't studied engineering? Or chemists haven't studied chemistry? And what about accountants? Or real estate agents? And medical doctors? Theoretically, there aren't any who haven't studied their professions. And those who do practice without educational credentials are labeled quacks, amateurs, or professional outlaws.

What about project managers? How many of them are practicing the profession without having studied it? Certainly tens of thousands manage projects although they haven't cracked a book on the basics of the profession. Does that make any sense? Is there any justification for it?

There are indeed historical reasons. For one, project management has been perceived as a profession only since the beginning of the 1990s, when professional organizations identified the "body of knowledge" necessary to practice the profession and established the criteria for competence in project management. Even today many project managers aren't aware they practice a profession that has a huge body of knowledge associated with it.

Another justification for "undereducation" on the subject is that project management is practiced in conjunction with other professions—engineering, architecture, computer science, research and development, environmental sciences, and business administration. Studying a second profession perhaps doesn't excite many project managers, particularly since they may be up to their elbows in alligators back at the office or project site.

Certainly those project managers who lack a formal education in the profession are not quacks, as would be the case if they were practicing medicine. Some of these project managers, as a matter of fact, display world-class competence. They have come up through the ranks, graduated from the school of hard knocks, and used their superior intuitive, technical, and leadership skills to manage projects within budget, on time, and to quality specifications. The large number of practitioners still outside the formal professional ranks is justified by the youth of the profession and the relative newness of standards for the field. Yet as time goes on, the pressure to become formally educated and qualified will surely increase.

EDUCATION IS THE ANSWER

The obvious solution for organizations that have a vested interest in the subject is to get programs under way to educate people in project management. As the number of formally trained professionals increases, the overall ability of companies to deal with projects will naturally grow. In this initial phase, however, no sophisticated testing of knowledge or competence is proposed. The idea is simply to expose people to the concepts with information that is relevant and useful. Here are the areas of project management training that need to be developed and delivered:

1. *Fundamentals.* Seminars involving the ABCs of managing projects, including the project life cycle and project management body of knowledge areas, are an initial step. Other basic seminars target softer management skills and hands-on use of project management tools.

2. *Interactive Programs.* Intended for intact teams and merged groups, these programs involve integration concepts for project players and key stakeholders, as well as high-impact events such as kickoff workshops.

3. *Discipline-Specific Issues.* Custom-fitted courses are offered for audiences that deal with specialties, such as construction, software development, systems integration, and research and development. The customizing involves using detailed case studies, examples, jargon of the trade, and an instructor who knows both project management and the disciplines involved.

Aside from being educated in project management as such, those who operate in a project environment are expected to be knowledgeable in two other major areas:

4. *General Management Concepts.* Topics of general application include principles of business, organizational development, marketing, negotiation techniques, behavioral psychology, planning, and operations.

5. *Specific Technical Knowledge.* More than passing familiarity in the dominant project discipline, such as systems development, is required, including knowledge of systems development methodologies, programming techniques, principles of systems design, and productivity standards.

If knowledge in these latter two areas is lacking, then the project management education program should also address them. For instance, if financial management is particularly relevant for managing projects in a given setting, then course work in that area is essential.

So there's a wide range of subject matter to be addressed in project management education. All of these topics are not essential for every situation, of course; employees don't need to be exposed to course work that doesn't apply to their projects. On the other hand, some people will need to delve deeply into some subjects. To size up who needs to study what, you need to assess your public for the project management training program. Here are the groups of people who most likely need training in project management:

• *Project Managers and Key Project Personnel.* These are the players who make it happen. They are like the captain and team members of a soccer team: they're on the field and charged with producing results, while the spectators watch, cheer, or bewail. These project team members are the most important targets for the education program.

• *Directors and Top-Level Executives.* These are like the owners and head executives of the soccer franchise. Although they don't play ball or score any goals, they are ultimately responsible for everything, so they need to know the game and everything that makes it work. The same holds true of organization directors, who need to know how to support project management.

• *Program Managers or Other "Managers of Project Managers."* This group corresponds to the coaching staff. Ideally, they played the game in the past and excelled at it. But they need to know the fundamentals so they can supervise, coach, motivate, induce, or even coerce the team into doing what's needed to win. These managers in a business setting hold the same importance as the coach in the sports setting.

• *Partners, Clients, and Key Vendors.* This group corresponds to stadium owners, fans, and equipment suppliers. They need to have a keen awareness of the game and it is in the franchise's interest that they be fully integrated into the program. Partners, clients, and key vendors need to be educated in project management methodologies and strategies.

• *Functional Managers and Support Personnel.* These are the specialists who take care of medical services, physical conditioning, physical therapy, and logistics. Their expertise is basic, and they must be schooled both in their respective specialties and in how they relate to the game. In the business organization, the relationship of specialists to the implementation of projects is similar.

Exhibit 9-1 shows the type of educational programs suggested for increasing project management performance in an organization. The matrix clearly shows the need to customize and to aim specific education to given target audiences. The greater the degree of relevance perceived by those receiving the education, the greater the impact that education will have on the organization.

How to Set Up the Program

To do any good for the organization, educational efforts need to match what the company wants to accomplish. Thus, linkage with overarching strategic plans is a major factor in the success of the program. This means treating the training initiatives like any other project and setting up the activities as you would develop a project in any other field. At some point, of course, the project may become an ongoing program and no longer have the characteristics of a project. But your initial efforts to conceptualize the course of training and get it up and running follow the project management process. Here is a checklist for planning a project management educational project:

1. *Gather information.* Benchmark with other organizations. Do a literature search. Discover what's going on in your organization in terms of project management. Map the methodologies and tools in use—learn why things are being done as they are. Survey

Exhibit 9-1. Educational programs in project management and respective target audiences.

Educational Program (days)	Project Managers, Key Project Personnel	Directors, Top Management	Program Managers	Partners, Clients, Key Vendors	Functional Managers and Support	Intact Teams
1. Fundamentals						
Project management Basics (3)	X		X		X	X
PMBOK areas (8)	X					X
Management skills (2)	X		X		X	X
Tools (2)	X				X	X
Enterprise project management overview (1)		X	X		X	
Fundamentals Summary (2)		X		X		X
2. Interactive Programs						
Kickoff workshop	X					X
Team integration	X			X		X
Group integration	X				X	
3. Specific Discipline Project Management issues						
Information technology	X					
Construction	X					
Research & development	X					
Product development	X					

the current practitioners and clients. Consult with internal and external experts.

2. *Set objectives.* Establish the program's mission (the "cause") and the vision (what you want project management to look like in the future), and determine the specific objectives to be met.

3. *Establish strategies.* Obtain strong sponsorship and determine how the program should be carried out. For instance, should you use internal or external trainers? Design the programs for intact teams or mixed groups? Customize the content or use a "one size fits all" approach? Offer a crash program or an extended training session?

4. *Develop and implement the plan.* Define the program components and related activities, establish the budgets and schedules, and mobilize the necessary people to carry out the work. Make allowance for modifications and build in flexibility by including review points along the way.

When IBM revamped its project management program in 1997, the information-gathering stage included mapping what was going on project-wise in its various business units. The mapping pinpointed differing project methodologies in use. To come up with a consistent educational program, it was necessary to develop a common methodology. The new educational program focused on *consistency* throughout the organization, such that all business units would speak the same project language. Regarding *competence*, the new program aimed at boosting overall results. A consistent methodology and a project management approach make the educational program cost-effective; at the same time, productivity is boosted when cross-functional teams get together (they don't waste time learning one another's methodology).

Education strategies for project management at IBM, as presented at a 1997 AMA Executive Forum on the Project Organization, include three levels: (1) project management fundamentals; (2) workshops on specifics such as team leadership, tools, contracting/subcontracting, and financial management; and (3) applied project management aimed at the issues of specific disciplines. Since IBM has as many as twelve different "flavors" of projects, these strategies entail customizing applied management courses during the third stage for each of those project types.

This strategy is somewhat different at Hewlett-Packard, where the assumption is that a project is a project, and therefore project management training need not address the peculiarities of specific disciplines. Courses offered to project managers at H-P include project techniques, behavioral aspects, organizational issues, business fundamentals, marketing, and customer issues. Mentoring is also part of the educational process at H-P.

During the planning stage for any educational program, aside from the activity, budget, and schedule issues, be sure the aim of each course or workshop is clear. Both the individuals taking the course and the sponsoring parties should know the expected outcome. For that to be the case, provide a clear statement or description of the course or workshop, along the lines of "These courses produce these skills at these proficiency levels. . . ."

BUILD OR BUY?

Early on in the planning stage, you need to consider whether to build your own training program in-house or buy one from a vendor. If the in-house option is selected, you need to focus attention on finding and mobilizing the right people to support and carry out the educational effort. If outside consultants or trainers are used, other issues need to be managed, such as selecting the right vendor, deciding on outside-produced or in-house materials, and form of contracting for services. Another possibility is to mix and match the options and have part of the training done by inside people, so as to get involvement and maintain the company flavor, while the rest is done by outside consultants, so as to have outside expertise and attenuate the demand on the time of internal personnel. Here are considerations for dealing with the build-or-buy question:

- *Go outside.* For small organizations, the outside approach tends to be most cost-effective, since such businesses lack expertise in both educational program development and project management. Colleges, consultants, and professional organizations are good sources for educational development and instruction in project management.

- *Mix and match.* Medium-size and large organizations are well served by using both internal personnel and outside support for developing and delivering educational programs. This combination provides the synergy and guarantees that the parent company can maintain the educational know-how to keep the program going.

- *Stay inside.* For mature organizations that know their needs and have people available to structure the programs and deliver them, there's solid logic to keeping the educational effort inside, even though many companies prefer to outsource. In this situation, however, someone in the organization has to be charged with knowing what's going on in the outside world, through benchmarking programs and professional organizations.

WHAT ABOUT THE CONTENT?

What should be included in a project management education program? Obviously any program will have to be tailored to meet the needs of the specific organization, but all should take into account the following factors: present company strategies and objectives, degree of organizational maturity regarding project management, degree of urgency, previous training programs, program mission, and objectives. The suggestions given below cover a broad scope of project management educational options with a suggested course content.

Programs Covering Fundamentals

1. *Project Management Basics.* Covering the techniques for managing project activities, this three-day course includes a project life-cycle overview, a review of project breakdown structure and network techniques, and a walk through the knowledge areas, including scope, time, cost, quality, communications, procurement, human resources, risk, and integration. Also covered in the fundamentals is a step-by-step project methodology outlining how to do project management in your company.

2. *PMBOK Areas.* This in-depth journey into the project management body of knowledge involves four two-day workshops in which topics are dealt with in detail and content guides are supplied for outside study. This series of workshops is aimed at people who plan to become certified as PMPs (project management professionals), or the equivalent. Scope, time, cost, quality, communications, procurement, human resources, risk, and integration are reviewed, as well as integration management of all these knowledge topics, with coverage of planning, execution, and change administration.

3. *Management Skills for the Project Manager.* Reviewing the techniques for managing people, this course targets leadership and management issues and uses practical templates that help ensure alignment of the project management community. The program surveys development of the project charter, the communications matrix, techniques for dealing with different behavioral types, the stakeholder management plan, and conflict management.

4. *Tools*. These techniques for speeding up project management tasks are presented as "how to use" and hands-on instruction in support instruments like project control and tracking software, cost control systems, risk management, and decision-making tools. The seminar shows how to input data and use tools in support of project management.

5. *Enterprise Project Management Overview*. This one-day briefing summarizes the basics of managing an organization by projects. It shows the relationship between single-project and multiple-project management, and it explores the essence of the "portfolio of projects" concept. It also covers how organizations can support project work in the form of the project support office, project management center of excellence, the program management office, and the chief project officer.

6. *Summary of Fundamentals*. This workshop is for people who don't have hands-on responsibility for projects but who need to understand the principles. It is a capsule version of the three basic seminars, or an extended executive briefing.

Interactive Programs

The following are examples of programs designed to promote integration among team members. The kickoff workshop, which is aimed at getting the project off to the right start, stimulates integration since the event is highly interactive. Team integration can also be generated through team-building events aimed specifically at developing behavioral and interactive skills.

1. *Kickoff Workshop*. This seminar follows a two-day plus one-day format. The idea is to bring together conceptual and planning information and to use the workshop to "massage it"—put it in its final form. The project team and other stakeholders are taken through the paces by a trained internal or external facilitator. The first two days involve reviewing the project charter, which includes mission, assumptions, constraints, and stakeholder expectations. Basic technical plans (what to do) and management plans (how to do) are also discussed. The second day wraps up with a size-up of any "missing pieces" in terms of project kickoff. Then there is a two- week span for everyone to pull together the pending information and plans and do the internal negotiation necessary for convergence on outstanding items. The third day is for finalizing project technical plans (including the project charter, project breakdown structure, schedule, budgets) as well as project management plans, outlining strategies, and

how the project will be performed, including all the interfaces with the parent organization.

2. *Team Integration.* For teams to work, there are issues that go beyond who does what, when, and where. These are behavioral questions involving trust, commitment, and synergy. There are three schools of thought on how the project team can obtain this behavioral buy-in:

1. *Head-On Attack.* If the team were to engage in an interactive team-building workshop, that might involve communications and conflict simulations, insight into personality profiles, strategic team initiatives, and basic challenge courses—or, for the more adventuresome, a ropes course or wilderness-survival adventure. GM's small-car chief Mark Hogan, who spent part of his career overseas, strongly supports outdoor team activities. He commented at a Latin America Conference of American Chambers of Commerce, "Our Excell team-building program has been one of the most important factors in attaining global productivity."

2. *Show-by-Example Approach.* If people are not "touchy-feely," says Debbie Hinsel, who headed Training and Development at Pfizer Global Health Care, then "you have to find another way to build team unity." Since dealing directly with the integration issue is often perceived as "touchy-feely," more conventional approaches for achieving a team-based culture are performance management, rewards and recognition, titles and roles, and career development.

3. *Group Integration.* Major outsourcees such as IBM, EDS, and the Dutch-based Origin share an integration challenge when it comes to education and team building. When they absorb dozens, sometimes hundreds, of employees from clients who have decided to outsource information technology services, these companies must integrate people who have worked for the client company for years and are not familiar with the culture of the new company. A combination head-on attack and showing by example is recommended for these situations.

Discipline-Specific Issues

When custom-building educational programs for specific disciplines, be mindful of the differences in risks, skills, and costing for each area. Those differences can be reflected in the training programs through case studies, precourse interviews, and instructors who speak the language of the discipline. The foundation elements to be factored into custom-tailored educational programs are as follows:

- Type of business (construction, systems integration, software development, product development, manufacturing, network services, retail)
- Type of project (high-tech "intelligent building," hardware manufacturing, modern furniture products, systems application development)
- Competencies required (capable at project cost control, able to deal with adversarial situation, strong negotiator, good risk evaluator)

Yet another element of discipline-specific education is the special audience. Certain hierarchical audiences, such as top management, functional management, or people indirectly involved in supporting projects, may call for a special approach. These groups may avoid project management education if not specifically targeted. Intact teams are another group that may require customization, particularly when the project team needs to be integrated.

COACHING AND OTHER NONCLASSROOM TECHNIQUES

Learning about project management is not limited to the classroom; there are other ways to go about obtaining the education. For example, coaching, mentoring, and on-the-job training are effective ways to develop skills in the trade. These can be complements to or, in some cases, in lieu of formal training classes.

Coaching is done by a person trained in the art of conducting one-on-one sessions with the purpose of improving a player's performance. The coach can be an outside consultant or a trained internal professional. Normally, a sponsor identifies the need and articulates a first meeting between the player and the coach. The initial sessions, usually two-hour periods, involve a dialogue and an informal size-up of the individual's knowledge and capability in the field. A typical program involves the following steps:

1. Identify the need and objective for the coaching.
2. Select a qualified coach.
3. Agree on a program, objectives, and a time frame.
4. Carry out the program.
5. Monitor progress and adjust.
6. Evaluate results.

In addition to teaching basic skills, coaching provides another benefit too: development of general life (and, consequently, management) skills. The person learns to apply project management techniques to his or her own "life project." That is, the project breakdown structure is used to define all major areas of the person's life. For instance, the components of a person's life might be broken down into its physical and health, family, work and professional, financial, education and intellectual, and spiritual aspects. Each of these aspects in turn can be subdivided into smaller activities that the person needs to reach his goals in life.

I started using project management techniques in coaching in the late 1980s. One of my "coachees" at the time was Edson Bueno, a Brazilian doctor who owned a couple of hospitals and a fledgling health insurance plan in Rio de Janeiro that sold about $50 million annually. His business objective was to grow as fast as possible, to build a truly excellent company, and to expand internationally. We decided to use a project breakdown structure to get a big-picture view of his life as a project, and then focus on the business side. Since medical doctors are trained to be analytical, Bueno took to the structured technique and quickly developed a project view of his life.

This project view of a life became a turning point in Bueno's career as an entrepreneur. A confirmed workaholic, he began delegating authority, spending more time on strategic issues, rethinking his priorities, and living a more balanced life. Although other reasons explain Bueno's success—his ambition and drive, a highly talented and dedicated executive team, an intense management training program, extensive use of international consultants, and an intuitive vision—he ascribes much of his success to the executive coaching sessions, which helped him gain a structured view of his life. Says Bueno in a handwritten note to me ten years later, "I owe much of my success to the coaching sessions and the structured project planning approach used to organize my life." Of course, Bueno knew how to take a simple project management concept and make it pay off. His Amil group now includes twenty companies in Latin America and the United States, with billings exceeding $1 billion. Bueno spread the concept throughout his executive ranks and even instituted structured life planning techniques for the children of his collaborators in a series of juvenile seminars.

So coaching and project management tie in to each other in two ways. First, coaching is applicable for project players who need to be brought up to speed rapidly, and for seasoned managers who want to rethink and update themselves on how to "quantum leap" their projects in these changing times. Second, project planning techniques can be used in a "project of my life" approach for conventional coaching that starts with life planning. The fringe benefit of this partnership is that players not only gain the fruits of the planning but also become familiar with techniques like project breakdown structure and life-cycle planning.

In addition to coaching, mentoring, and on-the-job learning are other nonclassroom approaches to education. *Mentoring* involves an in-house professional, trained in the art of nurturing professionals, who acts as advisor, counselor, and teacher, with the objective of bettering the player's development and performance. *On-the-job training* means putting players in situations where they perform tasks they need to learn or develop additional expertise.

NO GUARANTEES

As mentioned at the beginning of this chapter, project professionals who haven't studied the field will tend to become a phenomenon of the past. Those who continue to practice the profession without formal training will be perceived as less prepared than those who have had the education.

While education programs are no guarantee of achieving competence, they will certainly boost the knowledge base of both those new to the profession and practicing project people. Greater knowledge spread across the company makes for a more "learned" organization and for professionals who will be more "employable," both within and outside the organization. Education in project management is a cause that will always yield benefits to the professionals involved, to clients, and to the company's bottom line.

Principle
No.10

The measurement of individual competence in managing projects calls for reaching beyond knowledge-based testing, into the field of competence assessment.

10
CHAPTER

Competence in Project Management: Do People Know What They Are Doing?

Back in 1995, an article in *Fortune* magazine first spotlighted project management on a international scale as the number one profession in terms of employability. The article, "Planning Your Career in a World Without Managers" by Tom Stewart, pointed out that project manager was "the career of the decade." As Stewart noted, project management personnel have the capability and flexibility to respond to new situations; their fixation on bringing projects in on time, within budget, and to quality performance standards means that a company putting its initiatives in the hands of project professionals comes out ahead.

About the same time, the question of competence began to be addressed by various project management associations, such as the Australian Institute of Project Management, the International Project Management Association, the British Association of Project Managers, and the Project Management Institute. Both individuals and corporate members started pressuring the associations to come up with a way to measure an individual's competence at managing projects. If indeed this was to be the coming profession, there needed to be some way for people to show they had the qualifications, and some way for a company to screen and select candidates based on factors other than résumés, interviews, and gut feelings. Thus, individuals had a growing interest in testing their skills and enhancing their employability, while companies wanted criteria for gauging competence.

The assumption behind competence standards in project management is that both project and organization performance is boosted if projects are staffed with competent leaders and team members. This premise raises questions such as:

1. What is competence in project management anyway?
2. Why bother? What are the benefits?
3. How do you determine what to include in a project management competence model?
4. Is competence enough to produce successful projects?
5. Who needs to be competent?
6. Can competence be measured? How?
7. What is the best path to competence?

Here are the answers to those questions:

WHAT IS COMPETENCE ANYWAY?

Competence means possessing sufficient skills and abilities to perform a job. It involves observable evidence of performance and includes practices used in the selection and recognition of people within a work classification. The inference is that once competence has been determined regarding an individual, future levels of performance can be predicted for that person.

Competence must be measurable against some acceptable standard and be free of inference, assumption, and interpretation. That standard must be approved by a recognized entity. When competence is measured against that standard, candidates either pass or fail: they are either competent or not, as in the case of obtaining a driver's license.

To get a driver's license, a person is tested on his or her knowledge of traffic rules and regulations, procedures for operating a vehicle, skill obtained through practice, and ability to perform on a hands-on driving test. The candidate passes or fails. However, different levels of competence are required for different types of driving. For instance, the standards of competence differ for a learner's permit, a regular license, a professional taxi or limo license, and a trucker's or bus driver's permit. Required knowledge, skill, and the ability to apply that knowledge and skill all increase as greater competence is required.

Competence in project management is like driving competence, in that varying levels of ability are called for and standards must be measurable. For instance, a project manager must possess a level of competence superior to that of a team member. A project sponsor or other interested executive may not require the hands-on competence of a project manager, but surely needs a minimum level of knowledge to be able to interact with project personnel. So project competence models are similar to other competence models.

WHY BOTHER? WHAT'S IN IT FOR EVERYBODY?

Why go through the effort to perform competence testing in project management? There are sundry stakeholders involved, but competence testing appears to be a win-win situation for all those who are serious about the profession and about producing results through projects. Here are the stakeholders and some of the benefits they stand to reap from competence testing:

• *Project Managers and Project Team Members.* Competence testing focuses on project management as a profession and brings it from under the shroud of an "accidental profession." Recognized competence means that professionals are prepared for the job, and that there are agreed-upon standards for competence in the field. Project members certified as competent in the profession have a feather in their cap when jockeying for positions within or outside the company. Certification implies that project professionals will, on the average, outperform noncertified project professionals.

• *Project Sponsors and Corporate Executives.* Senior executives are winners when it comes to supporting competence in project management. Validated competence assures company executives that projects are more likely to succeed. Thus, the approach taken by project leaders will be predictable and consistent in different settings, from project to project, in differing time periods and in different environments. Since ultimate responsibility for project success rests with upper executives, competence testing for project professionals puts an additional safeguard into the process.

• *The Company.* Competence testing is a valuable tool in a company-wide professional development program. It can be used for career guidance, for performance measurement, and for compensation and reward plans. It can also be used to identify strengths and weaknesses and to tailor training. Indeed, competence assessment is a major factor in conjunction with project performance when evaluating project manager performance. For example, formal certification is a heavily weighed factor for promotion at AT&T, as it is at Lucent Technologies. Project management professionals at both AT&T and Lucent number in the hundreds. Also, a competence assessment lends greater breadth to the professional evaluation, since individuals may be assigned to projects with a high probability for failure (such as pure research projects) or "rescue" situations to reduce an inevitable loss (such as a year 2000 date-conversion project).

- *Clients.* With competence standards, clients and other external stakeholders are assured that the project leader and team members are capable of choosing and implementing the best practices. Stakeholders know that certified professionals have the traits, skills, and ability to apply the tools and methodologies of good project management practice. Certification also provides a certain peace of mind when project team members come from consultants or professional service firms.

- *Professional Organizations.* Validated competencies make it possible for professional organizations to play a significant role in helping both individuals and project organizations to zero in on what good project management is all about. Solid competence models, sponsored by professional project management organizations, make it possible to compare project professionals on different continents, based on generally accepted best practices in the profession. And professional organizations benefit by becoming the guardians of the conceptual framework and body of competencies and best practices that can be passed on, in the form of training, to future project professionals.

- *Consultants, Educators, Academics.* These professionals have an inherent interest in bettering individuals' competence levels. Not only is promoting improvement in the performance of project work part of this group's professional mission, but also the quest for competence opens doors of opportunity for all involved in training and education aimed at boosting that competence. Related research on competence is frequently of interest to consultants, educators, and academics.

What to Include in a Competence Model

The competence model spells out the capabilities to be measured, how they are to be measured, and what constitutes acceptable and superior ratings. If competence calls for knowledge, skill, and the ability to apply, then obviously any model must include standards for these three factors.

The DEC model, based on Digital Equipment Company's overview of competence, as shown in Exhibit 10-1, assumes that increasing knowledge ("I know") and skills ("I can do") are the foundations for increasing performance. Once those foundations are in place, the application abilities ("I can apply") become responsible for quantum leaps and bounds in project performance and consequently in meeting company bottom-line goals.

Organizations may establish their own model for evaluating competence or choose an independent assessment validated by an association of project management professionals or other outside entity. A formal model, recognized by the parties, has to be in place before proceeding to the assessment stage.

A competence model for project work requires identification of specific competencies (planning and contract administration, for instance). These agreed-upon competencies represent the starting point for development of a full competence program. Ways to arrive at a listing of competencies include using a panel of experts, hold-

Exhibit 10-1. DEC competence model.

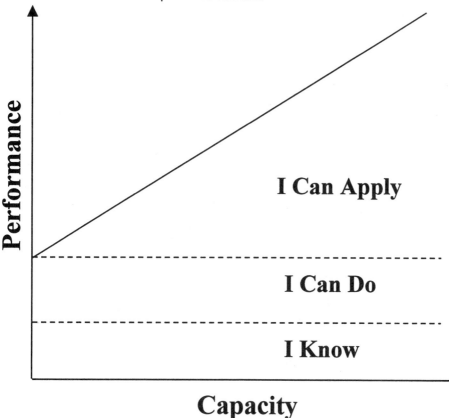

ing interviews with practitioners, doing a literature search, and benchmarking existing models and practices.

Once the listing has been compiled, there must be consolidation and workplace testing to fine-tune the list. Note that whether the organization chooses to elaborate its own model or validate an existing one, this final step of consolidation and workplace testing is fundamental to ensure that the competence model is applicable to the projects and culture of the organization.

Knowledge-based testing is the first major building block of competence models. For instance, the Project Management Institute's project management professional (P.P.) certification program is a set of widely recognized criteria for proof of a candidate's knowledge of project management activities. Yet knowledge-based testing does not certify that the candidate can actually perform the tasks effectively. Skills and the ability to apply knowledge also need to be assessed before competence can be determined.

An organization steeped in the art and science of developing sundry competence models might find preparing such a model for project management a routine task, yet most companies discover that developing a competence model is a sizable undertaking. Should a company develop its own competence model for competence in project management or use a model available in the marketplace? It all depends on how good the company is at developing its own models and what the company culture dictates. IBM has done internal certification of its project managers for years and has been looking increasingly to broader-based instruments for some of the testing, like the knowledge-based part of the certification requirements. For example, several divisions of IBM have augmented their internal training processes with study for the P.P. certification exam offered by the Project Management Institute. This knowledge measurement was felt to be so universally applicable that IBM translated the P.P. study course into several languages to implement the training worldwide.

For most organizations, however, an off-the-shelf, research-based product makes the most sense. So if buying is the logical way to go, how do you make the choice? Before a competence model is chosen by a company, a number of questions need to be answered.

1. What is the stated purpose of the model under review?
2. How was the model validated?
3. What do you wish to accomplish by applying the competence model: selection? appraisal? development?

4. How does an individual go about acquiring the desired characteristics that the model requires?
5. How easy is the model to apply?

These questions are aimed at making sure the competence model fits what the company has in mind. There may be questions of applicability depending on the field of specialization. For instance, if it is a generic model, will it fit the needs of, say, software development project team members? Remember, competence assessment calls for a considerable investment in time and effort on the part of the company and its project-related people.

IS COMPETENCE ENOUGH TO PRODUCE SUCCESSFUL PROJECTS?

Competent project managers and team members make large contributions to successful projects, but factors other than competence also strongly influence results. Researcher Frank Toney has listed some of the other factors that need to be monitored as the project progresses, and should be taken into account at evaluation time:

1. Upper management support and project management experience
2. Strength of the global and local economy
3. Company's position in the marketplace
4. Host organization's degree of maturity with respect to project management
5. Any tendency of the market that affects the project; for example, expansion or retraction
6. Financial stability of the organization and project clients
7. Company's competence in the basics of management: strategic planning, product mix, marketing, production, quality, sales

Thus, realizing project success is not simply a matter of bringing competent leaders and team members onboard. The successful completion of projects resides squarely with corporate management, which has reasonable control over all factors that affect a project—including appointing the right people for the job.

This accountability hasn't been fully appreciated in the past, but it is key to successful enterprise project management. Although senior managers have largely abdicated responsibility for projects in the past, they cannot do that anymore; there are fewer managers to go around, and project success directly impacts the company's bottom line.

WHO NEEDS TO BE COMPETENT?

For organizations moving toward a projectized structure, the question of project competence takes on particular importance. Remember, however, that not all competent project management leaders are willing to subject themselves to competence assessment. Those who are truly outstanding may reason, rightfully perhaps, that they don't need it. They know their worth and so do those who matter in their careers.

Here are some competency questions that bear answering in terms of enterprise-wide project management:

1. How competent in project management does the president of the company need to be?
2. How about the vice presidents and other principal corporate players?
3. What about the project manager for a mega-project? And the managers of smaller projects? And for multiple projects?
4. How competent at managing projects should the team players be? And project support personnel?
5. To what extent do clients and suppliers need to be project-management competent?

Obviously the degree of competence required varies depending on the function. Some needs are easy to pinpoint: team members need to be competent team members, project managers should be certified as project managers. And if mega-projects or full-fledged programs are involved, then genuine program managers are called for.

If the competencies of key players have been formally assessed, so much the better. In actual practice, however, many of the people involved in an enterprise project management transition will not be certified as competent in project management. This means that the principal change agent—be it the project manager, the project sponsor, or the director of human resources—has the job of boosting the competence of all those involved in project work. Here's what can be done to educate and stimulate those stakeholders who need to know more and do more about managing projects in the company:

- *Presidents, Vice Presidents, Higher Executives.* Use executive briefings by internal or external consultants. Distribute literature that addresses the management of projects from a high level. Get them involved in high-level external forums where the topic is likely to be discussed.

- *Managers of Projects.* Whether handling large, small, or multiple projects, these people are best reached by appealing to professional pride and employability to stimulate participation in external seminars and symposiums.

- *Team Players and Project Support Personnel.* Workshops (start-up and otherwise) are superb ways of bringing people up to speed on the basics of project management and thus boosting competence. On-the-job-training and planning sessions are also effective, as well as participation in external seminars.

- *Clients and Suppliers.* Briefings, planning sessions, and project integration workshops are ways to stimulate the interest among these important stakeholders, who have such a strong impact on the results of a project.

CAN COMPETENCY BE MEASURED?

The Australian Institute of Project Management launched its certification system in 1997, based on the Australian National Competence Standards for Project Management. This certification system is available both in and outside of Australia. The AIPM certification covers three levels—project team member, project manager, and program manager—and requires individuals to prepare portfolios showing output competence. The AIPM was supported and driven by a nationwide government initiative to establish competence standards for all professions in Australia.

Competencies, according to the AIPM model and as illustrated in Exhibit 10-2, fall into three categories (plus, they require individuals to prepare portfolios of evidence showing performance of output competence):

1. Input competencies, including knowledge as tested by PMI's Project Management Professional exam or other similar test and qualifications and experience as documented by curriculum vitae.
2. Process competencies, involving underlying enabling attitudes and behaviors, as tested by a personality profile test.
3. Output competencies, which are the results of project work

performed by the individual and formally documented and attested to by an appropriate professional entity, such as the Association of Project Managers (England), the Australian Institute of Project Management, or other professional group.

Exhibit 10-2. Australian competence model.

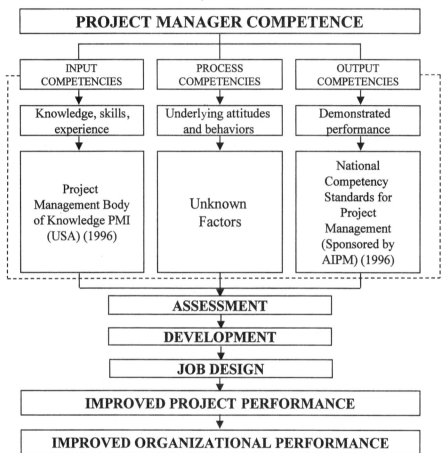

THE PATH TO COMPETENCE?

Measuring competence brings about the benefits detailed earlier in this chapter. Project team members, sponsors, the company itself, clients and external stakeholders, professional organizations, consultants, and educators and academics all stand to gain from the development and application of a competency model. And, indeed, the mere existence of certification is a stimulus to pursue excellence in project management.

Yet measuring competence alone isn't the answer to achieving it. It takes a structured program to stimulate individuals to achieve competence. Here are some of the components needed to ensure that individuals in an organization strive for competence:

- *Heightened Awareness.* Awareness of the importance of achieving competence can be stimulated through literature on the topic and participation in professional associations, which emphasize the benefits of greater employability and better career planning.

- *Facilitated Study Policy.* The discipline-specific part of the competence assessment requires study time, varying from a brief brush-up to a full review that includes study groups, computer-based learning materials, and test simulations.

- *Incentive to Participate.* Companies interested in boosting the competence level of project personnel need to provide some stimulus to sign on to the program. Financial incentives are good, but not always available. Other options are recognition, trips, heightened employability, and the de facto demonstration that certified professionals go further in the company than noncertified professionals.

COMPETENT PEOPLE IMPROVE PERFORMANCE

Knowledge, skill, and ability to perform are necessary to achieve competency. A given minimum standard is required, such as that involved in obtaining a driver's license. But once competence has been determined, future levels of performance can be predicted. If that premise is true, then the more competent project people in the organization, the greater the possibility that the organization will perform project work within budget, on schedule, and up to quality standards.

Principle
No. 11

Boosting the level of project management maturity across the enterprise increases productivity and contributes to the company's bottom line.

CHAPTER

How Grown Up Is Your Organization?

Just as human beings go through stages from infancy to maturity, companies travel a path from their smallest beginnings to full-fledged organizations. And just as people's behavior depends on where they are along the pathway of life, companies' actions and decisions reflect their maturity levels. An organization's project management maturity (PMM) level is a measure of its effectiveness in delivering projects.

Organizational maturity in project work is not necessarily related to the passage of time. A company may have been around for 100 years, be highly mature in marketing and customer relations, yet be caught in toddler stage when it comes to managing projects. Age relative to project management has to do more with the nature of the business and the forces of the marketplace than with time. Another organization may be a few years old, enterprise-driven, and projectized from the beginning, thus ranking high on the maturity scale.

The PMM reflects how far an organization has progressed toward incorporating project management as a way of work. Depending on a company's history in managing projects, its swing to increasing those applications on a broader scale may vary from a short leap to a very long "row to hoe." So how fast can a company incorporate project management into its way of doing business? It depends on a combination of factors:

- External market pressure to work faster, cheaper, and better
- Internal dissatisfaction regarding the present organization, systems, and procedures
- Major commitment by the principal players in the organization
- A clear vision and plan for changing to a new way of doing business

It takes the combined pressure of these factors to jump-start the transformation to management by projects. Since you are reading this book, it is a safe bet that the first two factors—external pressure and some degree of internal dissatisfaction—are probably already at work. The last two depend on initiatives taken within the company.

The degree to which the company's business is project dependent also influences its position in terms of project management maturity. For instance, many of the project-driven organizations described in Chapter 1 are, by nature, well along the way to PMM. Most require some updating or fine-tuning, but no major revamping. On the other hand, a traditional company, just beginning to sense the winds of change, requires an organizational rethink, as well as a powerful program to change the mind-set of functionally oriented people to a project-slanted approach. So before an organization begins projectizing, someone needs to determine the starting point for the change project.

A Scientific Approach or a Superficial Review?

Common sense says that a company with a purely intuitive, random approach to managing projects merits a lower maturity rating than, say, a company at an integrated stage, where multiple projects are controlled and managed using tried-and-true methodologies. Thus, a general assessment of project management capability within the organization can pinpoint strengths and weaknesses in project management while offering a glimpse of the organization's PMM level. Benchmarking with other organizations also reveals comparative data on project management that lead to conclusions regarding the sophistication of project management efforts.

A formal maturity model is one way to judge how much an organization has incorporated project management as a way of doing its work. Maturity can also be measured in a less formal way, via rule of thumb; this is discussed later in this chapter. The maturity model requires identifying relevant project management topics, such as standards, work authorization, mission, training, and risk management. One model groups these topics into major sections, such as leadership and management, performance management, and management information. Other maturity models use the groupings defined in the PMBOK *Guide*. Questions like "Is the work breakdown structure technique applied to projects during the planning stage?" yield yes or no answers; those answers are then tabulated to give numerical results.

THE PROJECT MANAGEMENT MATURITY MODELS

Existing models for project management maturity are based on the Carnegie-Mellon University Capability Maturity Model (CMM) for software development, prepared in conjunction with the Software Engineering Institute. The model was developed with initial funding by the U.S. Department of Defense and thus rests in the public domain. The CMM establishes five levels of maturity: initial, repeatable, defined, managed, and optimizing. The levels were developed as progressive standards to help organizations improve their software practices.

The models have in common the five levels of the software model. The higher the level of maturity, the greater the project management performance, as shown in Exhibit 11-1. As opposed to the CMM, however, no one generally accepted model exists for measuring project management maturity. Because of the lack of an accepted model, the Project Management Institute's Standards Committee plans to develop and issue an organizational project management maturity model as a PMI Standard, according to Bill Duncan, director of standards for PMI.

Here is a summary of the levels used in a sampling of available PMM models. The CMM level titles are maintained for lack of an industry-wide consensus (some alternative titles are given in parentheses).

- *Initial (ad hoc)*. No formal project management processes are in place. Success at this level depends on individual effort, since systems and procedures are poorly defined. Each project is perceived as unique. The project management process is unclear and projects are marked by cost, quality, and schedule problems. There is no historical reference and little attention is given to risk factors or lessons learned from previous projects. Schedules are often established on a top-down basis, with inadequate regard for resources and previous experiences. Interfacing with functional

Exhibit 11-1. Levels of maturity shown in terms of performance and time.

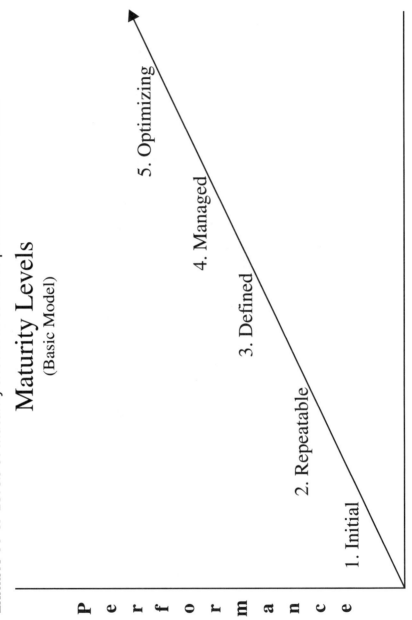

Maturity Levels
(Basic Model)

areas within the company is usually laden with communications problems.

• *Repeatable (abbreviated, planned)*. Project management systems and processes for planning, scheduling, tracking, and estimating are in place and perceived as important. The tools are seen as a solution to some of the performance problems, yet they are not used in a fully integrated form. Project success continues to be unpredictable, and cost and schedule fluctuations persist throughout the projects. Project management software is in place but results are not evident because of lack of experience and overall project management view. There is no integration of databases, although schedule information is generally abundant.

• *Defined (organized, managed)*. There is a standardized approach to project management within the organization. The project management systems, defined and documented, are integrated into the company systems and procedures. Input into the tracking and control systems is more reliable. Project performance is predictable, with a high degree of accuracy. Schedule and cost performance tend to improve. Strong emphasis is placed on scope management, which is perceived as a fundamental part of managing projects. While databases are used, they tend to be difficult to manage. Much time is spent maintaining the models used in managing the projects, to the detriment of analysis and problem solving.

• *Managed (integrated)*. Process management is measured and controlled. Management is linked with the information flow on major projects and knows how to use and interpret the information. Systems are able to generate integrated management-level information without reprocessing and reformatting. Project performance tends to conform to plans, thus the project success rate is high. There is a consolidated project database, which can be accessed for estimating and benchmarking purposes. Because this approach also involves management-level reporting, the level of the work packages in the system (lowest relationship level) is not always sufficient to adequately plan the work to be performed. Therefore, in some cases it is necessary to do a more detailed breakdown or work with complementary checklists to get the projects done.

• *Optimizing (adaptive, sustained)*. Project management processes are continuously improved. Project teams naturally use models to develop schedules and budgets, and to process project information. A historical database can be consulted on-line to obtain lessons learned, reference data, and estimating criteria. A sophisticated system exists such that both top-level management reporting requirements and in-the-trenches tracking needs are met. Resource optimization is a reality, not only at the project level but also on an enterprise basis. There is strong integration of schedule, cost, and scope requirements. Reliable information can be rolled up across all projects and analyzed from a company-wide standpoint.

One logical approach is to evaluate the maturity level of the organization with respect to its execution of the project management body of knowledge (PMBOK) areas, shown in Exhibit 11-2. Ideally, the established project management knowledge areas can be used as components in project management maturity models. In other words, how well does the organization manage cost, time, quality, and so forth on its projects during the classic project phases of initiating, planning, executing, controlling, and closing? Such an approach, it can be argued, covers the essence of project management.

Yet, aside from an indication of how individual projects are handled, the organization itself needs sizing up, as illustrated in Exhibit 11-3. Basic questions need to be answered regarding the organization's maturity. For instance, how does the company track multiple projects? Does it use an integrated system? How are projects supported within the organization in terms of tools, administrative, and contractual assistance? How does the company keep up to date with the latest tools and trends in project management? How does a global organization, for instance, keep ever-changing techniques and tools compatible around the world? How are the project managers managed—to whom do they report and how are they kept current on new techniques?

Evaluating Maturity Using a Model

For a maturity model to be complete, it must focus on both the competencies involved in managing a project and broader organizational issues. This means making sure that all areas of the PMBOK are covered in the classic project phases. It also calls for a review of the business unit that backs up the projects. One such approach involves making a survey matrix that crosses the PMBOK areas with the project management processes plus the organizational issues. This results in a structure shown in Exhibit 11-4, which was used in a benchmarking questionnaire included in the PMI Educational Institute's research study, "The Benefits of Project Management."

A model developed by Micro-Frame takes a different tack and gives more attention to broad organizational issues. The project management maturity categories in this model are:

Exhibit 11-2. Knowledge areas that can be used as components in project management maturity models.

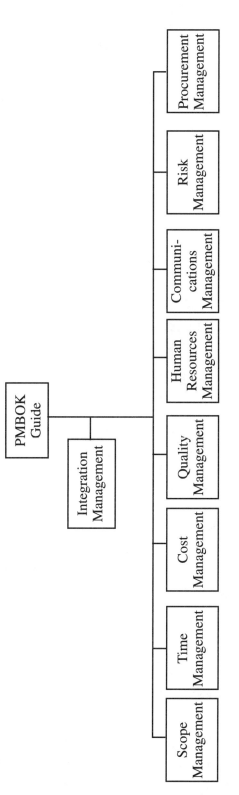

Exhibit 11-3. Project management for projects and for organizations.

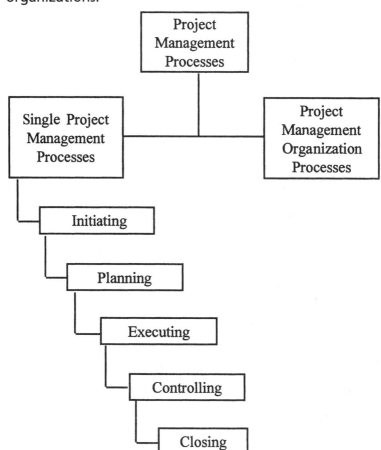

1. Leadership and management: the human factor and cultural environment that determine the ultimate effectiveness of the project management function.
2. Project performance management: the management and control of individual projects within the multiproject organization.
3. Problem/risk/opportunity management: a formal process describing analysis of project data; identification of potential problems, risks, and opportunities; and a structured approach for managing problems, mitigating risks, and leveraging opportunities.
4. Multiproject management system: the multiproject process and system—that is, the institutional framework of project management.

Exhibit 11-4. Sample project management benchmarking questionnaire.

Project Management Processes and Knowledge Areas	Initiating	Planning	Executing	Controlling	Closing	Project Management Organization Environment
Scope management	6	7	8	3	3	3
Time management	1	2	12	1	1	1
Cost management	2	2	2	1	1	3
Quality management	1	2	3	3	3	1
Human resources management	2	4	5	2	2	7
Communications management	5	3	12	7	2	1
Risk management	1	1	7	6	1	1
Procurement management	1	1	1	1	1	2
Integration management	*	*	*	*	*	*

Structure of project management benchmarking questionnaire used for survey results published in "The Benefits of Project Management." (Numbers represent how many survey questions were directed at the subject matter of each matrix cell.)
*Not included as the study was initiated prior to the inclusion of "Integration Management" as part of the PMBOK model.

This figure is reprinted from "Benchmarking PM Organizations," by William Ibbs and Young Hoon Kwak (1998) with permission of the Project Management Institute, Four Campus Boulevard, Newton Square, PA 19073–3299, a worldwide organization of advancing the state-of-the-art in project management. Phone: (610) 356–4600. FAX: (610) 356–4647.

5. Management information: the flow, timing, content, and medium of project information throughout the multiproject organization.

6. Policies and procedures: the documents describing "the way things get done around here."

7. Data management: the standards for project management data.

8. Education and training: the training course material and program used to perpetuate sound project management practices.

These eight sections are then broken down into the forty-two categories shown in Exhibit 11-5, which are graded, resulting in a numerical maturity ranking. The exhibit shows a model developed by Micro-Frame that gives more attention to broad organizational issues, as opposed to concentrating principally on the knowledge areas that relate to the management of singular projects.

Special Situations

Some situations call for special attention. For instance, take the famous Y2K challenge faced by major corporations in the late 1990s to keep computers from going berserk at century's turn by reading the digits 00 in an MM/DD/YY pattern as the year 1900 instead of 2000. The implications for those companies caught behind the eight ball on this matter are millions of dollars in claims and legal costs brought on by dissatisfied clients, who will have been misserviced, harassed, or just plain ignored by a highly confused data system. This project management situation is so peculiar that a general survey on project management maturity probably wouldn't contribute to solving the question in a timely manner.

It takes something more specific to bring order to such mayhem. One solution is a certification program aimed specifically at this type of project. In the case of Y2K projects, the Information Technology Association of America developed a program called ITAA*2000 in conjunction with the Software Productivity Consortium to identify the "best of breed" companies in addressing the year 2000 issue. By contracting companies or purchasing products that are duly certified, senior executives are assured that the right procedures and processes are in place—that if these are properly and diligently applied, projects will be brought to a successful and timely closure.

Exhibit 11-5. Sample of project management maturity categories.

Leadership and Management

- Mission
- Customer focus
- Career path involvement
- Organizational structure

Data Management

- Accountability
- Skills
- Career path

Project Performance Management

- Architecture
- Project decision support
- Scope management
- Work authorization
- Performance standards (metrics)
- Baseline control
- Estimating
- Resource management
- Schedule development
- Schedule management
- Budget development
- Cost management
- Performance measurement and forecasting
- Change control
- Quality management
- Subcontract management
- Project application tools

Problem/Risk/Opportunity Management

- Management process
- Risk management
- Opportunity management

Multiproject Management System

- Linkage to organizational goals
- Data integrity
- Decision support
- System scalability
- Knowledge capture and reuse
- Interproject integration
- Manpower and resource management
- Enterprise tools and processes

Management Information

- Relevance to operations
- Cross-functional data integration
- Performance capture
- Timeliness and accuracy

Policies and Procedures

- Process templates
- Standard procedures
- Project management documentation

Categories used in maturity model developed by Micro-Frame Technologies.

This figure is reprinted from "Adding Focus to Improvement Efforts with PM3," by Ron Remy (1997) with permission of the Project Management Institute, Four Campus Boulevard, Newton Square, PA 19073–3299, a worldwide organization of advancing the state-of-the-art in project management. Phone: (610) 356–4600. FAX: (610) 356–4647.

The Process of Determining Project Management Maturity Levels

To assess an organization's maturity, it is a matter of applying a procedure and communicating the results. Here's the basic approach:

1. *Initial Assessment.* This includes reviewing the overall PMM process to be applied, becoming familiar with the organization assessed, determining the distribution of survey material, and reviewing previous related assessments.
2. *Kickoff Meeting.* This meeting includes key stakeholders involved in the assessment and covers the following topics: objectives and scope of the assessment, agreement on the timetable for completing the surveys, and confirmation of survey distribution strategy.
3. *Information Gathering and Initial Analysis.* This phase consists of distribution and collection of the survey material and holding complementary interviews.
4. *Consolidation.* This involves data analysis and drafting and finalization of a written report, which also may be presented verbally.

MEASURING MATURITY BY RULE OF THUMB

If company decision makers prefer not to invest the time and resources, or don't have the inclination to invest in a formal study of project management maturity, an off-the-cuff size-up takes only several hours of review and reflection. An internal or external consultant, schooled in project management and in organizational behavior, can readily do a quick overview. Here is how to make a speedy but reliable assessment:

1. *Framework, Methodology, Procedures.* Use the PMBOK *Guide* as a base for assessing project management capabilities. How are projects done in the organization as compared to the PMBOK procedures? Use the questions outlined in Chapter 7, "The Fine Art of Asking Questions," as a reference.

2. *People's Knowledge and Capability.* Determine to what extent managers and professionals are knowledgeable and competent in managing projects. Use the criteria given in Chapter 10, "Competence in Project Management," as a basis for determining how knowledgeable and competent players are.

3. *The Organization Basics*. Assess if the organization has the basics of project management in place: technical and administrative support, focus on promoting the cause of project management, an organizational reporting system, and a system for managing project managers. Refer to Chapter 5, "Oh, Give Me a Home," for material on organizing project management support functions.

THE NEXT STEP

Once the maturity level has been established, then what? Let's say the organization's sponsoring parties conclude, either by rule of thumb, scientific model, or independent assessment, that it is about halfway along the pathway—around level three—to full project management maturity. What are the next steps?

• *Create awareness, spread the word, generate involvement.* An assessment of project management maturity is akin to a reading on a GPS (Global Positioning System, the satellite-based geographic locating device): it tells you where you are, but it doesn't get you where you want to go. Knowing the organization's maturity level provides an orientation so you can travel the most efficient route to full project management. A PMM assessment doesn't improve the management of projects, yet it can be used as an awareness-raising tool. And although raised awareness doesn't solve the problem either, it is a great place to start generating interest in improving project management practices within the organization. Talk up the topic in meetings and discussions, and use the house organs and such to spread the word.

• *Develop a plan.* An assessment pinpoints areas that are below par. For instance, if the company's risk management is nonexistent, procurement management is shaky, and the project support office is understaffed and behind on technology, then these areas are prime targets for improvement. The plan to raise project management maturity needs to include all the fundamentals of any good project plan, including a clearly stated objective, implementation strategy, stakeholder management plan, a communications plan, and a schedule of activities.

• *Implement, control, and adjust.* Since everything is changing in most organizations, the project management maturity improvement project will likely be hit with a barrage of happenings that might push it off track—things like an announced merger or buyout, a reorganization, a change in the stakeholders, or a cut in funding. As on any project, corrections and adjustment have to be made to ensure the project is completed on time, within budget, and meets the stated objective with the desired quality.

In summary, the project management maturity level measures an organization's effectiveness in delivering projects. It sizes up how far an organization has progressed toward incorporating project management as an effective way of work. The assessment provides an initial awareness for the status of project management in the organization and at the same time helps set the stage for making it better.

Principle
No. 12

Compensation packages consistent with the importance of projects to a company's success are fundamental for retaining project managers and top team members on projects.

12

CHAPTER

Money and Other Turn-Ons for Project Managers

Money talks; it can promote skills acquisition, lateral career development, team flexibility, continuous learning, and superior performance—all strongly related to success in managing projects. How can you make sure your cash incentives speak fluent project management? Let's look at reward systems in the workplace.

Compensation used to be aligned with the career ladder. As you ascended rung by rung within a company, your titles grew more impressive, responsibilities broader, status symbols more posh—and, of course, your salary kept pace with your climb. Now the ladder's lying on the ground with the rungs broken, and the old salary paradigms have been called into question.

Hierarchical pay structures rarely fit the team-based work environment. A project team needs to be rewarded for getting the job done and not for striving to reach the next rung on the organizational ladder. Because of the differing nature of project work, traditional functional hierarchies and narrow pay scales limit an organization's efforts to keep pace with the marketplace. Hence the issues to be taken into account in designing team compensation packages are shown in Exhibit 12-1. The primary questions that need to be considered in designing project team compensation packages can be identified and used as a basis for designing the approach.

Exhibit 12-1. Major issues in designing team compensation packages.

- Type of team pay contemplated: gainsharing, competency, team-based merit, fixed-based, hybrid
- Alignment of project results with organization results
- Source of funding for team-incentive pay
- Relationship of team pay and individual pay
- Policy for people participating on multiple teams
- Fairness among teams faced with differing challenges
- Relationship between core team members and noncore support staff
- Policy for team members versus people not on teams

The trend toward flat, flexible structures has induced organizations to adopt a broad-band approach for compensation, steering away from narrow, restrictive salary grades. This has resulted in a reduction in the number of levels and titles, broader salary ranges, and alternative career tracks for nonmanagers. There are three pay-delivery systems that work well in a broad-banded environment.

1. *Skills-Based Pay.* This form of compensation rewards people for competence and the skills they learn and apply rather than only for the jobs they carry out. The company must take special care to align the compensatable skills with the requirements of the work. A skills-based pay program communicates to employees that they will advance if they grow in their capabilities. It also guides them toward working on their development needs. Development in project management skills would be part of the basis for skills-based pay in a projectized company.

2. *Career Development Pay.* Career development pay, under a broad-band pay structure, allows the company to compensate employees for increasing their flexibility, experience, and knowledge through lateral job shifts. These moves can be made in role (from manager to individual), professional function (from sales to production), product line (from A to B), and type and magnitude of project (from a small administrative project to a large construction project). The reward is generally made at the time of the move, and is associated with the degree of change. The average increase for these lateral moves is generally about 10 percent. Career development pay can be highly effective in a team-based environment since, like skills-based pay, it provides an incentive for workers to

broaden their knowledge of the business, thus developing more flexible work teams.

3. *Merit Cash.* A one-time cash payment for individuals who meet given performance expectations, this payment form creates a very direct relationship between performance and pay. To be effective, the size of the merit award must be big enough to get the employee's attention. And it must be clear to all that the merit cash is linked directly to performance of a specific task or project. This is particularly applicable to people who are at the top of a pay band, yet who deserve additional stimulus based on superior performance.

These three compensation forms provide incentive for skills acquisition, lateral career development, team flexibility, continuous learning, and superior performance, all of which are strongly related to success in managing projects. Properly articulated, these payment forms can contribute substantially to successful projects and consequently to achieving the organization's performance goals.

Research by Hewitt Associates, in cooperation with the University of Chicago's Graduate School of Business, demonstrates this point. In this study, data obtained from 437 publicly traded companies showed that those with programs that managed the performance of their people and rewarded them for superior performance tended to significantly outperform those that used traditional management and compensation approaches. Specifically, the 205 companies that had performance management programs outshone the 232 that did not, showing better profits, improved cash flows, stronger stock market results, greater sales growth per employee, and improved financial performance and overall productivity. The study also found that troubled companies with newly installed implemented performance management systems were able to do turnarounds within about three years, increasing total shareholder return by 24.8 percent and boosting sales per employee from an average of $99,000 to $193,000.

Project environments fit the classic conditions for incentives to be effective: tasks and functions are interdependent, group interaction is essential for success, there's a strong focus on team problem solving, and results are (usually) measurable. The challenges, however, in putting team-based incentives into place are considerable. Employees and supervisors tend to resist the new concept. Success depends strongly on picking the right performance measures and in setting achievable standards for performance. The accountability for the work process and expected results must also be well assigned and the system needs to fairly reward individual performance.

THE IMPLICATIONS OF SKILL-BASED PAY

Skill-based pay is often used in conjunction with other reward-system practices, such as gainsharing, team incentives, flexible benefits, profit sharing, stock ownership, individual incentives, and nonmonetary incentives. Most notably, skill-based pay is commonly associated with gainsharing.

According to studies, companies that use or are increasing the use of skill-based pay schemes are those subject to foreign competition, companies with strong speed-to-market concerns, and those attempting to increase the effectiveness of TQM movements and self-managing teams. Those that are under heavy competitive pressure, be it foreign or domestic, are also much more likely to use skill-based pay and experiment with other innovations.

Jobs as permanent fixtures are dying out, so pay structures must reflect the shift toward dynamic, project-driven business practices. Since traditional compensation packages focus on the job (a concept in extinction) and not on the person, those forms of the past are bound to be inadequate in these new settings. With the focus away from the job and on the person and the project assignment, the challenge is to compensate people for having the skills to carry out their assignments and for their performance in terms of measurable results. A simplified matrix is shown in Exhibit 12-2. In a projectized organization, hierarchical pay structures are particularly out of place. This matrix shows the recommended compensation policy for combined competency and performance variables in relation to market rate.

While improved results and boosted incentives constitute the

Exhibit 12-2. Compensation policy matrix.

Pay based on individual competency and project performance (M.R. = market rate).

	Low Performance	*Medium Performance*	*High Performance*
Low competency	Below M.R.	Below M.R.	Below M.R.
Medium competency	Below M.R.	M.R.	Above M.R.
High competency	Below M.R.	Above M.R.	Above M.R.

upside of pay based on skills and performance, this policy is not without its pitfalls. Here are some of the dangers:

1. *The company isn't ready yet.* If the organization hasn't made the shift from hierarchical process to a team-based business, then an innovative pay scheme will likely run into snags. It is best to disassemble the layers of the organization and make the cultural shift before making major shifts in pay policy.

2. *The company has no superstars to model the advantages of the new incentive system.* Without some frontrunners, the revised payment structure may have no effect. If that's the case, competency-based benchmarks can be obtained from high-performing organizations, which in turn can be used as an ideal standard for competence and performance.

3. *Pay ranges may get out of control in relation to overall company policies.* Outstanding performers may wreak havoc with what's considered reasonable and acceptable within the company. If market pricing is used to fix limits, without sabotaging the intent of rewarding exceptional performers, then pay policy can still be kept within certain boundaries. The concept, however, of pay based on skills and performance is to loosen up limited structures and broaden the bands for compensation.

Projects by nature are performed by teams, so team-based pay issues come into play when the project and organization results need to be optimized through a compensation program. There's no known magic formula, however, to apply to the compensation of project team members since each organization has its own set of peculiarities.

The primary questions that need to be considered in designing project team compensation packages, however, can be identified and used as a basis for the system. Those design issues are shown in Exhibit 12-1.

Money isn't everything, but as some wit once remarked, it gives you some clout with your teenagers. Of course, there are many other factors that drive productivity. But without a compensation program that makes sense in the project-driven organization, other incentives will fall flat or be perceived as window dressing.

IF YOU HAVE TEN BUCKS TO SPEND

Common wisdom in the executive suite has it that if you have limited resources, you need to spend them wisely before you put together an ambitious compensation package. If the human resources area has limited money to spend, it should do so on selection first, as opposed to forking out funds for compensation packages, benefits, training, and such. Selecting the right project manager accounts for 70 percent of the success in managing a project. Once the right project manager is selected, the pay factor becomes relevant, so the person will be attracted to the project and carry it through to completion.

Criteria for selecting project managers are discussed in Chapter 10, on competency. All of the pay-based and other motivating factors discussed in this chapter are dependent on making the right choice. No amount of pay or motivating skills at the executive level will be enough to offset an individual's characteristics that aren't right for the job. Once the choice is made, however, upper management can help project managers boost their performance by designing the right pay package and by making sure that the classic motivating factors are dealt with.

TURN-ONS BESIDES MONEY

An appealing pay package is a step in the right direction for turning on project managers and other important players. It makes them feel secure, signals that their work is appreciated, and lets them know how much the company values them as compared to the marketplace. If there's truth in the expression "You get what you pay for," it also ensures that the company is getting quality people for the key slots on the project.

The right pay should be enough to stimulate project managers, boost productivity, and promote an atmosphere of diligence and well-being. At least common wisdom would have it so. After all, in consumer-based societies, the money factor is high up on most people's list when it comes to deciding where to work.

Yet studies on motivation claim that money isn't the real turn-on at all. Frederick Herzberg's classic survey puts money together with other maintenance-type factors that are expected by the worker. Rather, the lack of these factors (which include adequate lighting and physical items related to the work setting) are turn-offs. So the theory is that folks don't get excited because they have a decent work setting, and that the lights work and that they are being paid at market level—they expect those things. They're not happy because those things are in place. But they become unhappy if those components are missing.

Assuming there's some credence to Herzberg's time-tested theory, this means a powerful pay package won't result in increased productivity—at least not by itself. It takes a healthy mix of motivating factors to make productivity soar. Project managers like challenges, they like to work on things that interest them and create new opportunities, and they like situations that generate synergy. Most project managers are self-achievers, so they like situations that will allow them to achieve results. Some project managers yearn for recognition; if that's the case, then medals, back-patting, and plaques may be important. Here are some of the keys for stimulating project managers and other key players:

• *Positive Feedback.* Even gruff and tough project managers like to know they are appreciated. And the appreciation doesn't need to wait for the annual awards banquet. Informal "atta-boys," literal or virtual pats on the back, a friendly note, and generally appreciative body language go a long way toward fueling the project manager's desire to stretch for excellence and achieve outstanding results.

• *Status.* Project managers make things happen in organizations. They are responsible for virtually all change that goes on. They deserve to be given treatment consistent with that position, in terms of elbow rubbing, benefits, and work setting.

• *Involvement in Strategic Planning.* Project managers like to feel they are at least partially in control of their destiny. Involving them in the strategic, preimplementation phases helps mitigate the "we planned it, now you go do it" syndrome that many project managers face and complain about.

• *Support.* For project managers to make it through the turbulence that surrounds most projects, they need support. This means support from above in terms of power and politics, and from the organization itself in terms of systems, procedures, and resources. The project manager who feels supported is likely to be motivated toward meeting project goals.

• *Clear Guidelines.* Project managers like to know what the ground rules are and how those rules are made and how they can be changed. Clarity of purpose and clarity of direction are fundamental building blocks to carry out their mission.

• *Personal Style.* The "different strokes for different folks" principle applies here. Each project manager has a way of doing things. If the manager is a "go away and let me do my job" kind of person, then upper management needs to get strong buy-in on a very clear project charter, which spells out responsibilities and scope clearly. If, on the other hand, the project manager is a participative "let's work it out together" type, then executives need to be prepared to sit together with her from time to time. Project managers expect people to be able to adapt to their style.

An increasing body of research shows that work-life issues are more important than money to today's job candidates—and that includes project managers. The U.S. Labor Department's unemployment rate figures are the lowest they've been in about a quarter-century. "Job seekers today are more concerned about corporate culture and long-term growth than about accepting the highest offer," according to Lynn Taylor, director of research at Robert Half International, Inc., a staffing services firm specializing in the accounting, finance, and information technology fields.

This same logic applies to keeping motivated those project managers already on staff. For many project managers, a high salary will not offset a negative, rigid work environment. Many talented people would prefer to work for a company offering less money but better future prospects and a more progressive corporate culture.

As baby boomers age, long-term potential and stability are top concerns for many workers, in light of the last decade's merger mania and downsizing. Rather than seeking the most money in the shortest time, many project managers are considering a range of benefits, including career advancement opportunities, stock options, tuition reimbursement, training, bonuses tied to personal or company performance, and retirement savings plans. They also place a higher value on a "kinder, gentler" workplace—one that offers such "human factor" perks as flex-time, casual dress days, telecommuting, job-sharing, extended vacation time—even on-site gyms and child-care facilities.

But these tangible components are only part of a friendly work environment. Some of the less tangible aspects, such as support, mentoring, and teamwork, are just as important. It has become a truism that employees who feel they are valued are more loyal and will work harder, so the provision of a relaxed work environment is simply smart business. Even temporary professionals—a category that project managers sometimes fall into—are looking for the same kind of positive work environments. By focusing more on the qualitative versus quantitative aspects of compensation, a company adds depth to the merely "hygenic" salary and benefits package and has the opportunity to create a profoundly motivating environment.

Exhibit 12-3. Guidelines for engagement.

Relative Influence of Incentives to Other Managerial Factors

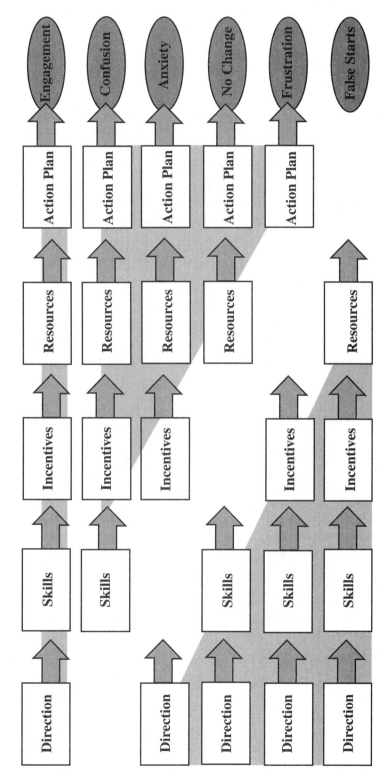

KEEPING COMMITMENT UP IN CHALLENGING TIMES

Even when a company is struggling to keep pace with change and is faced with reorganization, reengineering, downsizing, and other morale busters, it is possible to keep project managers coming back for more by engaging them in the process of change. Dutch Holland and Sanjiv Kumar, in a *PM Network* article (June 1996), laid out a model of engagement that keeps the morale of team members and managers alike high during difficult periods of transition—such as the transition from a traditional organization to one governed by the principles of enterprise project management. According to these authors, individuals in an organization need direction, or a picture of where the organization is going. They also need skills to do work in new ways, incentives to get refocused in the desired direction, access to resources to ensure their success, and an action plan to provide a starting point. Only when all these pieces are in place can the members of an organization feel fully engaged in the work of transforming the way they do business (see Exhibit 12-3). Note that when the incentives, or compensation package, are the missing factor, things basically just stay the same.

MONEY IS GOOD, BUT THERE'S MORE

Project managers are turned on by a number of factors, including money. Money can provide stimulus for superior performance, as well as motivation for skills acquisition, lateral career development, team flexibility, and continuous learning. Good pay is a move in the right direction for stimulating project managers and other important players.

On the other hand, a powerful pay package won't increase productivity by itself. Studies on motivation claim that money isn't the real turn-on at all. It takes a mixture of other factors to make a quantum leap in productivity for project managers and teams. Those factors include positive feedback, providing status to the position and work, involvement in strategic issues, availability of support, clear guidelines, and allowance for personal style.

Principle
No. 13

Communication in enterprise project management covers the spectrum from alignment of company-wide goals on one end to interpersonal communication on the other.

13

CHAPTER

Communication: Wired or Unplugged?

Ray Boedecker, a senior manager with KPMG/Peat Marwick, gives his secret formula for successfully developing and implementing highly complex business processes involving hardware, networks, software, applications development, and technical experts: "Pray. Run hard. Constantly reset expectations. And learn to communicate."

On high-technology projects, it is often assumed that the methodologies and tools will take care of communicating data through processes that have logical relationships. In fact, those tools and methodologies are rarely fully integrated in systems that take into account the complexity of communications on a project. And they certainly don't consider the subtleties and frailties of the human element and the impact these have on communication.

Communication is *so* basic that everything in project management depends on it. The initial project concept starts out in somebody's head and, through successive iterations of communication, gathers enough steam to be formally proposed as a project. Project approval represents another communications hurdle, as sundry parties have to buy in to the idea. The kickoff and planning phases are, in essence, exercises in communication involving the exchange and organization of information so decisions can be made. Successful implementation is also communication dependent because of the need for timely data transfers and daily fine-tuning. Project wrap-up and turnover to client also depend on close interfacing between the project team and the people who will operate the finished project. So success on projects is in direct proportion to the quality of communication.

Most everything that goes wrong on projects can be traced to a communications glitch of some sort. Communication gone awry can be downright embarrassing. For example, a field memo from a copper plant under construction contained the question: "Has the second overhead crane been bought yet?" The engineering design people thought the memo amusing until they discovered that, owing to a lack of civil-mechanical engineering communication, the single crane specified would not make the transition from one section of the plant to another. This resulted in major rework and a lot of red faces.

PREMISE HUNTING: WORTH THE TIME AND EFFORT

The first step toward establishing a solid base for communication is to pinpoint basic assumptions. This is like looking for gold within all the communications that goes on in organizations. When communication is based on the correct common assumptions, the odds for clear, noise-free transmission and reception are boosted: that is pure gold for the communicating parties, who free themselves from errant decisions and costly rework caused by operating on mixed premises.

Finding the proper assumptions and making them known to the interested parties are theoretically an easy task—as simple, say, as ensuring that members of a rowing team are in the same boat before they start rowing. Or that singers in a barber-shop quartet are side by side so they can harmonize. When parties share the same basic premises, understanding tends to happen. The shared assumption, or premise, is what makes good communication possible. Yet finding the shared assumption is tricky because assumptions are believed to be self-evident truths by those who hold them. An assumption is so obvious to the person attempting to communicate a thought that no effort is made to make that assumption clear to others. And that's where the problems in communication arise.

Tiny Projects, Product Launch Projects, and Mega-Projects

Our first case of mixed premises spotlights the U.S. supplier of technology for a "challenge ropes course" to be built in Brazil. The specifications included details for miscellaneous planks and blocks, as well as material for a wall that was to be constructed of locally available "high-quality wood." The best-quality Brazilian wood, however, has a density much greater than that of the pine the U.S. supplier had in mind, which meant the planks were too heavy to be used as designed. Also, the wooden "climbing wall" took three times longer to build than anticipated. The incorrect premise was that the wood was the same; that wrong premise cost extra drill bits, time, money, and anguish. In this case, there was no common assumption regarding the density of the wood.

The second case involves the launch of a product for which there was no apparent demand. Art Fry of 3M started in 1974 to overcome numerous barriers to get Post-its through the corporate maze and into the marketplace. After heroically maneuvering around numerous technical and political roadblocks, he faced the results of a market survey that indicated no interest whatsoever in his Post-it "stick-ons." The marketing department's premise was that a conventional survey could adequately gauge the potential for a product of this nature. Fry was finally able to shed new light on that premise, reasoning that the product was so different that people would be unable to visualize its use unless they actually tried it. Ultimately, the commercial launch became successful when 3M began generous distribution of samples.

The last example involves a mega-project. On October 19, 1993, the U.S. Congress pulled the plug on the Superconducting Super Collider Project, the gigantic $11 billion subatomic particle smasher designed to obtain answers to fundamental questions about the formation of the universe. At least three incorrect premises were largely responsible for major communication breakdowns during the project, and ultimately for the project's demise:

1. That scientists who had successfully managed similar projects of a smaller nature would be able to successfully deal with the peculiar challenges of a mega-project. In fact, the combination of scientists and Department of Energy overseers proved themselves incapable of dealing with both basic project management issues and political pressures.
2. That the general public would be supportive of the project. The public was basically indifferent and often perplexed by the vagueness of the project's objective.
3. That team-building and behavioral issues were not pertinent to a science project. Only in 1992, a year before the project was axed, did the SSC begin to timidly contract some "team integration seminars," and these seminars did not involve the higher management team, where most attention was needed.

PREMISE HUNTING: AS SIMPLE AS ABC

Uncovering the premises behind decisions is the key to effective communication. It is the obvious first step, like putting the horse before the cart. "Premise awareness" is not an intuitive ability, but rather one that requires detective work to ferret out the assumptions governing decisions.

Here are the ABCs for bringing premises out into the open:

• *My/Our Premises.* When faced with a new situation, look beyond your gut feeling and write down the premises behind your initial position. If you are part of a group making a decision, do a "groupthink" and get your assumptions out front.

• *Your/Their Premises.* When you negotiate with other parties, you are at an advantage if you learn where they are coming from. In some cases, up-front questions will clarify things; in other situations, probing questions are required to get a feel for the other side's assumptions.

• *Other Premises.* There are probably other valid premises that no one has thought about, and a brainstorming session can bring out possibilities for review.

DO CLEAR PREMISES MEAN CRYSTAL COMMUNICATIONS?

Having clear premises, recognized by all involved, can be likened to a land-based observatory that makes long-range observations into the universe. Telescope experiments conducted on a cloudy day are doomed to failure, just as are communications based on fuzzy assumptions. Yet unclouded days and crystal-clear premises aren't enough to make for successful experiments or guarantee glitch-free communications. Both are much more complex processes.

The theory of communication is simple and well known, yet this very simplicity may jade the communicator's thought process and hide the high probability for error. Communication starts as an abstract mental concept in someone's mind. That concept is then translated through another mental process into a code, usually verbal or written words or data. The code is transmitted through some medium to whoever is destined to receive the message. In the transmission stage, factors such as volume, diction, and speed come into play. Media, such as telephone lines or air and radio waves, affect the communication process as noise in the communications channel distorts or interferes to some degree with the message. The receiver then has to be tuned in and paying attention to extract the message from the medium. Once the message has been received, it is decoded and interpreted by the receiving party, and reconstructed in the form of a mental concept.

Although the process is almost instantaneous, these distinct steps exist, and each one represents a potential roadblock to communication. The probability of achieving efficient communication is extremely low. A partial breakdown in the conception, coding, transmission, medium, reception, decoding, or interpretation can set off a colossal communication crash, even if the premises are fully convergent. For effective communication to exist, there must be great care to ensure that all the communication phases are effective.

Since the cards are stacked against good communication, a pro-active stance is required to care for this delicate process. After all, the failure or success of a project rides on the communication waves that dart, swirl, and twirl about an organization. Here are some ways to shift the odds in the other direction, toward healthy and productive communications:

From the Project Perspective

The project manager takes on the role of master communicator. The classic route to effective communication is through the project communication plan, which outlines the actions necessary to guarantee a smooth and accurate information flow. The project communication plan can be developed on two levels to separate the general principles and concepts from the nitty-gritty of sharing information:

• *Level I Communication Plan.* This plan consists of a listing of communication premises, such as: "Intranet communication is the preferred channel; action items will be determined at weekly coordination meetings; follow-through on communication is a project communication policy, meaning that recipients of communication are responsible for complying with, rebutting, or proposing revision to the initial communication." Once the premises are established, then overall communication flow is defined in terms of who, what, when, and how. *Who* is a listing of the project stakeholders, such as project manager, project sponsor, client, functional managers. Then for each stakeholder, the plan outlines *what* kind of information is pertinent for that individual, *when* the information should be sent or received, and *how* the communication should take place.

• *Level II Communication Plan.* This plan lays out the communications flow in great detail. It is presented in matrix form showing all project players and the precise role of each player (sends, approves, becomes informed). Whereas the level I plan provides a background sketch for communication, level II tells exactly what action is to be taken by whom.

From an Organization Standpoint

In a projectized organization, senior executives are responsible for establishing a healthy communication ambience that will ensure appropriate communication processes are in place. The very essence of managing an enterprise of projects is ensuring that communication is effective at both the project level and the organization level. How that communication will happen depends on how the organization is structured for projects. Whoever has the strongest project focus in the organization needs to take the initiative to develop a level I plan for the management of projects. If there is a chief project officer, as outlined in Chapter 5, then the responsibility for the plan lies clearly with the CPO. Otherwise, this task must be picked up by someone carrying out the duties of the program management office, the project management center of excellence, or the project support office.

SOME SUBTLETIES OF COMMUNICATION

Communication is a complex process that involves different approaches for differing objectives. It calls for overcoming a wide variety of barriers. And it means being able to communicate well in widely varying situations. Here are tips for dealing with some of these subtleties of communication.

Gauging the Energy Level for Data, Compliance, or Commitment

The energy level required to communicate varies in accordance with the purpose of the communication. If data flow is the sole purpose of the communication, then a system that accurately transmits data through a relatively noise-free medium will suffice. A step up in terms of energy is required, however, if the purpose is to communicate information that guarantees compliance with a preestablished goal or objective. In this case, feedback loops are needed to check whether the receivers are, in fact, using and interpreting the information for the good of the cause. To guarantee compliance, then, greater effort is required than simply to transmit data. An even greater level of energy is required when the purpose of the communication goes above and beyond compliance. When the communication goal is to achieve commitment, buy-in, or heart-and-soul participation, the energy put into the communication has to be top level.

Such was the case for Phil Condit and Alan Mulally as leaders of the 777 team that successfully managed to keep Boeing a step ahead of its European Airbus competition. Much of their leadership effort was aimed at gaining commitment—convincing the team that the world aviation market had undergone unprecedented change and that they faced an exciting challenge that involved the very future of Boeing.

"You get out of communication what you put into it," goes the popular saying. So obviously a data-level effort will not produce compliance. Nor will a compliance-level communication effort bring people to commit heart and soul to a cause. The secret to getting what you want out of your communication is to state the upfront purpose of the communication—data, compliance, or commitment—and put the energy needed into the communication to meet that objective.

Communication Roadblocks

Roadblocks abound along the routes of project communication. They pop up individually or collectively, and set off detours and wild goose chases. Here are some of the barriers that get in the way of communication on projects:

• *Geography.* Project work is increasingly being spread about to different locations. The reasons for this include friendlier telecommunications and pressure to keep travel costs down. While, in theory, communications can be dealt with over the airwaves, the geographic spread of project work cuts down on face-to-face communication and thus on an important component of managing projects. Solutions to the geographic challenge include communications audits, videoconferences, and periodic everybody-present meetings

• *Personal Agenda.* Individual interests, ego, and personal style are major pieces of the project communication puzzle. They manifest themselves in the form of power and politics and have a striking effect on stakeholders, as discussed in Chapter 6. Since everybody comes from a different background and processes information in different ways, a special burden is placed on project communicators. The varied personal agendas require a customized approach—one that takes into account the individuality of project players.

• *Culture*. When Romanians nod their heads up and down, they are signaling no; when they shake their heads back and forth, they mean yes. For non-Romanians, however, it takes major concentration to distinguish yes from no because of cultural convention. The Japanese are formal when compared to people in many parts of the United States, who like to deal with everybody, even perfect strangers, on a first-name basis. Since most Japanese don't use first names outside family circles, some Japanese executives in the States take nicknames like "Bob" or "Ted," thus reserving the privacy of their Japanese given names while conceding first names to the local culture. The Itaipu Binacional Hydroelectric Project connects Paraguay and Brazil, which are otherwise separated by the Paraná River. When the dam was under construction in the 1980s, language and culture also strongly separated highly industrialized, 130-million-strong, Portuguese-speaking Brazil from agrarian-based, Spanish-speaking Paraguay with its only 3 million people. The differences in the cultures turned out to be so great on the binational project team that a formal "cultural project" was developed to help develop language and intercultural skills.

Different Situations

Communication takes place in various contexts and settings, and each situation offers its own set of challenges. The project communication plan needs to take into account the very different requirements of distinct settings. Here are clues for dealing with each of those situations:

1. *On Stage, Live (same time, same place)*. These settings include meetings, presentations, one-on-one discussions, and any other event that is going on live and where the parties are in the same place. Being organized in this setting calls for using the right tools, such as electronic copy boards and other audiovisual resources or standard flip charts. A functional layout that blends easy communication with needed privacy is also an organizational requirement, along with fully equipped conference rooms, meeting rooms, and team rooms. Other necessities are training in presentation skills, meeting management, and individual coaching skills.

2. *Out of Synch (different time, different place)*. This is where answering machines, E-mail, computer conferencing, and the like

come into play. These tools make it possible to organize interactions in spite of the fact that people are geographically distant from one another and send and receive information at different times. Much of the training is on-the-job. Some basic rules, however, are important: what can be sent and what can't, guidelines for responding, and preferences of some people for E-mail over voice mail and vice versa.

3. *On–Line (same time, different place).* The telephone has long helped us deal with real-time reactive communication from afar. Videoconferencing is another way to link up from a distance. The challenges here involve actually making the connection with the other parties and the normal difficulties of telephone protocol. Also, in the case of videoconferencing, geographically split meeting management becomes an issue. Computers can also "converse" with one another on-line, if needed.

4. *Shift Work (same place, different time).* Offices where everyone is not in the office at the same time are typical of the shift work situation. Although the place is the same, people are on flextime or shift rotation, or the nature of the work is such that people are in and out of the office a lot. The out-of-synch tools are useful in this situation (E-mail, voice mail, etc.); so is a formal way of passing information on a daily basis (shift report, routine notes on a board, and checklists).

ON PROJECTS AND ACROSS THE ENTERPRISE

The quality of communications is a key success factor in project work. Virtually everything that goes on in project management depends on effective communications. This means that, on a project level, there needs to be special care taken so that free-flowing, accurate communication takes place. A two-level project communication plan is a good way to make that happen. On a larger scale, communication can be ensured by applying the same principles to enterprise-wide project management—in other words, ensuring that the same communication principles are applied at the organization level.

Principle
No. 14

Project management will continue to take on new forms to
meet the demands of change.

CHAPTER

Where Is It All Going From Here?

Author Tom Peters has said that no matter how zany his prognostications have been about the "wacky future," reality eventually proved that he had actually been conservative, in spite of the apparent brashness of his initial vision. Things happened at a faster pace and in a more surprising manner than he had originally envisioned. So crystal-balling the future is a challenge even for those who do it for a living.

Peters has been preaching the glories of project management for some time now. He sees project management as a way of getting things done, of jolting companies into a results-based mind-set. He cites companies that are project-based or are in the process of making the transformation to enterprise project management. Among them are EDS, CNN, Imagination, Oticon, Ingersoll-Rand, and Union Pacific Railroad.

As far back as 1992, Peters pointed out that project management was the "coming" premier skill. Since the third millennium is now upon us, based on what is going on in the industry in terms of growth, it is evident that project management is no longer coming and has indeed arrived. It is spreading across organizations and is increasingly perceived as a fundamental skill for managing in these times of constant change. The tendency is for this spreading of the project management word to grow and adapt to the changing scenario. Here's what is likely to happen in the first part of the twenty-first century.

GLOBALIZATION

The globalization upswing has been going on for years and has touched business in all corners of the globe. On this vast playing field, world-class players in the best-in-industry category tend to prosper and perpetuate themselves. Smaller companies have the option of joining international networks and alliances to keep abreast, or being alienated from the global marketplace and trying to survive locally among the tentacles of the world's giants. Projects tend to grow in size as they are driven by sociopolitical factors. The greater dispersion throughout the global marketplace makes the timeliness and accuracy of information critical and places a heavy burden on the coordination of cross-cultural teams. For major functional organizations, this means having world-class project management in place and contributing to the bottom line. The same is true for projectized organizations like Bechtel, EDS, IBM, and ABB, which make their living by delivering successful projects and project-related equipment. Smaller organizations like ESI (associated with George Washington University), which offers training programs, and Primavera, supplier of project management software, are also under pressure to keep pace with the demand for world-class support and expertise.

Entities like the Project Management Institute are working on expanding the formal body of knowledge to ensure that all the member-parts of the creature we call project management are taken into account. The Global Forum, a group loosely connected with PMI that meets before or after most international symposia on project management, is also addressing the cross-cultural issues of managing projects globally. An ad hoc Global Project Management Standards Committee, involving standards organizations from around the world, including PMI, is making moves toward global standardization. Project management organizations around the globe will tend to network ever tighter to mitigate the challenges of globalization.

WHO WILL BE DOING IT? AND HOW WILL IT BE DONE?

Project management is changing faces. Based on trends at PMI, more women will practice the art (18 percent of the responses to a survey of PMPs (project management plans) by PMI's Certification Committee were women). That percentage at the general membership level is certainly on the rise. Forecasters of social mega-trends have been forecasting the blossoming of female power in the marketplace since the early 1990s. This trend will continue into the next millennium, to the point where women will outnumber men on many project management endeavors.

In 1995, a survey indicated that the typical reader of *PM Network* magazine was a forty-four-year-old male. A major downshift from this age bracket is also going on. A stroll around the hallways at any project management convention will prove the point, as will a visit to project sites, especially when those projects involve software development or other emerging technologies.

Teams will tend to be more cross-cultural, especially as projects are managed virtually by multidisciplinary groups scattered about the globe. This means that project personnel will require greater awareness of diversity and more capability in managing intercultural settings. The population of the United States is predicted to continue becoming more racially diverse, to the degree that by mid-century, "white" Americans will actually be in the minority. The plurality of black, Asian, and Hispanic Americans will outnumber them significantly. So even within national boundaries, diversity among team members will tend to grow.

Project junkies will be increasingly part of the scene. They are like NBA players who loyally play to win for their team, no matter who their team may be at the time. Project junkies will continue to take the "employability" concept to heart, preparing themselves for employment both within the company and outside in the marketplace. The project junkie, like an artisan in a medieval guild, owes allegiance not to a company or a job but to a profession: the profession of project management. This makes him or her much more mobile, not only across company lines but across industries, sectors of the economy, and national boundaries.

"FASTER THAN THE SPEED OF LIGHT"

Since time is ubiquitous, everywhere at the same time, deadlines all around the globe clamor for timely completion, often simultaneously. The impact of this accordion squeeze on completion time is more concurrence—more parallel activities going on at the same time—and a faster response to events. Globalization works in favor of meeting the growing time crunch. Projects can now churn out results twenty-four hours a day, by having the right parts of the project strategically farmed out around the globe: design can be done in India, while procurement is handled from Europe and fabrication takes place in Argentina. So like the old British empire, the sun never sets on project work. This trend to take advantage of the twenty-four-hour day in this manner will tend to grow.

This tendency is consistent with project management, since the race against the calendar's flipping pages and the ticking of the clock sets the tone for project work. This start-to-finish characteristic makes projects stand out from other types of operations; as time becomes an important measuring stick for assessing success, projects will become more and more recognized as the path to success.

TECHNOLOGY

Technology will continue to have a speeding-up effect on project management. As telecommunications systems become more reliable, particularly worldwide, projects will be managed better and quicker. Quality of images and paperless office capabilities will also keep bureaucracy down and productivity up. Fax machines will be museum pieces and the Internet will not only provide the highway but also will place amazingly powerful software just a few keystrokes away. Stand-alone souped-up microcomputers will be rare, as the Internet will become as reliable as a utility power grid, and up-to-date software can thus be accessed from the network at any time.

Project management software will get even more user-friendly, particularly for the management of a single project. More complex software will also be available for multiple-project situations and enterprise-wide settings. Although some software packages now propose to control projects on an enterprise-wide basis, the packages of the future will provide interface with other company systems and will offer an integrated view of multiple projects. These systems will be highly flexible yet will require considerable customizing upon installation to interface with related ongoing company systems.

On the other hand, while technology will make communications and data handling on projects an easier task, the projects themselves will be increasingly complex. This calls for a higher degree of specialization and at the same time requires all involved in the project to broaden their knowledge base. They will have to be knowledgeable about a number of topics: the base technology, project management systems, and the organizational aspects of the implementation of projects. Expanded complexity in terms of technology means greater risk if the technology doesn't fully meet the project's needs. It also creates a greater burden in terms of the integration of the project technology, the support systems, the project team, and the parent organization.

TOWARD A CORPORATE PROJECT MANAGEMENT CULTURE

The surge in project management is following a track similar to the quality movement of the 1980s. Quality control (rejecting the parts that weren't up to snuff) evolved into quality assurance (inspecting the processes as opposed to the individual parts) and finally into various forms of total quality management (managing all the pieces of the organization correctly, to achieve quality results).

In project management, the thrust has been on how we manage a single project effectively. Lately there is more concern for the management of multiple projects. And the future points toward a more holistic view, like enterprise-wide project management. While the awakening of major corporations regarding the organizational applications of project management may be perceived as new, in fact the concept has been around for a long time—at least since the early '90s. In spite of this fact, it will take a few more years before most companies jump on the bandwagon.

This means that in the future companies will perceive themselves not as hierarchical, functional organizations but as fast-tracking entrepreneurial enterprises made up of a portfolio of projects—ever-changing and ever-renewable—all of which need to be done faster, cheaper, better. Companies thus will embody a project management culture. Project managers have long replaced middle managers. Company team members at all levels will be versed in the basics of project management and will naturally apply the concepts both for single projects and across the company. Project management will be part of the company culture. That culture will be reinforced by institutionalized support, in terms of integrated systems, trained personnel, and a corporate culture that will perceive itself ever more as an enterprise, as opposed to a traditional corporation.

PAST EXPERIENCES ARE LIKE LAST YEAR'S CHRISTMAS DINNER

What worked in the past might not work in the future. What didn't work last time might be a great solution. Just like last year's Christmas dinner that's done and gone, so is last year's project. Some lessons were learned from last Christmas, but this year is to be very different. For instance, Grandma, who always brings the special apple pie, can't make it for Christmas this year; two Muslim Egyptian exchange students will be at the table; cousin Frannie has developed an allergy to turkey; and Dad, who usually does the cooking, will be on call at the hospital. Just like the Christmas dinner, this year's project is subject to changes, even if it is an apparent remake of last year.

Five years from concept to market was still a reality in the automobile industry in the 1980s. Incremental improvement would never have brought the industry to the under-twenty-four-month level achieved in the 1990s. It took tossing away old methods and coming up with new quantum-leaping techniques to obtain the quicker response required to cut the cycle time by 60 percent. Agility and contingency planning become factors when navigating in unknown waters. Risk assessment grows increasingly complex. Strategies have to be flexible to adapt to the ever-changing situations.

In many projects, the changes are far more dramatic than this year's Christmas dinner or next year's new car model. Some manufacturers had to scrap entire fabrication lines to come up with completely new products. Put yourself in the situation of manufacturers of these products: carbon paper, typewriters, carburetors, bound-copy encyclopedias. Past experience was probably useless in coming up with new replacement products. It takes a whole new view to survive and prosper in the new projectized world.

BACK TO THE JUNGLE

Ferocity promises to be on the upswing in all project endeavors. Competition springs at businesses both from the neighborhood garage and from around the globe, demanding new products and services to meet emerging needs. Environmental instability sets off the need to adapt to not only changing physical settings but also to the economics related to those changes. It is a back-to-the-jungle world, where part of a company's time has to be spent looking over its shoulder to keep from being eaten and the other part preparing to pounce on new opportunities.

Survival in this adrenaline-packed scenario calls for flexible political strategies, operational agility, highly efficient information systems, and internal processes. Contingency planning is a must in this savage setting, as is a special instinctive leadership attuned to the beat of the jungle drums. Projects need an increasingly strategic focus to ensure that they are aligned with the company's strategic direction. This responsibility is shared by project managers, who must become more strategy aware and by senior executives who must increasingly think and breathe projects.

A LOOK FROM INSIDE THE PROFESSION

Chief project officers. Project managers as teachers and mentors. "Everybody in the company is a project manager." Things are changing radically. The field is making a giant leap from a basic set of tools for tracking projects to one of the most dynamic career paths of the future. For people within the profession, this comes as no surprise. Here are some of the messages *PM Network* columnist Greg Hutchins heard when he asked people within the profession what they thought the future would hold:

> "Project management in the 21st century will be marked by two paradoxical trends . . . an emergence of new technologies [that] will allow project team members to function globally in increasingly effective ways . . . a movement to reemphasize the art of project management—active listening, negotiating, conflict resolution, problem solving, communication, influencing, and other leadership skills."—William S. Ruggles, PMI Chairman, Ruggles & Associates

> "Because of the sheer numbers of people who will become involved in projects in the near future, lots of people—managers, engineers, administrators, and even secretaries—will become project managers."—Bruce Taylor, Vice President, GTW

> "The future of project management will belong to those who lead geographically dispersed or virtual teams. It will be commonplace to have project teams all over the world, working 24 hours a day, shipping their work effort from India, Europe, North America."—Steve Weidner, Manager, Boeing

> "Traditional long-term planning seems more and more irrelevant to day-to-day work, maybe impossible or even dangerous. Who will take responsibility for the evolution of organizations over time? It has to be project managers . . . [because] messy situations encountered in the heat of complex projects present the best real opportunity for organization development."—Bob Dressler, OD Consultant

"In terms of the future, teachers may be our most important project managers. Our future depends upon their ability to focus on the development of individual students while planning lessons, managing classrooms, participating in quality improvement teams, and exploring new technology."—Hank Lindborg, President, National Institute for Quality Improvement

"The term 'project management' will become an oxymoron. The need to change things in existence and to create new things will continue into the far future, but technology is altering the way those changes are implemented. Many left-brain functions, which are logical, rule-based, and highly structured, are giving way to computer-embedded analogs. These structures will eliminate the need for many of the management functions currently performed by project managers. Information-intensive projects will be among the first to take advantage of the new technologies. Over time IT projects will require fewer people to complete—and that includes project managers."— Stan Smith, President, Millennium Marketing

"Tomorrow's managers will be specialists in facilitating and integrating resources. They will not direct nor will they be technical problem solvers. They will be 'project managers.' This type of manager will need to understand system and process development, resource development, accountability, and team dynamics."—Page Carter, Educator, City University

"The future need of project management will be the ability to manage people. . . . What's needed is a new project manager who can extract what the client really needs and get the technologists to deliver it."—John Rall, Rall and Associates

"The future of project management I see as rings of interacting systems: More individuals telecommuting, consulting. Quality-of-life issues becoming increasingly important . . . fewer hours working on-site and more at home. Work will be process-oriented. More workers will have professional status. There will be strong 'big big' companies, strong 'small small' companies, not much in the middle. Project management works because it is a way for the bigs to use the strengths of the smalls. . . . There will be clear divisions between those who know how to make good use of emerging technologies and

those who refuse to change with the technologies."—
Pen Stout, Principal, Stout Consulting

KEEPING UP

Keeping up with trends in project management can be done on a daily basis, or stretched out over the year. There is enough news breaking to track the topic on the Internet every day, or for those who prefer to group their news in batch form, monthly meetings, magazines, and newsletters are a feasible alternative. On a quarterly basis, there are sundry standards committees and benchmarking forums that get together to take the pulse of what's happening. And then, on an annual scale, yearly conventions pull together the status quo of the profession and what is foreseen for the future.

Certainly a way to keep pace with changes in project management is through the professional associations. The best known are the Project Management Institute, based in the United States, and the International Project Management Association, based in Europe. These two reach out farthest in terms of global coverage. From its U.S. base, PMI has chapters as far away as New Zealand, South Korea, and the Arabian Gulf. The IPMA is a federation of European associations (basically one for each country) that also has members around the world. Other countries have their own independent associations and maintain affiliations with international entities like PMI and IPMA. Such is the case of Australia, India, and South Africa.

These professional project management associations have a lot of keeping up to do. The need of both individual and corporate members not only to keep up with but stay ahead of the game places a special responsibility on the associations. Although a lot of good work has been done, much is left. Says Bill Duncan, director of standards for PMI, "There are over 100,000 copies of *A Guide to the Project Management Body of Knowledge* in print. Each month, nearly 4,000 people register to download the document from PMI's Web site. Maybe we should leave well enough alone. Rest on our laurels for a while. Tempting, but not what we are going to do."

Here are some of the issues that are under discussion in project management forums and committee meetings in associations around the world.

- *Enterprise-Wide Project Management Standards.* Most project management literature and guides focus on the management of a single project. As organizations move toward management by projects, a guide addressing project management from the corporate view is needed.

• *Project Management Maturity Models.* There is still no industry-wide consensus that defines the parameters for judging the maturity of project management in an organization, as discussed in Chapter 11. Although several models are on the market, a professional organization–sponsored movement is needed to provide an industry-wide standard.

• *Competency of Project Managers.* Standards have been published by the Australian Institute of Project Managers (AIPM) and the Association of Project Managers (APM) in the United Kingdom, describing project manager competencies. Yet there is no global agreement as to the applicability of these standards across industries. Continued work is required on competency standards.

• *Project Categories or Project Typology.* A project typology is a classification and description of project types that have common traits, such as construction projects, software development, and organizational change. Such a project typology needs to be in place to properly certify project managers. Although some industry-specific books address the issues, an across-the-board professional association view is called for to focus on a standard set of terms.

• *Updates and Extensions.* Existing standards need to be questioned and updated periodically. Some specific industries prefer to adapt standards to a specific project typology. Once again, professional organization guidance is required to facilitate future professional practice and dialogue.

• *Product Recognition.* For vendors of project management products and services, formal recognition or certification of products by a recognized professional association is desirable. The organizations that purchase such products may feel reassured also in knowing that their supplier is duly certified. Yet not all professional organizations are willing or prepared to provide a product certification service.

This list of topics on the agenda of international project management associations promises to spark new developments in project management applications. Keeping up with what's going on in the profession is fundamental for companies that plan to use project management as a strategic weapon. One practical way to keep up is to benchmark with other project-interested professionals and organizations.

BENCHMARKING

Since 1994, a group called the Fortune 500 Project Management Forum has been meeting three to four times a year to compare data and exchange experiences. The group, which is partially supported by PMI, is largely composed of Fortune 500 companies. Some of the organizations that have been actively participating over the years are Northwestern Mutual Life, Motorola, FedEx, American Airlines, Citibank, Sprint, AT&T, IBM, Allied Signal, Eli Lilly, Fujitsu, Intel, NCR, Nynex, Honeywell, Bell Atlantic, General Motors, Dupont, and EDS. This benchmarking group, which was pioneered by Ray Powers, then of US West, and Bob Teel of Disneyland, and supported technically by consultant Frank Toney, has based itself on the following assumptions:

1. The focus is on the use of project management in large functional organizations, ranging from $1–$155 billion in annual sales. Generally the participants in the benchmarking forum are not project driven—that is, they use project management only as a means to produce some other final product.
2. The primary interest of the forum is in large projects that require a full-time manager. Therefore this forum doesn't include any weak matrix or committee-type situations.

The Forum publishes its findings from time to time through the Project Management Institute. The first book-length publication was released as *Best Practices of Project Management Groups in Large Functional Organizations* (1997, PMI) and documents the key success factors that provide practitioners with information for replication of best practices in their own workplace and students, teachers, and other project management professionals with basic benchmarking data.

Most benchmarking projects strive to identify a "benchmark organization," which is then used as a model for others to try to emulate. Since the concept of using project groups to better functional effectiveness is relatively new, there is no generally accepted information source from which to draw conclusions. The objectives outlined in the study are as follows:

- Provide benchmarking comparisons so people can evaluate their company's performance against other project management leaders.
- Create a database that can provide comparisons with other companies involved in similar situations.

- Define problems and difficulties encountered by participants.
- Identify key success factors and core business practices that result in project management success in functional organizations.
- Expand the body of knowledge to benefit all groups involved.
- Provide value to each participant.

Targeted Benchmarking

A spin-off from the Fortune 500 Project Management Benchmarking Forum was a group interested in comparing data and practices of project management for information technology projects. This involves both companies whose end product is information technology and major users of IT as a means for doing business. That group desired a focused discussion aimed at the issues peculiar to the field.

Other groups are available for a targeted approach to benchmarking. Organizations such as the American Association of Civil Engineers and the Institute of Electrical and Electronics Engineers have forums for project management within their associations, as does the construction industry, the software industry, and cost engineers. Independent groups can also be set up through informal networking channels, by placing ads in appropriate industry trade journals, or through Internet postings.

No Surprise

The fact that project management has spread across organizations at all levels comes as no surprise. After all, the race against the calendar's flipping pages and the clock's ticking set the tone for project work. This start-to-finish characteristic makes projects stand out from other operations; time becomes an important measuring stick for assessing success. The time-pressured and information-packed setting promise to keep accelerating into the future, where products that meet the faster-cheaper-better triad will continue to have a strong competitive advantage. Companies that keep up with, and apply, the ever-evolving trends in project management increase their odds not only for surviving but also for prospering in the exciting times of the third millennium.

Notes and Sources

Chapter 1

"The Software Selection Project," *PM Network,* September 1996. Max Feierstein was interviewed by Jeannette Cabanis of PMI.

ISO Guide 10006: Quality Management: Guidelines to Quality in Project Management. For more information, go to http://www.ansi.org.

A Guide to the Project Management Body of Knowledge, by the PMI Standards Committee (Project Management Institute, 1996).

The Global Status of the Project Management Profession. Proceedings of the 1995 Global Forum in New Orleans (Project Management Institute, 1996).

"Make Projects the School for Leaders," by H. Kent Bowen, Kim B. Clark, Charles A. Halloway, and Steven C. Wheelwright. *Harvard Business Review,* September-October 1994.

Information derived from the Fortune 500 Benchmarking Forum is based on my notes from the meetings of the Forum. The results of these Forums have also been gathered into a book, *Best Practices of Project Management Groups in Large Functional Organizations,* by Frank Toney and Ray Powers (Project Management Institute, 1997).

Chapter 2

The concept of MOBP was first laid out in my *PM Network* column "Up & Down the Organization," during 1996. See "On the Leading Edge of Management: Managing Organizations by Projects," March 1996, pp. 9–11;

"Toward Corporate Project Management," June 1996, pp. 10–13; and "Tom Peters Is Behind the Times," September 1996, pp. 10–11.

"Management of Projects: A Giant Step Beyond Project Management," by Rudolph G. Boznak. *PM Network,* January 1996.

Chapter 3

Information about Promon is from a personal interview with Carlos Siffert, January 27, 1998.

The concept of aligning projects with corporate strategy was first discussed in my column "Lining Up the Corporate Ducks," *PM Network,* February 1997, pp. 17–18.

Chapter 4

The outline for the executive session was first published in my column "Socking Project Management to Your Organization: First, You've Got to Get Their Attention," *PM Network,* October 1997, pp. 22–23.

Chapter 5

A discussion of the various types and sites of project offices was first published in my column "O Give Me a Home," *PM Network,* August 1997, pp. 18–19.

Personal notes from the Forum 500 Project Management Benchmarking Forum, Milwaukee, September 19, 1997.

Chapter 6

The basics of stakeholder management were discussed in my column "Will the Real Stakeholders Please Stand Up?" *PM Network,* December 1995, pp. 9–10.

Chapter 8

A Guide to the Project Management Body of Knowledge by the PMI Standards Committee (Project Management Institute, 1996).

Chapter 9

Notes from AMA's Executive Forum on the Project Organization, "Transitioning for Maximum Corporate Agility," November 17–18, 1997, Miami Beach. Presentations cited included "Project Management Education: Consistent and Flexible for Bottom-Line Value," by Sue Guthrie, Manager, IBM Project Management Center of Excellence; "Creating an Environment for Successful Projects: The Quest to Manage Project Management," by Randy Englund, Hewlett-Packard Company; and "Effectively Building and Managing a Team Culture," by Debbie Hinsel, Pfizer.

Chapter 10

"A Project Manager Competency Model," by Ron Waller, PMP. *Proceedings of the 28th Annual Project Management Institute Seminars & Symposium* (Project Management Institute, 1997), p. 453.

"Project Management Competence for the Next Century," by Lynn Crawford. *Proceedings of the 1997 Project Management Institute Seminars & Symposium* (Project Management Institute, 1997), pp. 411–416.

Information on APM and IPMA models was derived from materials posted to the Project Management Forum Web site at www. pmforum.org/prof/standard.htm#CERTIFICATION, January 24, 1998.

Chapter 11

"Adding Focus to Improvement Efforts With PM3," by Ron Remy. *PM Network,* July 1997, pp. 43–47. Micro-Frames Technologies developed a PM maturity model called PM3, which uses a similar five-tiered approach.

"Project Management Maturity Model," by Anita Fincher. *Proceedings of the 1997 PMI Seminars & Symposium* (Project Management Institute, 1997), pp. 1028–1035.

"760 Days and Counting . . ." by Jeannette Cabanis. *PM Network,* December 1997, p. 46.

Capability Maturity Model for Software, *SEI Technical Reports 91-TR-024* (Software Engineering Institute, August 1991).

"Benchmarking Project Management Organizations," by C. W. Ibbs and Young-Hoon Kwak. *PM Network,* February 1998, pp. 49–53.

Chapter 12

"A Proven Connection: Performance Management and Business Results" by Danielle McDonald and Abbie Smith. *Compensation & Benefits Review,* January-February 1995, pp. 59–64.

"One More Time: How Do You Motivate Employees?" by Frederick Herzberg. *Harvard Business Review,* 46, 1 (1968), pp. 53–62.

"Employee Engagement in Reengineering," by Dutch Holland and Sanjiv Kumar. *PM Network,* June 1996, pp. 35–39.

Chapter 13

"Communications: The Project Manager's Essential Tool," by Ray Boedecker. *PM Network,* December 1997, pp. 19–21.

"Communication, Commitment, and the Management of Meaning," by Bud Baker. *PM Network,* December 1997, pp. 35–36. Baker is head of the MBA Project Management Program at Wright State University.

Chapter 14

"Envisioning the Next Century," by Jeannette Cabanis. *PM Network,* September 1997, pp. 25–31.

"Toward a Corporate Project Management Culture: Fast-Tracking Into the Future," by Paul C. Dinsmore. *Proceedings of the 1997 PMI Seminars & Symposium* (Project Management Institute, 1997), p. 447.

APPENDIX

Professional Organizations That Support Project Management

Project Management Institute
Four Campus Boulevard
Newton Square, Pennsylvania 19073-3299
Tel: 610/356-4600; Fax: 610/734-4647
E-mail: pmieo@pmi.org
World Wide Web: www.pmi.org

PMI also has cooperative agreements with the following organizations:

AACE International
Tel: 304/296-8444; Fax: 304/291-5728

Australian Institute of Project Managers (AIPM)
Tel: +61-02-9960-0058; Fax: +61-02-9960-0052

Construction Management Association of America (CMAA)
Tel: 703/356-2622; Fax: 703/356-6388

Engineering Advancement Association of Japan (ENAA)
Tel: +81-3-3502-4441; Fax: +81-3-3502-5500

Institute of Industrial Engineers (IIE)
Tel: 770/449-0460; Fax: 770/263-8532

Institute of Project Management (IPM-Ireland)
Tel: +353-1-661-4677; Fax: +353-1-661-3588

International Project Management Association (IPMA)
Tel: +45-45-76-46-76; Fax: +45-45-76-80-20

Korean Institute of Project Management and Technology (PROMAT)
Tel: +822-510-5835; Fax: +822-510-5380

Performance Management Association (PMA)
Tel: 714/443-0373; Fax: 714/443-0374

Project Management Institute of Canada
Tel: 403/229-9708; Fax: 403/281-3068

Russian Project Management Association (SOVNET)
Tel: +7-095-133-24-41; Fax: +7-095-131-85-29

Western Australian Project Management Association, Inc. (WAPMA)
Tel: 619/383-3849; Fax: 619/383-3849

In addition, there are numerous other organizations in related fields that may be able to provide information about project management. Current contact information for these and other professional and technical organizations worldwide can generally be found in your local library or by searching the World Wide Web.

American Society for Quality Control
American Society of Civil Engineers
Construction Industry Institute
National Association for Purchasing Management
National Contract Management Association
Society for Human Resource Management

Sources of Project Management Expertise

The following list of project management consultants and trainers was compiled by PMI Publications in 1997. PMI publishes a similar list annually in *PM Network* magazine.

21st Century Management Inc., William A. Zimmer, 10537 B. Green Valley Rd., Union Bridge, MD 21791, 410-775-1467

ABT Corporation, Christine Chevaux, 4747 E. Elliot Rd., PO Box 29-485, Phoenix, AZ 85044, 602-496-9131

ABT Corporation, Harriet Girdley, 361 Broadway, New York, NY 10013, 212-219-8945, 212-219-1589

ACA Consultants, Keith Linton, 342 Main St., Rochester, MI 48307, 810-650-1112, 810-650-1731

Access Project Management, Chris Johnston, 4/1 Charles St., South Perth, 6151, Australia, 61-9-367-1572, 61-9-367-3737

ACM—Administrative Controls Mgmt. Inc., Anthony J. Werderitsch, 525 Avis Dr., Suite 2, Ann Arbor, MI 48108, 313-995-9640, 313-995-9638

Acquisition Management Institute, Al Caflith, 7432 Alban Stablup, Suite B252, Springfield, VA 22150, 703-440-5000, 703-440-5005

This list is reprinted from "1997 Project Management Consultants & Trainers Survey," by PMI (1997) with permission of the Project Management Institute, Four Campus Boulevard, Newton Square, PA 19073–3299, a worldwide organization of advancing the state-of-the-art in project management. Phone: (610) 356–4600. FAX: (610) 356–4647.

ACT Project Management Inc., Barbara Hoganson, 5829 Jeff Place, Edina, MN 55436, 612-926-9654, 612-926-1810

Adaptive Project Management, Henry E. Mensing, 112 W. Campus View Blvd., Columbus, OH 43235, 614-885-2118

Administrative Controls Mgmt. Inc., Tony Werderitsch, 525 Avis Dr. #2, Ann Arbor, MI 48108, 313-995-9640, 313-995-9638

Africon, Dr. P. S. Viljoen, PO Box 905, Pretoria, 0001, South Africa, 27 12 427 2521, 27 12 427 2540

Afterimage, Ande Gromosky, 5200 DTC Pkwy., Suite 260, Englewood, CO 80111, 303-220-9992, 303-220-0854

Air Force Institute of Technology, Robert R. Bergseth, 2950 P St., Wright-Patterson AFB, OH 45433, 937-255-7777 ext. 32

Akkon, Christopher B. Burch, 407 S. Gummon St., Pittsburgh, PA 15232, 412-361-5325

ALF—Tech Consulting, Alfred Mitterdorfer, PO Box 166649, Brackendonns, 1454, South Africa, 27-11-868-1820

Alfa Management Group Inc., Ed Elgerzawy, 239 Parkview Ave., Suite 200, North York, ON, M2N 3Z2, Canada, 416-730-0305, 416-730-0239

Allen & Affiliates, Inc., Edward S. Allen, 3491 Emerson Dr., Roseville, CA 95664-7905, 916-781-2802, 916-783-4699

American Graduate University, Paul McDonald, 733 N. Dodsworth Ave., Covina, CA 91724, 818-966-4576, 818-915-1709

AMS User Services, Inc., Jim Dubbert, 2000 West Loop South #2150, Houston, TX 77027, 713-871-0363, 713-871-9513

AMX International, Inc., Glen Boyls, 1050 17th St. NW, Suite 600, Washington, DC 20036-5503, 202-223-1444, 202-466-6780

Anderson McLean Associates, Inc., R. Alan McLean, 10220 129th St., Edmonton, AB, T5N 1W7, Canada, 403-452-1735

Angel Group, Ann Miller, 6605 Rolling Vista, Suite 101, Dallas, TX 75248, 972-458-7052, 972-458-7053

Angeles Crest Consulting, Donald J. Martinelli, 5221 Vista Lejana Lane, La Canada, CA 91011, 818-790-1128

Apex Project Management Ltd., Ron Eckman, PO Box 10778, Wellington, New Zealand, 64-4-499-8162, 64-4-499-8164

Applications Management Group, Robin Morris, 4 Lyons Terrace, Kinnelon, NJ 07405, 973-838-8758, 800-299-3432

Applied Integration Management, Mark Patlan, 200 Pine Ave., Suite 200, Long Beach, CA 90802, 310-983-6727, 310-983-6730

Applied Management Associates, Dr. Larry A. Smith, 9611 Conchshell Manor, Plantation, FL 33324, 954-370-7507, 954-473-8308

Arthur Andersen, Rian Gorey, 225 Peachtree St., NE Suite 505, Atlanta, GA 30303, 404-658-1776, 404-221-4300

AT&T, Ron Sedlak, 19 School House Rd., Somerset, NJ 08875, 908-302-3285, 908-560-2879

Athena Consulting, Inc., Gary Nelson, 4008 Bienvenue Dr., Greensboro, NC 27409, 910-605-0220, 910-665-1402

Atkey Consulting, Allison Atkey, 151 Oak St., Winnipeg, MB, Canada, 204-489-4234

Atocrates Project Academy, W.G.M. (Bud) Lush, PO Box 30540, Oshawa Centre, Oshawa, ON, L1J 8L8, Canada, 905-723-7444, 905-723-1564

August Star, Inc., Terry Kolz, 2645 Holly Lane North, Plymouth, MN 55447, 612-473-4242

Austen Taylor Corporation, Dan Klein, 300 G. 5th Ave., Suite 330, Naperville, IL 60563, 630-717-7700, 630-717-7373

Axis Consulting International, Lars Sundstrom, One Maritime Plaza, 24th Floor, San Francisco, CA 94111, 415-434-2947, 415-434-2951

B.A.S.I.C., George Wilson, 2720 Asbury Dr., Aurora, IL 60504, 630-820-0835

B.D. Lyons & Associates, Barry D. Lyons, PO Box 1004, Hailey, ID 83333, 208-788-6357, 208-788-4490

Baker Consulting Group, A.C. Fred Baker, 113 Escher Lane, Cary, NC 27511, 919-467-1411

Bakrie Management Group, Paul D. Giammalvo, J1. Sisinqaman-qaraja #23, Jakarta, 1212, Indonesia, 62-21-725-1966, 62-21-724-6807

Barrington Consulting Group, Inc., Scott A. Beisler, 1114 Ave. of Americas, 41st Floor, New York, NY 10036, 212-819-9300, 212-819-9818

Barton Consulting Corp., Jack S. Barton, 130 Buttonwood Circle, Tequesta, FL 33469, 561-746-2252, 561-746-7779

Bates Project Management Inc., Sandy Heard, 190 Somerset St. West, Suite 208, Ottawa, ON, K15 3S3, Canada, 613-567-2060, 613-567-2061

The Battle Group, Roger K. Battle, PO Box 4572, Incline Village, NV 89450, 702-832-0113

Beekay Systems International, Kumar Bhagavatheswaran, 7200 Bollinger Rd., Suite 702, San Jose, CA 95129-2744, 408-252-8441, 408-252-8442

Bell Atlantic, Jonita Mitchell McCree, 11720 Beltsville Dr., Beltsville, MD 20705, 301-595-1224, 301-595-1260

Ben Lao & Associates, Inc., Ken Thayer, 2350 Airport Fwy., Suite 440, Bedford, TX 76022, 817-354-6644, 817-354-5898

Bernate & CIA, German Bernate, Calle 130 N 33-19 T-I (403), Bogota, Colombia, 57-1-615-8323

BEST Practice Group, Dr. Paul O. Ballouir, 12011 Calie Court, Fairfax, VA 22033, 703-805-4479, 703-805-2178

Beyond Expectations Inc., Vicky Jarosz, 39 S. Main St., Suite 25, Clarkston, MI 48346, 810-625-8100, 810-625-2020

Bit of Technology, Laura L. Beiman, 1475 Stoney Wood Way, Penryn, CA 95663, 916-955-9454, 915-663-3333

Blue Planet Engineering, Don Merrik, 2422 Leach Court SE, Olympia, WA 98501, 360-753-6300, 360-753-6240

Boeing Info. Services, Pete Joodi, 77 Outerbelt St., Columbus, OH 43213, 614-575-4914, 614-575-4901

Boston University Corp. Ed. Ctr., Mark A. Gould, 72 Tyng Rd., Tyngsboro, MA 01879, 508-649-9731, 508-649-6926

Both Belle Robb Ltd., Frank Di Ciocco, 4898 de Maisonnevve West, Westmount, QU, H3Z 1M8, Canada, 514-488-8130, 514-488-5063

Bridge the Distance, Inc., Dr. Jacklyn Kostner, 8378 East Jamison Circle SO, Englewood, CO 80112, 303-694-9099, 303-694-9091

Brownstein & Associates, Barry Brownstein, 682 Autumn Tree Place, Westerville, OH 43081-3114, 614-882-1080, 614-882-5155

BRP Project Management, Bruce Rodriguez, 83 William Nicoa Dr., PO Box 68858, Johannesburg, South Africa, 27-11-463-1022

BRTRC Institute, Dawn Sheppard/Kelly Drinkwine, 8260 Willow Oaks Corp. Dr., Suite 800, Fairfax, VA 22031, 703-205-1593, 703-204-9445

BRTRC Technology Research Corp., Bill Baun, 8260 Willow Oaks Corp. Dr., Suite 800, Fairfax, VA 22031, 703-205-1520, 703-204-9445

Buhler & Associates, H. Coyle Buhler, PO Box 1111, Lockhart, TX 78644, 512-398-4414

Building Consulting Services, Jim Van Lente, 24025 SW Newland Rd., Wilsonville, OR 97070, 503-638-5243

Building Project Admin. Services, John R. Tanton, Box 83, Irene, 1675, South Africa, 27-12-667-1009, 27-12-667-1059

Business Improvement Architects, Michael Stanleigh, 302-85 Scarsdale Rd., Don Mills, ON, M3B 2R2, Canada, 416-444-4108, 416-444-6743

Business Management Consultants, Dr. Tom Jones, 17523 Sugar Pine, Houston, TX 77090, 281-440-0455, 281-440-0704

BVI Consulting Engineers, J. R. Barnard, PO Box 2967, Pretoria, South Africa, 27-12-34-91211, 27-12-34-91219

C&C Consultants Inc., Dr. Calin Popescu, 211 Bee Caves Rd., Austin, TX 78746, 512-471-4638, 512-471-3191

C.R. Jean, 37 Av Dr Picaud, Cannes, 06400, France, 33-49-347-6575, 33-49-348-8562

C.W. Costello & Associates, Ify John Dchiagha, 1539 Oak Ave., Arden Hills, MN 55112, 612-513-9000, 612-513-9897

CADENCE Management Corp., Connie Plowman, 9020 SW Washington Sq. Rd., Suite 460, Portland, OR 97223-4426, 503-641-4300, 503-641-4345

Calibre Consulting, John M. Bradley, PO Box 711, Cramerview, 2060, South Africa, 27-11-807-2262, 27-11-807-2263

Cambridge Group, Eugene G. Spiegle, 37 Pine Court, New Providence, NJ 07974, 908-665-1415, 908-665-2269

Cardinale Construction Services, John A. Cardinale, 617 Sartori Dr., Petaluma, CA 94954, 800-883-5646, 707-769-0173

Carlton Consulting & Arbitration Services, Ltd., W. (Don) Stenson, Suite 101, 9618 42nd Ave., Edmonton, AB, T6E 5Y4, Canada, 403-490-1400, 403-465-9297

Carson Group, Ben Mitchell, PO Box 1872, Christchurch, New Zealand, 663-374-9600, 643-376-9601

Carson Group Pty Ltd., Richard Hawkins, Level 8, 52 Alfred St., Milsons Point, 2061, Australia, 02-9956-7033, 02-9956-7186

Cashman Associates, Inc., James H. Cashman, 19 Orchard Hill Rd., Canten, CT 06019, 860-693-6067, 860-693-1717

Cataysis Group, Payson Hall, 1224 Fall Creek Way, Sacramento, CA 95833, 916-929-3629

Caupin Et Associes, Gilles Caupin, 3 Rue Creuse, Treuy, Levelay, 77710, 33-1-64-29-01-11, 33-1-64-29-05-21

Center for Systems Management, James L. Brownlee, 19046 Pruneridge Ave., Cupertino, CA 95014, 408-255-8090, 408-255-5180

Centre for Excellence in Project Management, Adesh Jain, A48, Sector 5, Noida, 201301, India, 91-11-852-6673, 91-11-646-4481

CERA Consult, Arild Sigurdsen, POB 581, Lierstranda, 3412, Norway, 47-92-48-86-58, 47-32-84-14-48

CEW Engineering, Charlotte Wiley, 14729 62nd Ave. North, Maple Grove, MN 55311, 612-559-8674, 612-559-9225

Chamberlain Consulting, Charles Chamberlain, 1416 Hayes St., Orleans, ON, K1E 3M6, Canada, 613-841-0250, 613-841-0251

Chicago Management Consulting, Gene Greiner, 3530 N. Lake Shore Dr., Chicago, IL 60657, 773-665-9015, 773-665-9831

Christopher G. Rotas, 11 Rue Rotheschilo, Geneva, 1202, Switzerland, 41-22-731-5039

Claremont Consulting Group, Arnold M. Ruskin, 4525 Castle Lane, La Canada, CA 91011-1436, 818-249-0584, 818-249-5811

Combase, Ray Shilling, 1611 Telegraph Ave., Suite 512, Oakland, CA 94612, 510-238-0711, 510-238-0717

Commint Inc., Doug Davidson, 1511 Katy Fwy. #450, Houston, TX 77079, 281-558-2433, 281-870-9376

COMP-U-LINK, James Bulmer, 331 Cooper St., Suite 600, Ottawa, ON, K2P 0G5, Canada, 613-237-8200, 613-235-7250

Compuware Corporation, Phil Simpson, 7475 Wisconsin Ave., Suite 306, Bethesda, MD 22102, 301-652-1143, 301-654-1590

Concepts Dynamic Inc., Jim Letterer, 1821 Walden Office Square, Suite 500, Schaumburg, IL 60173, 847-397-4400, 847-397-0575

The Constell Group, Inc., Mark Wakelin, 619 River Dr., Elmwood Park, NJ 07407, 201-703-8300, 201-703-8855

The Constell Group, Inc., Ronald J. Jotz, 619 River Dr., Center 1, Elmwood Park, NJ 07407, 201-703-8300, 201-703-8855

Construction Management Consultant, Phil Lanterman, 5844 Mathiloe Dr., Windsor, CA 95492, 707-838-9630

Construction Management Services, John F. Kovacs, 10 Winthrop Rd., Carnegie, PA 15106, 412-276-6031, 412-276-6105

Construction Management Services Co., Seif Kanaan, PO Box 5235-Zahram 11183, Amman, Jordan, 962-6-682-846, 962-6-690-838

Construction Performance Specialist, Inc., Donald F. McDonald, Jr., 5528 Old Bullard Rd., Suite 103, Tyler, TX 75703, 903-581-0200, 903-581-0393

Consultant, Roger F. Trandell, 1700 Sea Spray Court, Suite 2137, Houston, TX 77008-3145, 713-862-7373

Consultants to Management, Inc., W. Stephen Sawle, 20 N. Walker Dr., Suite 2250, Chicago, IL 60606, 312-357-0857, 312-332-3707

Consulting and Audit Canada, Marion Dempsey, 112 Kent St., Tower B, Ottawa, ON, K1A OS5, Canada, 613-995-8237, 613-943-8364

Consulting and Audit Canada, Vernon R. Miller, 112 Kent St., Tower B, Ottawa, ON, K1A 0S5, Canada, 613-996-7627, 613-943-8364

Consultoria Y Servicios Interdisciplinarios, SC, Jose Kramis, Presa Las Pilas N:25, Mexico, 11500, Mexico, 525-557-1234, 525-395-7913

Coopers & Lybrand, Gustave H. Murby, One International Place, 8th Floor, Boston, MA 02110, 617-478-3616, 617-478-3900

Coopers & Lybrand Consulting, Rip Greenfield, 14800 Landmark Blvd., Suite 300, Dallas, TX 75240, 972-448-5081, 972-701-0828

Coopers & Lybrand LLP, Evandro F. Braz, 1301 Ave. of the Americas, New York, NY 10019-6013, 212-259-2979, 212-259-4009

Cornelius and Associates, Kelly C. Steinhilper, 631-G Harden St., Columbia, SC 29205, 800-200-1104, 800-500-8818

Corporate Educational Services, Eric Munro, One Tower Lane, Suite 1000, Oakbrook Terrace, IL 60181, 800-831-1831, 630-574-1991

Corvelle Management Consultants, Inc., Yogi Schulz, 700, 400 5th Ave., SW, Calgary, AB, T2P 0L6, Canada, 403-249-5255

Cressmere Pty Ltd., Chris Henshaw, 23 Balmerino Dr., Carina, 4152, Australia, 61-7-3899-2767, 61-7-3899-4767

CSC Artemis, Dave Reinmuth, 1415 Lakeshore Dr., Irving, TX 75060, 972-986-7991, 972-986-0313

CSC Artemis, Richard Hayden, 10530 Rosehaven St., Suite 600, Fairfax, VA 22030, 703-293-4400, 703-277-1052

CSC Artemis Products & Services, Paul McGough, 10530 Rosehaven St., Suite 600, Fairfax, VA 22030, 703-293-7414, 703-277-1052

CSC Continuum, Robert A. Mozgawa, 9500 Arboretum Blvd., Austin, TX 78759, 512-338-7899, 512-338-7730

Cushman & Associates, Inc., Michael A. Cushman, 100 Pecaniere, Mandeville, LA 70471, 504-845-9965, 504-845-1955

Cuthbertson Project Management, Kelly Cuthbertson, 3672 19th St., San Francisco, CA 94110, 415-255-1743, 415-255-8005

D. B. Crane and Assoc. Inc., David Crane, 78 Oak Hill Rd., Southborough, MA 01745, 508-229-0147

D. N. Frank Associates, Don Frank, PO Box 295, Flurham Park, NJ 07932, 973-377-6782

Dais Systems, Inc., William F. Mosca, 455 Champions View Dr., Alpharetta, GA 30201, 770-475-5876

Dames & Moore, Steve Swenning, 1200 Jadwin, Suite 102, Richland, WA 99352, 509-946-4833, 509-943-4449

Dar Al-Handasah Consult., Dr. Hosni M. Fahmy, PO Box 895, Cairo (11111), Cairo, Egypt, 202-346-3934, 202-346-1170

Data Analysis & Results, Inc., Darrel A. Raynor, 1030 W. Main, Waxahachie, TX 75165-2949, 972-935-9525

Davcar Inc., David Carroll, PO Box 8592, Austin, TX 78713, 512-426-3008, 512-280-3052

Davenport College Corporate Services, Doug Hentschel, 643 S. Waverly Rd., Holland, MI 49423, 616-395-4600, 616-395-4698

David A. Connell & Assoc., Dave Connell, 749 Dividing Rd., Severna Park, MD 21146, 410-647-3889, 410-647-4957

David Cole Consulting, Dave Cole, 2564 N. 150 Ave., Alpha, IL 61413, 309-529-9745

David Hamburger Mgt. Consult, Inc., David Hamburger, 19 Zabe La Dr., New City, NY 10952, 914-352-1564, 914-356-2726

Davis Systems, Darryl L. Davis, 238 Northwood Dr., Harvest, AL 35749-9795, 205-837-0058, 205-895-9178

De Carlo Paternite & Associates, Joe LaMontia, 22526 Center Ridge Rd., Rocky River, OH 44116, 216-524-2721, 216-524-2845

Deanna R. Doherty, 1617 Central Ave., Alameda, CA 94501, 510-769-2115

Decision Precision®, John R. Schuyler, 15492 E. Chenango Ave., Aurora, CO 80015-1703, 800-214-3916, 303-693-2827

Decision Sciences Corp., Michael W. Curran, PO Box 28848, St. Louis, MO 63123, 314-739-2662, 314-536-1001

Defense Systems Management College, Fred Ayer, 9820 Belvoir Rd., Ft. Belvoir, VA 22060-5565, 703-805-4611, 703-805-2215

Defense Systems Mgmt. Corp., Dr. Jay Billings, 555 Sparkmon Dr., Suite 1218, Huntsville, AL 35816, 205-864-0232, 205-830-4979

Delcan, Charles Orolowitz, 133 Wynford Dr., Toronto, ON, M3C 1K1, Canada, 416-441-4111, 416-441-4131

Deloitte & Touche, Karim Al-Husseim, 3854 Baird Rd., Stow, OH 44224, 216-328-0945, 216-328-0857

Demand Const. Services, Jeff Jackmond, 7430 E. Caley Ave., #350, Englewood, CO 80111, 303-740-8647, 303-796-8714

Denmark & Associates, Robert E. Denmark, 38 Digby St., San Francisco, CA 94131, 415-584-4567, 415-337-9280

Desarrollo Tecnologia Y Planeacion, Melesio Gutierrez Perez, Filadelfia Col. Napoles, 03810, Mexico, 525-543-86-58, 525-682-34-70

Dinsmore Associates, Paul C. Dinsmore, Rua Primeiro de Marco 21-12, Rio de Janeiro, Brazil, 20010-000, +5521 221 7622, +5521 252 1200

DJS Business Services, Inc., Denise J. Schweinsberg, 3333 Todd Rd. SW, Prior Lake, MN 55372, 612-440-7360

DMR Consulting Group, Germain Huppe, 1200 Megill College, Montreal, QU, H3B 4G7, Canada, 514-877-3301, 514-877-3351

Dodge & Associates, Ltd., Terry Dodge, 81 Sycamore Dr., Reading, PA 19606, 610-779-1869

Dominick Project Management, Leon Dominick, 6473 Jefferson Hwy., Baton Rouge, LA 70806, 504-926-9145, 504-928-3772

Domino Crest Pty Ltd., Peter Grant, PO Box 1012, Research, 3095, Australia, 613-9719-7108, 613-9719-7112

Doren Associates, David S. Jacob, 32 Dewberry Way, Suite 250, Irvine, CA 92612, 714-786-0052, 714-552-4033

Douglas Business Systems Consultants, Inc., Patricia C. Hess, 307 Yoakum Pkwy. #1826, Alexandria, VA 22304, 703-370-3078, 703-370-2630

Dozal & Associates, Inc., Frank Dozal, 370 17th St., Suite 3170, Denver, CO 80202, 303-446-8464, 303-446-9177

Dr. Jean Couillard, Project Management Consultant, 33 Bear Brook, Gloucester, PQ, Canada, 613-837-2380, 613-837-7406

Dressler & Associates, Robert F. Dressler, 1117 Jefferson Ave., Louisville, CO 80027, 303-666-4515

Dries Associates, Dr. William Dries, 1600 H. High Point Rd., Middleton, WI 53562, 608-831-5542, 608-831-5598

Duhig Berry Inc., Tom Caprariello, 90 Park Ave., Suite 1600, New York, NY 10016, 212-984-1060, 212-984-1061

Duncan-Nevison, Steve Spring, 114 Waltham St., Lexington, MA 02173, 617-861-0124, 617-861-2006

DVIR Dov Consultant, 5 Shturman St., Herzelia, 46311, Israel, 972-9-9573616, 972-9-9586837

Dyer Associates, Philip Dyer, 607 Summit Forest Dr., Marietta, GA 30062, 770-977-8260

Eagle Enterprises, Charles Huston, 26200 W 108th St., Olathe, KS 66061, 913-829-5099

Ed Petrick Consulting, Inc., Ed Petrick, 14706 Shirley St., Omaha, NE 68144, 402-334-9381, 402-697-0455

EDS, Jim Kelley, 5400 Legacy Dr., Plano, TX 75024, 972-604-1412, 972-604-9448

EDS, Walter Taylor, 3715 Northside Pkwy., Bldg. 100, Suite 600, Atlanta, GA 30327, 404-812-2245, 404-812-2466

EDS Project Management Consulting, Scott Webb, A5N-D51, 13600 EDS Dr., Herndon, VA 20171, 703-742-1775, 703-904-8906

Edward (Ed) Chapman, 1301 Harrison Lane, Austin, TX 78742, 512-385-2481

EIG, Gary De Spain, 13333 Dorset Way, Poway, CA 92064, 619-675-2090

EII, Inc., Bob Wysocki, 4 Otsego Rd., Worcester, MA 01609, 508-791-2062

Electronic Data Systems, Kevin Wille (Detroit Office), 5555 New King St., Troy, MI 48098, 810-578-4268, 810-578-3532

Electronic Delivery Consulting, Inc., Fadi Samafa, 16 Relpuy Court, Scarborough, ON, M1W 2X7, Canada, 416-499-1714, 416-499-0430

Employee Empowerment, Inc., Jerry Touslee, 616 SW 3rd St., Lee's Summit, MO 64063, 816-525-5550, 816-525-5666

Engineering Resources, Inc., Joseph P. Dougherty, 32 Sally Harden Rd., Sussex, NJ 07461, 201-875-7916, 201-702-7965

Engle Asociados, Federico Zambra, Serrano 240-5, Madrid, 28016, Spain, 34-1-345-7276, 34-1-457-2079

Enterprise Management Systems, Alan Teyssier, 359 Saybrook Court, Wallingford, PA 19086, 610-872-5405, 610-872-2307

Env. Strategies & Mgmt., Cliff Harper, 65 D Hale Hollow Rd., Bridgewater Cors, VT 05035, 802-672-6112, 802-672-6227

Environmental Management, Inc., Michael B. Malady, 835 Terminal Dr., Suite 190, Richland, WA 99352, 509-946-1686, 509-946-4194

Envision Consultants, Ltd., Tracey Blackwell, 115 White Horse Pike, 2nd Floor, Haddon Heights, NJ 08035, 609-547-5888, 609-547-5885

EPCG Enterprise Perspectives Consulting Group, Judy Ambler, 11560 West 95th #320, Overland Park, KS 66214, 913-888-3903, 913-888-3613

EPM Consultancy, Prof. Adel El-Samadony, 13 El-Zafrast, Agouza, Egypt, 00202-344-2460, 00202-302-0121

Equinox Limited, Paul Ramsay, PO Box 10-089, The Terrace, Wellington, 6036, New Zealand, 64-4-499-9450, 64-4-499-9510

Erika Jones & Associates, Inc., 7801 Academy Rd. NE, Building 2, Suite 103, Albuquerque, NM 87109, 505-856-1265, 505-856-1018

ES—Consultoria, Carlos Eduardo De Souza, Rua Pedro Osvaldo Venturini 134, Sao Paulo, 04445-140, Brazil, 55-11-522-9295, 55-11-246-6199

ESI International, Ben Sellers, 7814 Odell St., Springfield, VA 22153, 703-558-3000, 703-558-3001

ESI International, Dr. Curtis R. Cook, 4301 N. Fairfax Dr., Suite 800, Arlington, VA 22203, 703-558-3000, 703-558-3001

ESI International, Jim Duncan, 4301 N. Fairfax Dr., Suite 800, Arlington, VA 22203, 703-558-3000, 703-558-3001

ESI International, Simon S. Begg, Pantiles Chambers, 85 High St., Tunbridge Wells, TN11YG, England, 44-0-1892-513191, 44-0-1892-547120

Evans Technology, Inc., Deane Evans, 1335 Northmeadow Pkwy., Roswell, GA 30076, 770-751-9950, 770-751-9619

Executive Coach LTD, Ken W. Hill, 148 Varsity Cres. NW, Calgary, AB, T3B 2Z3, Canada, 403-288-2456

Facility & Relocation Services, Inc., Andy Howell, 2704 12th Ave. South, Nashville, TN 37215, 615-383-3044, 615-298-1611

Fair Canada Engineering Ltd., John E. Fair, 810, 602 12 Ave. SW, Calgary, AB, T2R 1J3, Canada, 403-269-5311, 403-265-5559

Farid & Associates, Dr. Foad Farid, PO Box 99, Santa Monica, CA 90406, 310-573-4110, 310-828-3155

The Federal Market Group, Daniel M. Jacobs, 124 Park St., SE, Suite 201, Vienna, VA 22180, 703-242-9650, 703-242-9652

Filupeit & Associates, LLC, Donald Filupeit, 7587 E. Milton Dr., Scottsdale, AZ 85262, 602-585-3238, 602-502-2470

First Mark Technologies Ltd., S. Michael Faulkner, 16 Concourse Gate, Suite 300, Ottawa, ON, K1Z 8L2, Canada, 613-723-8020, 613-723-8048

Fissure Corporation, Jesse Freese, 12751 Nicollet Ave. South, Suite 201, Burnsville, MN 55337, 612-882-0800, 612-882-9067

Fleming Management Consultancy, Quentin Fleming, 14001 Howland Way, Tustin, CA 92680, 714-731-0304

Fouquet & Associates, Gregory Fouquet, 3282 Rutledge Dr., Las Vegas, NV 89120, 702-897-5340

G.A. Development Group, Inc., Joseph E. Gaudet, PO Box 817, Washington Crossing, PA 18977, 215-493-5191, 215-493-9163

G.E. McCoy & Assoc., Gerald McCoy, 835 18th Ave., Salt Lake City, UT 84103, 801-328-8986, 801-575-8314

G.H.Q., Ltd., Gerald H. Quinn, 1082 Grand Oaks Glen, Marietta, GA 30064, 770-426-4466

Garold D. Oberlender & Assoc. Inc., Garold Oberlender, 23 Yellow Brick Rd., Stillwater, OK 74074, 405-377-2774, 405-377-1678

General Physics Corp., Jim Teer, 11455 N. Meridian #250, Carmel, IN 46032, 317-843-5800, 317-843-5808

General Physics Corp., Tony Skubi/Fred Frendo, 580 Kirts Blvd., Suite 310, Troy, MI 48084, 810-244-9870, 810-244-9793

General Physics Corp., W. Lee Harper, 27 W. Queens Way, Suite 203A, Hampton, VA 23669, 757-727-9477, 757-727-9472

George E. Dew, 287 Levis, Hull, QU, J8Z 1A3, Canada, 819-772-9332, 819-772-9392

Gerencia De Proyectos, Arcesion Lopez-Prieto, Carrera 50 137-43, Bogota, Colombia, 57-1-271-1318, 57-1-222-5503

Gestion De Projects Mentor, Inc., Benoit Lalonde, 15 Rue Jacques—Cartier Nord, St. Jean Sur. Rfchelien, QU, J3B 8R8, Canada, 514-358-6500 ext. 5771, 514-358-6555

Gestion DJR Plus Inc., Denis Martineau, 3475 Rue Meilleur, Brossard, Quebec, QU, J4Y 2A7, Canada, 514-656-8263, 514-656-6821

Gestion Ecosys Inc., Guy Messier, 634 St. Jacques W, Suite 303, Montreal, QU, H3C 1C7, Canada, 514-874-0077, 514-874-0660

GFM, Jochen Platz, Gross Hesse Loher Str 19A, Munich, D 81479, Germany, 0049-89-79-17-174, 0049-89-79-17-183

Giorgio Sartori, Ave. Des Traquets 151, Brussels, B-1160, Belgium, 32-2-675-3185, 32-2-673-3800

GL Consulting, Gary Shaff, 47 Eastwood, Medford, OR 97504, 541-773-6471

GLH, Inc., Dr. G. T. Haugan, PO Box 730, Heathsville, VA 22473, 703-821-3947, 703-821-8112

GLH, Inc., Dr. Ginger Levin, 2900 NE 46th St., Lighthouse Point, FL 33064, 954-783-9819, 954-783-9235

Global Project Management Group, Ltd., James Klanke, PO Box 6641, Lee's Summit, MO 64064, 816-525-0747, 816-524-4626

Global Quality Management Associates, Paul Gladeux, 3355 SW Upper Dr., Lake Oswego, OR 97035, 503-697-8429, 506-697-8429

GMP Associates Inc., Max M. Shoura, 95-325 Kahikinui Court #219, Mililani, HI 96789, 808-623-0057, 808-538-3269

Godcharles Goulet & Associates, Denis Godcharles, 582 Somerset St. West, Ottawa, ON, Canada, 613-237-9331, 819-246-9030

Goff Associates, Inc., Stacy Goff, 6547 N. Academy #534, Colorado Springs, CO 80918, 719-488-3850, 719-488-9375

Goodine-Hellberg Consulting Services, Jack Hellberg, 25 Scarborough Ave., Scarborough, ON, Canada, 416-283-0529, 416-283-6369

Gordon L. Tucker, 4608 Glenwood Hills Dr. NE, Albuquerque, NM 87111, 505-292-6182

GPMT, Inc., Lee Ekstrom, 5404 W. Elm St., Suite C, McHenry, IL 60050, 815-385-2944, 815-385-2963

Grander Services Inc., David Russell Grander, PO Box 1737, Boise, ID 83701-1737, 800-211-4726, 208-331-2818

Granot-Striechman Management Consultants Ltd., Mickey Granot, PO Box 2353, Rishon Le Zion, 75121, Israel, 972-3-648-7868, 972-3-648-6689

The Griffin Tate Group, Karen Tate, 3604 Carpenter's Green Lane, Cincinnati, OH 45241-3219, 513-984-8150, 513-984-8151

Growth Performance, Craig Wydell, 610 Ivy Court, Lake Zurich, IL 60047, 847-726-2830

Grupo Aconsa, Jose A. Cortina, San Francisco 1374, Mexico, DF, 03210, 525-575-2093, 525-559-8970

Grupo Rioboo, Rodolfo Ambriz, Insurgentes Sur 1194-301, Col. Del. Valle, 03100, Mexico, 525-559-1381, 525-559-1575

GTW Corp., Barbara Andersen, 500 S 336th, Suite 204, Federal Way, WA 98003, 206-874-8884, 206-838-1798

GTW Corp., Bruce Taylor, 500 South 336th, Suite 204, Federal Way, WA 98003, 206-874-8884, 206-838-1798

HAAS Associates Inc., John J. Haas, 23 Attwood Dr., St. Albert, AB, T8N 2T4, Canada, 403-458-9322

Haessler Software Canada Ltd., G. Schmitt, 108 Beaconsfield Ave., Toronto, ON, M6J 334, Canada, 416-533-7540

The Hampton Group, Dick Billows, 3547 S. Ivanhoe, Denver, CO 80237, 303-756-4247, 303-727-4105

Hans Thamhain Associates, Hans Thamhain, 25 Lanewood Ave., Framingham, MA 01701, 508-620-0370, 617-891-2896

Hanscomb Inc., Paul T. McDermott, 225 West Wacker Dr., Suite 825, Chicago, IL 60610, 312-332-0070, 312-332-0071

Hayworth Consulting Services, Scott Hayworth, 301 13th St. SW, Ruskin, FL 33570, 813-641-1783, 813-641-1532

HIFAB, Johan Low, PO Box 19090, Stockholm, 10432, Sweden, 46-8-674-6600, 46-8-673-2023

High-Point Rendel, James G. Zack, Jr., 4199 Campus Dr., Suite 650, Irvine, CA 92612, 714-854-5237, 714-854-5239

High-Point Rendel, John A. Smith, 600 N. Pine Island, Plantation, FL 33324, 954-424-6363, 954-424-6365

Hilary Carlile & Associates Ltd, Hilary Carlile, PO Box 99-023, Newmarket, Auckland, New Zealand, 64-9-5222053, 64-9-5221332

Hill Walker Inc., John H. Walker, 960 Rice Rd., Edmonton, AB, T6R 1A1, Canada, 403-988-5905, 403-439-1132

Holly & Rose Pty. Ltd., Roger Worthy, 10 Holyrood St., Hampton, 3188, Australia, 61-39-521-6370

Hood Avers, Dr. Joseph L. Hood, 4404 Stars Jordan Dr., Annandale, VA 22003, 703-978-5716, 703-323-8462

HPI Associates, Stephen F. Stofanak, 4 Jewett Ave., South Berwick, ME 03908, 207-384-1975, 207-384-0114

Hulett & Associates, David T. Hulett, 318 14th St., Santa Monica, CA 90402, 310-395-9866

HVR Canada Inc., Alan Mayer, 255 Albert St., Suite 902, Ottawa, ON, K1P 6A9, Canada, 613-230-5004, 613-230-0559

I.S. Management and Methods, Kathleen Hohner, 147 Brenda Cres., Scarborough, ON, Canada, 416-269-4904, 416-269-2324

I.T. Business Consultants, Colleen Johnson, 30 Heather Rd., Toronto, ON, M4G 3G3, Canada, 416-322-0329, 416-322-9780

ICF Kaiser, Peter Bonner, 9300 Lee Hwy., Fairfax, VA 22031, 703-934-3815, 703-218-2662

ICF Kaiser Engineers, Said E. Fraij, 5949 E. Colonial Dr., Orlando, FL 32817, 407-380-3333, 407-380-3008

ICS Group, Ronald J. Yelin, 40 Richards Ave., Norwalk, CT 06854, 203-838-1150, 203-886-7170

IDP—Instituto de Direccion de Proyectos, Norberto R. Figini, Ciudad de la Paz 2238—7 A, Buenos Aires, 1428, Argentina, 541-784-9577, 541-544-8410

IFIP Institut F. Internat. Projekte, Prof. Dr. Gerald Adlbrecht, Fichtenweg 21, Mudersbach, D- 57555, Germany, 49-271-382179, 49-271-3829696

Illinois Institute of Technology, Dr. David Arditi, 3201 S. Dearborn St., Chicago, IL 60616, 312-567-3540, 312-567-3519

IMS Group, Stan Zawrotny, PO Box 2381, Ponte Vedra Beach, FL 32004, 904-273-9400, 904-273-6283

Independent Consultant, Wayne L. Hinthorn, PO Box 176, Half Moon Bay, CA 94019, 415-726-9413, 415-726-6218

Industra, Inc., Dan Burciaga 15055 SW Sequoia Pkwy., Suite 100, Portland, OR 97224, 503-620-5333, 503-620-0120

Industrial Cost Management, Jerry D. Canezaro, 5723 Superior Dr., Suite B-2, Baton Rouge, LA 70816, 504-292-1910, 504-292-2325

Inform Worldwide Inc., Darren Dambly, 5600 Greenwood Plaza Blvd., Suite 150, Englewood, CO 80111, 303-689-9200, 303-689-9222

Informatics Corporation, Dale L. Stewart, 6006 Jordan Dr., Loveland, CO 80537, 970-663-4573, 970-593-9490

Infotech Management Inc., Russ Choyce, 2418 Cales Dr., Arlington, TX 76013, 817-861-2296, 817-861-0405

Innovative Project Management, Jack N. French, 10297 E. Inspiration Dr., Parker, CO 80134, 303-840-1260

Innovus Ltd., Muzzay Dill, PO Box 10-547, Wellington, New Zealand, 64-4-472-0877, 64-4-472-0858

Institute of Global Competitiveness, Viral Chokshi, 125 Edinburgh St., Suite 200, Cary, NC 27511, 919-462-6699, 919-462-6284

Instream Management Group, Ltd., William Kronemeyer, Box 2243, Bankers Hall, Calgary, AB, T2P 4J1, Canada, 403-531-1795, 403-531-1798

Integrated Management Associates, Kanan Alhassani, 17 Aqueduct Rd., Natick, MA 01760, 617-930-0507, 508-655-6540

Integrated Process Developers, Douglas B. Bosenger, 313 Buckingham, Canton, MI 48188, 313-317-4686, 313-337-9572

Integrated Project Systems, Inc., Cathy Tonne, 1070 Sixth Ave., Suite 110, Belmont, CA 94002, 415-802-1020, 415-637-1724

Integrated Technology Group, Inc., Owen McGovern, 500 Park Blvd., Suite 70C, Itasca, IL 60143, 630-616-2200, 630-616-2206

Intelligroup, Inc., Ashutosh Yadav, 517 Route 1 South, Iselin, NJ 08830, 908-750-1600, 908-750-1880

International Institute for Learning, Inc., E. LaVerne Johnson, 110 E. 59th St., 6th Floor, New York, NY 10022-1380, 212-758-0177, 212-909-0558

Interpro ADF Corporation, Elie Asmar, 3569 Mt. Diablo, Suite 210, Lafayette, CA 64569, 510-299-8500, 510-299-8511

Intersect International Incorporated, Frank Fletcher, PO Box 54, Hampden, MA 04444-0054, 207-862-3837, 207-862-2101

Interwest Construction, Inc., James H. Confer, Sr., 2253 NE Cornell Rd., Hillsboro, OR 97124, 503-640-4112, 503-640-0342

Ira Bitz & Associates, Ltd., Ira Bitz, 9007 LeVelle Dr., Chevy Chase, MD 20815, 301-654-1119, 301-656-3229

Iris Technologies, Corrado Viganoi, Via Filzi 41, Milano, 20124, Italy, 39-26-713-171, 39-26-707-555

J.D. Garner & Associates, Inc., Jeff Garner, 2201 Fourth Ave. North, Suite G, St. Petersburg, FL 33704, 813-823-0427, 813-822-1621

J.F. Burke Consultants, Jack Burke, 16 Harwood Ave., Harvick, MA 02645, 508-432-4043, 508-432-8176

J.J. Glatt & Associates, Inc., Joe Glatt, PO Box 5366, Clinton, NJ 08809-5366, 908-735-8000, 908-735-0329

J.M. Peters & Associates, Jim Peters, 9513 Lucerne St., Ventura, CA 93004, 805-659-0280

James Bent Associations, Inc., James A. Bent, 697 E. Chelsea Dr., Bountiful, UT 84010, 801-295-6179, 801-295-6482

James Martin & Co., Kathy Lindstrom, 6133 N. River Rd., Suite 600, Rosemont, IL 60018, 847-292-5040, 847-292-5056

James McLaughlin, 29 Henry St., Sag Harbor, NY 11963, 516-725-7945, 516-725-2688

James W. Harte Consulting, James W. Harte, 74 Tanglewood Dr., Summit, NJ 07901, 908-273-4744

Jamison Group, Patti E. Jamison, 5004 NW 75th Lane, Gainesville, FL 32653, 352-376-0388, 352-375-1154

Jantesa, Rolando Martinez, PO Box 522237, Miami, FL 33152-2237, 562-285-2183

Jason Associates Corporation, Marc Zocher, 3250 Port of Benton Blvd., Richland, WA 99352, 509-375-0556, 509-375-0196

Jean Golonka, 5 Pheasant Run, Kinnelon, NJ 07405, 973-492-2447, 973-838-7593

Jean Tempke, 306 N. Mountain Ave., Claremont, CA 91711, 909-624-0299

Jean-Francois d'Entremont, 2022 Ave. De L'Eolise, Montreal, PQ, H4E 1H3, Canada, 514-761-7689

Jeffrey K. Pinto, 2832 Madeira Dr., Erie, PA 16506, 814-898-6430, 814-898-6223

Jenise N. Baber, 7699 Poplar Rd., Brownsburg, IN 46112, 317-852-4138, 317-852-2703

JF Thibodeau Inc., Joe Thibodeau, 490 West St., PO Box 425, Taylors Falls, MN 55084, 612-488-0610

JFR International, Arthur D. Tullett, Gogmore Lane, Chertsey Surrey, KT11 2ND, United Kingdom, 44-19-32-570604, 44-19-32-570365

Jim Spiller & Associates, Jim Spiller, 8004 Bottlebrush Dr., Austin, TX 78750, 512-342-2232, 512-342-2234

John M. Cotterell, P.E. Inc., John Cotterell, PO Box 440005, Houston, TX 77244-0005, 281-496-6666, 281-496-3299

Johnson & Associates Ltd., Richard A. Johnson, 125 Lincoln Ave., Suite 400, Santa Fe, NM 87501, 505-989-3514, 505-984-1202

Joy Luhman Consulting, Joy Luhman, 26 Fortification Rd., Seatoon, Wellington, New Zealand, 00-64-4-380-9490, 00-64-4-380-9497

K2 Project Control Systems, Paul Krogh, 4330 East West Hwy., Suite 320, Bethesda, MD 20814, 301-656-2228, 301-656-0229

Kaon Project Management, Roger Pither, 411 Roosevelt Ave., Suite 301, Ottawa, ON, K2A 3X9, Canada, 613-722-0114, 613-722-9059

The Karsten Institute Inc., Ron Karsten, 16400 S. Stoltz Rd., Oregon City, OR 97045, 503-650-5855, 503-650-7598

KE Group, Roger Kent, 112 Jefferson, Tiburon, CA 94920, 415-384-8864

Ken Colman Consulting, Ken Colman, 271 Ridley Blvd., Suite 1008, Toronto, ON, M5M 4N1, Canada, 416-485-2061

Kepner Tregoe Logicim AB, Henn Nystroum, Box 7057, Soterlalie, Sweden, 15207, 46-10-226-9145, 46-8-550-87902

Kern Konsult USA Inc., Ernst P. Harting, 1295 Texter Mountain Rd., Robesonia, PA 19551, 717-484-0253, 717-484-0234

Klohn-Crippen Consultants Ltd., Don Macintyre, 600-510 Burrard St., Vancouver, ON, V6C 3A8, Canada, 604-664-2000, 604-664-2051

Knowledge Alliance, Ger Maguire, 5160 Yonge St., North York, ON, M2N 6L9, Canada, 416-733-9509 ext. 332, 416-733-3255

The Knowledge Webb, Ken Whiting, 6901 S. Yosemite, Suite 207, Englewood, CO 80112, 303-793-9900, 303-793-9585

Koala-T Management Consulting, Inc., Larry A. Mars, 16748 E. Smoky Hill Rd., Suite 317, Aurora, CO 80015, 303-690-6360, 303-690-1888

Kraulis & Associates, Inc., Olaf E. Kraulis, 140 Holmes Ave., North York, ON, M2N 4M6, Canada, 416-225-1541, 416-226-4848

KRUSE, Inc., Wally Kruse, PO Box 2010, Sparks, NV 89432, 702-721-2189

L. Sanders & Associates, Lonnie Sanders III, PO Box 8246, Emeryville, CA 94662, 408-291-1115, 510-654-1952

L.I.S. Lavy Int'l Software Ltd., Hr. Giora Lavy, PO Box 325, Kiriat-Bi Alik, 27103, Israel, 972-4-8701026, 972-4-8236231

Lakie Associates, Mary Lakie, Marfield View, Kitleyknowe, Carlops, Edinburgh, EH26 9NJ, United Kingdom, 44-1968-661167

Laurent & Associates, Inc., Frank Laurent, 10826 Admiral Bend Way, Knoxville, TN 37922, 423-675-1963

Lawrence E. Long, 2026 Cliff Dr., Suite 170, Santa Barbara, CA 93109, 805-962-5438, 805-899-2198

LCS International Inc., David J. Lanners, 12140 Larchgate Dr., Dallas, TX 75243-5053, 972-690-1131, 972-690-3107

LCT Consulting, Louis C. Terminillo, 11 Bongort Dr., West Orange, NJ 07052, 201-575-4321, 201-575-1234

LD&M Consultores Associados, Lucio J. Diniz, Alaneda Da Serra, 420-CJ 510/511, Nova Lima, 34.000.000, Brazil, 031-286-3405

Leading Special Projects, Inc., W.P. Doc Holiday, 2722 Brookdale Court, Crestview Hills, KY 41017, 606-341-4924, 606-341-0605

Leah Paras & Associates, Leah Paras, 4305 Green Cliffs Rd., Austin, TX 78746-1244, 512-327-1915, 512-327-8802

Leshem-Nituv Engineers Ltd., Mottie Shwartz, PO Box 2108, Herzlia, 46120, Israel, 972-9-9585661, 972-9-9588648

Lewis P. Miller, 340 Hollyridge Dr., Roswell, GA 30076, 770-998-5312

LFJ Group, Larry F. Jones, 116 Albert St., Suite 814, Ottawa, ON, K1P 5G3, Canada, 613-760-8836, 613-841-6038

LGS Group Inc., Max Feierstein, 3007-201 Partage Ave., Winnipeg, MB, R3B 3K6, Canada, 204-989-0820, 204-989-0849

Lindberg Consulting, Lesley Lindberg, 309 St. Paul St., St. Adolphe, MB, Canada, 204-883-2784, 204-883-2239

LMond Associates, Laura Caughlin, 4333 NE 17th St., Renton, WA 98059-3942, 206-277-8779, 206-277-8727

Locher Interests LTD, J. S. McElroy, 406 W. Fireweed Lane #101, Anchorage, AL 99503, 907-258-2200, 907-258-5842

LOG/AN, Ed Fisher, 924 Westwood Blvd., Los Angeles, CA 90024, 310-208-3505, 310-824-4661

Logic Ability Inc., Adrienne Scott, 1875 Barsuda Dr., Mississauga, ON, L5J 1V3, Canada, 905-855-5191

Logicum Kepner Tregoe, Henrik Nystrom, Box 7057, Stockholm, 15207, Sweden, 46-10-226-9145, 46-8-550-87902

Logistics Redesign, Inc., Larry Rutledge, 8059 Andiron Lane, Jessup, MD 20794, 301-206-3024

The London Group, Sid Rimmington, PO Box 848, 29 Palms, CA 92277, 619-362-4201

Louise Novakowski, 5730 Ferguson Court, Delta, BC, V4L 2J4, Canada, 604-943-2731, 604-943-0952

Lucent Technologies, Harry Volpe, Room F132, 140 Centennial Ave., Piscataway, NJ 08855-1374, 732-457-7165, 732-457-7257

M&P Associates, Michael J. Tuckett, 2 Realm Place, Massey, Auckland, 1008, New Zealand, 64-9-832-4619

M.S.K. Heshev—Israel, E. Marshall, 5 Margalit St., Tel Aviv, Israel, 972-3-647-1550, 972-3-647-2291

MAC Technical Services, Troy Cowan, 2309 Renard SE, Suite 103, Albuquerque, NM 87106, 505-242-7525, 505-242-0328

MacAskill & Associates, Inc., Adele MacAskill, 63 Conference Blvd., West Hill, ON, M1C 2E4, Canada, 416-284-2790, 416-284-9874

Management & Computer Counselors, Francis M. Webster, Jr., PO Box 2257, Cullowhee, NC 28723, 704-586-8521

Management Directions, Inc., Richard L. Plasket, 200 Clark St., PO Box 235, Chapin, SC 29036, 803-345-6891, 803-345-6707

Management Planning & Control Systems, Robert Youker, 5825 Rockmere Dr., Bethesda, MD 20816, 301-320-5806, 301-320-2127

Management Technologies Group Inc., John Tuman, Jr., PO Box 160, Morgantown, PA 19543, 610-286-2178

Management Technologies, Inc., Steve Gress, 3331 W. Big Beaver Rd., Troy, MI 48084, 810-643-1915, 810-643-4934

Management Training and Development Associates, Dean Sotiriou, 3907 South Jasmine St., Denver, CO 80237, 303-758-1129, 303-871-2294

Mantix Systems, Inc., James P. Worley, 12020 Sunrise Valley Dr. #120, Reston, VA 20191, 703-715-2450, 703-715-2456

Mario Campero Q, Luis Zegers 119, Dep. 603, Santiago, Chile, 24-61-624

Mark Scholz, 8423 Fort Hunt Rd., Alexandria, VA 22308-1839, 703-779-0859

Marshall Technical Services (MTS), Robert M. Irwin, 2901 Riva Trace Pkwy., Annapolis, MD 21401, 410-224-0841, 410-224-8518

Marvin A. Datz, Inc., Marvin Datz, 4034 Silverwood, Houston, TX 77025, 713-667-2044

Master Systems, Stan Rifkin, PO Box 8208, McLean, VA 22106, 703-883-2121, 703-790-0324

MaxiComm Project Services Inc., Paul Shaltry, 71 E. Wilson Bridge Rd., Suite A-5, Columbus, OH 43085, 614-841-0867, 614-888-8731

MBA & Associates Ltd., Kenneth Mortimer, 51 Spencer St., Wellington, 6004, New Zealand, 64-4-479-5203, 64-4-479-7960

mbpNet, Ahmet Taspinar, 93 Thousand Oaks, Oakland, CA 94605, 510-569-7471, 510-569-4636

mbpNet, William Trnka, 1067 Discovery Way, Concord, CA 94521, 925-672-2672

The Meadowlark Group, Larry Coulter, 3634 Sunderland Circle, Atlanta, GA 30319, 770-457-5975

Media Consulting Inc., Don Barnett, 900 Senate Dr., Centerville, OH 45459, 937-435-2526, 937-435-2243

MetaVista Consulting Group, Charles Ritchie, 104 Falthorne Lane, Folsom, CA 95630, 916-351-9266

Michael A. Johnson, B.P. 4226, Noumea, New Caledonia, 68-7-26-11-15, 68-7-28-69-78

Microdata Systems, Inc., A. J. Haddad, 5 Talleyrand Dr., Colts Neck, NJ 07722, 732-308-0622, 732-308-1899

Micro-Frame Technologies, Jodi Sacco, 430 N. Vineyard, Ontario, CA 91764, 909-983-2711, 909-984-5382

Micro Planning International, Brad Pirrung, 3801 E. Florida Ave., #507, Denver, CO 80210, 800-852-7526, 303-757-2047

MIP-Tech. Inc., Dr. David R. Lee, 9073 Academy View Court, Dayton, OH 45458, 937-885-5444, 937-885-9915

MLLA & Associates, Inc., Serge Locas, 425 Viger West, Suite 400, Montreal, QU, H2Z 1X2, Canada, 514-875-0878, 514-871-1573

MMSS, Glen C. Veno, PO Box 605, Brighton, MI 48116, 810-227-9256

MPA Consulting, LLC, TS Hand, 4655 Cass St., Suite 309, San Diego, CA 92109, 619-272-6172, 619-272-6175

MTB Project Management Professionals, Inc., Stephen P. Felice, 8301 E. Prentice Ave., Suite 312, Englewood, CO 80111-2903, 303-741-9633, 303-741-9636

MTG, Fran Russell, 14 Inverness Dr. E. 100E, Englewood, CO 80112, 303-706-7140, 303-706-9088

MTS Associates, Jeff Kottmyer, 5709 Oak Green Way, Burke, VA 22015-2311, 703-426-4124, 703-426-4064

N.H. James & Assoc. Inc., Norman James, 25 Linden Rd., Narragansett, RI 02882, 401-782-4564, 401-789-9708

N.V. The STR Company, Steven Ryckebusch, Messem 1, Brugoe, B-8200, Belgium, 32-50-31-98-59, 32-50-31-92-19

Nabil MA Abras Consultants, Nabil Abras, PO Box 1448, Leddah, 21431, Saudi Arabia, 966-2-6711009, 966-2-6718613

NCR Corporation (Philippines), Luis Sp. Sison, 109 Alfaro St., Salcedo Village, Makati City, 1227, Philippines, 632-810-4551, 632-818-4499

NDV Project Management Services, Inc., Nghi M. Nguyen, 1610 Rigaud, Brossard, QU, Canada, 514-672-2693, 514-672-7922

The Neal Whitten Group, Neal Whitten, 335 Camber Trace, Roswell, GA 30076, 770-667-0881, 770-667-0588

North Highland Company, David Peterson, 550 Pharr Rd., Suite 850, Atlanta, GA 30350, 404-238-0600, 404-233-4930

Nutshell Productions, Ltd., Dr. David E. Weil, 3408 Brennan Dr., Raleigh, NC 27613, 919-846-9560, 919-870-1105

Oak Creek Group Inc., Robert Coleman, 31 N. Tejon St., Suite 410, Colorado Springs, CO 80903, 719-578-9683, 719-578-9685

Open Technology Limited, Gerard Fitzgibbon, CM5 Newton Rd., Abbey St., POB 6389, Auckland, New Zealand, 64-9-378-0280, 64-9-378-0293

Oracle 2000 Ltd., Douglas Layton, 2 Selwyn Place, Winnipeg, QU, R3T 3N1, Canada, 204-261-0512

Oracle Corp., Gabe Forray, PO Box 261119, Plano, TX 75026-1119, 972-964-7837, 972-985-1923

P&A Consultants Corp., Hans Picard, Fourth & Walnut Centre, Suite 1510, Cincinnati, OH 45202, 513-241-4242, 513-241-2232

P.M. Associates Ltd., Philip Cesario, 65 Dewdney Ave., Winnipeg, MB, R5B 0E1, Canada, 204-949-5150, 204-943-3700

P2E, Ulla Merz, 5501 Aztec Court, Boulder, CO 80303, 303-499-7301, 303-499-0607

Pace Consulting Group, Anil Kumar Sud, SPL Habitiat Apt. #A, Bangalore, 560002, India, 9180-555-9893

Pacific Contract Designs Inc., Jack Rodgers, 433 Clark Dr., San Mateo, CA 94402, 415-343-2630, 415-343-4466

Pacific Rim Architecture Ltd., 14439—104 Ave., Surrey, BC, V3R 1M1, Canada, 604-581-7750, 604-581-8870

Pacifica Companies, Janice Preston, 25031 Amberwood, Mission Viejo, CA 92692, 714-859-7004, 714-587-1022

PAL Business Advisors, Lloyd Brown, 2510 N. Grand Ave., Suite 200, Santa Ana, CA 90705, 714-639-2200, 714-639-1814

PARADIAM Professional Services, Lawrence R. Dunlop, L2, 76 Berry St., North Sydney, NSW, 2060, Australia, 61-2-9956-8388, 61-2-9956-8136

Paragon Consulting Group, Inc., Sally Love, 10 Lavinia Ave., Greenville, SC 29601, 864-233-8326, 864-233-4232

Pareo, Inc., Donn Wassink, 120 S. Sixth St., Suite 1901, Minneapolis, MN 55402, 612-476-8160, 612-371-0500

Partners in Management, Michael C. Monico, Box 1338, Carlsbad, CA 92018, 800-434-0501, 619-945-7725

Pathfinder Global Group, Inc., George H. Dewey, 328 Hobbes Lane, Rochester, NY 14624, 713-827-4481, 716-594-8213

Pathfinder Inc., Stephen L. Cabano, 11 Allison Dr., Cherry Hill, NJ 08003, 609-424-7100, 609-424-6414

PC Micro Consultants, Robert E. Widomski, 4333 W. 148th St., Midlothian, IL 60445, 708-489-6630

Penn State Ogontz Campus, Ralph Demarco, 1600 Woodland Rd., Abington, PA 19001, 215-881-7387, 215-881-7317

People Places LLC, Lawrence Stern, 2220 Glendaloch Rd., Ann Arbor, MI 48104, 313-668-6828, 313-665-8525

Performance Management Associates, Inc., James Wrisley, 15 Via Verona, Palm Beach Gardens, FL 33418, 561-694-1646/7, 561-694-1648

Perot Systems TM, Tom Block, 9101 Knoll Ron Lane, Marshall, VA 20115, 540-349-8528

Peters & Company Engineering & Management Services, Lee Peters, 70 North Main St., Zionsville, IN 46077, 817-873-0086, 817-873-0052

The Phoenix Index, Inc., Donald Reynerson, 5295 Hwy. 78, Suite 0183, Stone Mountain, GA 30087, 770-465-9129, 770-465-9712

Pinnell/Busch, Inc., Jeff S. Busch or Dragan Milosevic, 6420 SW Macadam Ave., Suite 330, Portland, OR 97201, 503-293-6280, 503-293-6284

Pitagorsky Consulting, George Pitagorsky, 153 E. 32nd St., Apt. 7E, New York, NY 10016, 212-696-9687, 212-696-9689

Plan Tech, Inc., Jim Bongiorno, 22000 Springbrook, Suite 201, Farmington Hills, MI 48336, 888-228-7676, 810-615-0292

Plan Tech, Inc., William A. Moylan, 22000 Springbrook, Suite 201, Farmington Hills, MI 48336, 810-615-0333, 810-615-0292

Planning Masters, Chase Lichtenstein, 3343 William Dr., Newbury Park, CA 91320, 805-499-7526, 805-499-8356

Platie Valley Consulting Inc., Daniel M. Priebe, 7835 S. Elizabeth Way, Littleton, CO 80122, 303-740-6935

Plexus Corporation, David A. Giardino, 1302 Elmwood Ave., Cranston, RI 02910, 401-467-1300, 401-467-1319

PM* Pharos Inc., E. D. Marion, 137 Cambridge Dr., Berkeley Hts., NJ 07922, 908-508-9294, 908-464-0630

PMA—Worldwide, Gunther Schoof, PO Box 536, Ausable Fords, NY 12912, 518-647-8144

PMCO Inc., Ben E. Voivedich Jr., 1373 Corporate Square Blvd., Slidell, LA 70458, 504-641-0477, 504-641-0659

PMP Consultants, Christian Maranda, PO Box 60001, Levis, QU, G6V 8W9, Canada, 418-837-1893

PNS Project Services Inc., K. Shankar, 3390 Chartrano Crescent, Mississauga, 905-820-9537, 905-820-7597

Poesys Associates, Robert J. Miller, 36 Whitney St., San Francisco, CA 94131, 415-468-8621, 415-695-0381

Predictive Technologies, Oleh Kostetsky, 560 Rustic Trail, Beavercreek, OH 45434, 937-320-9018, 937-320-9017

Primavera Systems, Andre Oporto, Two Bala Plaza, Bala Cynwyd, PA 19004, 610-667-8600, 610-667-7894

The Principal Financial Group, Mary Meier, 711 High St., Des Moines, IA 50392-1210, 515-283-5689, 515-362-0154

Procept Associates Ltd., Keith Farndale, 65 Front St., W. Suite 0116-110, Toronto, ON, M5J 1E6, Canada, 416-465-9373, 416-465-7870

Process Solutions, LLC, Louis B. Muench, 5401 N. Adams Rd., Bloomfield Hills, MI 48304, 810-540-6453, 810-540-1766

Procost, Michael S. Putzer, 4105 Ridgebrook, Raleigh, NC 27603, 919-779-2722, 919-779-3866

Procyon, Michael N. Wakshull, PO Box 2210, Moorpark, CA 93020-2210, 805-529-4610, 805-523-0864

Product & Process Innovation, Ray Sheen, 25 Field Stone Run, Farmington, CT 06032, 860-678-1064, 860-677-4677

Production Modeling Corporation, Susan Khoubyari, 3 Parkland Blvd., Suite 910W, Dearborn, MI 48126, 313-441-4460 ext. 118, 313-441-6098

The Professional Group, Inc., Dr. Philip A. Dillaber, 3003 N. Arkendale St., Woodbridge, VA 22193, 703-670-2088

Professional Training Associates, Susan M. Ashtianie, 4608 Briarclift Rd., Baltimore, MD 21229, 410-233-5159, 410-945-3899

Program Management Associates, Inc., Patrick K. Taylor, 1320 Fenwick Lane, Suite 510, Silver Springs, MD 20910, 301-608-3400, 301-608-0008

Program Planning Professionals, Briene Coleman, 2314 Monroe Blvd., Dearborn, MI 48124, 313-561-3134, 313-561-6836

Projacs Project Mgt. & Controls, Bassam A. Al-Samman, PO Box 7583, Dubai, United Arab Emirates, 971-4-822-327, 971-4-822-377

Projecktcknik Gunnor Selin AB, Gunnor Selin, Isbergsgarden, Avers Stychebrub, S-64060, Sweden, 46-159-303-27, 46-159-319-08

Project Administration Institute, Edward P. Mahler, 47 Echo Lane, Larchmont, NY 10538-2203, 914-834-4162, 914-834-5248

Project Coordinators Inc., Denis Conture, 900 Wilshire Dr., Suite 310, Troy, MI 48084, 810-269-4000, 810-269-4024

Project Force, Jim Downer, 9762 Broadmoor Dr., San Ramon, CA 94583-3551, 510-556-0810, 510-829-1512

Project International, Stephen McManus, 4931 E. Camino La Brinca, Tucson, AZ 85718, 520-219-1605

The Project Knowledge Group, Harvey A. Levine, 21 Pine Ridge, Saratoga Springs, NY 12866, 518-581-0661

Project Management & Engineering, Bruce Morn, 912 Hawthorne Dr., Walnut Creek, CA 94596, 510-943-2231

Project Management Advisors, Inc., Scott Gill, 333 Conventry Way, Noblesville, IN 46060, 317-637-0082, 317-753-3400

The Project Management Centre, Scott Hunter, 190 Bronson Ave., Ottawa, ON, Canada, 613-235-8075, 613-213-5158

Project Management Consulting, Andrej A. Cesen, Mlakarjeva 59, Trzin, Trzin, SI-1236, EU, 386-61-71-5598

Project Management Consulting Assoc., Charles Fletcher, 3526 Charleston Lane, Cibolo, TX 78108, 800-341-8850

Project Management Consulting, S.L., Francisco Perez-Polo, Arturo Soria, 320, Madrid, 28033, Spain, 34-1-302-1377

Project Management Group—UMIST, Stephen Wearne, PO Box 88, Manchester, M6D 1QD, United Kingdom, 44-1625-585536

Project Management International, Inc., Dr. Clifford Gray, 3735 NW Glenridge Dr., Corvallis, OR 97330, 541-752-5970

Project Management Professional Services LTD., Terrence G. Warren, PMP House, Gardner Rd., Maidenhead, Berkshire, Sl6 7RJ, England, 44-1628-75444, 44-1628-26203

Project Management Service Bureau, Inc., George T. Patton, 3608 South 12th St., Arlington, VA 22204-4256, 703-920-0874, 703-920-3127

Project Management Services, Kenneth L. Reese, 746 Cockrell Hill Rd., Red Oak, TX 75154, 972-217-1546, 972-217-1700

Project Management Services LTD, Fritz Ehrenreich-Hansen, 2219 Palisade Dr. SW, Calgary, AB, T2V 3V2, Canada, 403-281-4917, 403-255-3401

Project Management Solutions, Inc., Ms. Deborah Bigelow, 5114 Bond Ave., Drexel Hill, PA 19026, 610-853-0526, 610-853-0527

Project Management Solutions, Lisa Carpenter, 1781 Kingsdale Center, Columbus, OH 43221, 614-486-2420, 614-486-9003

Project Management Solutions, Jim Lyon, PO Box 583, Claremont, 6010, Australia, 61-9-385-3852, 61-9-385-3849

Project Management Tech, Inc., Dennis Busch, 8186 So. Logan Court, Littleton, CO 80122, 303-730-6291, 303-797-3334

Project Mentors, Carter Jerrett, 211 Sutter, San Francisco, CA 94108, 415-955-5770

Project Management Consultant, Kenneth F. Smith, 4517 Twin-brook Rd., Fairfax, VA 22032, 703-978-1876, 703-691-9022

Project Planning & Control, Monica A. Conover, 125 Lakebridge Dr. N, Kings Park, NY 11754, 516-544-6024

Project Planning Group, Inc., Edward Mislaysky, 1602 Lawrence Ave., Suite 113, Ocean, NJ 07712, 908-918-1700, 908-918-0188

Project Plus Ltd., Jain Fraser, PO Box 10-515, Wellington, New Zealand, 64-4-479-3014, 64-4-497-2412

Project Principles, Michael Lemiski, 1364 Glenburnie Rd., Missis-sauga, ON, L5G 3C8, Canada, 905-274-7214, 905-274-0840

Project Services Associates, Maris Cukurs, PO Box 51206, Idaho Falls, ID 83405, 208-522-8991, 208-522-4163

Project Solutions Unlimited, Edward Kilner, 3236 Trelawny Circle, Mississauga, ON, L5N 5G6, Canada, 905-824-0950, 905-824-8013

Project Strategies, David L. Neff, 10555 Foster, Overland Park, KS 66212, 913-649-2198

Project Technologies Corporation, Lew Ireland, 20290 Doewood Dr., Monument, CO 80132-8050, 719-481-9628, 719-481-9569

Project Technologies Inc., Thomas Sumter, PO Box 1714, Poulsbo, WA 98370-0227, 360-779-1844, 360-779-1850

Project Time & Cost, Inc., Clint Owings, One Precsto, Suite 1200, Atlanta, GA 30339, 770-444-9799, 770-444-9808

Project Time & Cost, Inc., Spencer Bryan, 2727 Paces Ferry Rd., Atlanta, GA 30339, 770-444-9799, 770-444-9808

ProjectWorks, Gerald W. Barr, 1183 Laurell Loop, NE Suite 215, Albuquerque, NM 87122, 505-856-1767, 505-856-1765

Pro-Link Ltd., Joseph Wudyka, 33 Carriage Lane, Bedford, NH, 03110, 603-471-0025, 603-471-2525

PSM Consulting Services, Michael W. Newell, 294 Lakeview Dr., Slidell, LA 70458, 504-643-7623, 504-826-1204

PT Susanto CiptaJaya Corp., Eddy Susanto, Taman Kedoxa Baru/Akasta 1/B3/41, Jakarta, 11520, India, 62-21-392-2183, 62-21-392-2185

Pyramid Computing, Inc., James L. Zeeb, 333 Red Lily Place #102, Evergreen, CO 80439, 303-674-2363

QC International, Jennifer Doman, 245 Holly Lane, Orinda, CA 94563, 510-254-7125

QdeQ—Consultoria de Gestar, Nuno Ponces de Carvalo, R. Freitas Reis 263 LL, Cascais, 2750, Portugal, 351-1-4865903

Quality Engineered Decisions (QED) Inc., Francis Hartman, 311 Ranch Estates Bay NW, Calgary, AB, T3G 2A3, Canada, 403-651-0666, 403-239-0207

Quality IS Projects, Inc., Ian Koenig, 238 Chimney Rock, Houston, TX 77024-5600, 713-465-3794

Quality Plus Engineering, Greg Hutchins, 4052 NE Couch, Portland, OR 97232, 503-233-1012, 503-233-1410

Quality Project Management, Inc., Chee Tan, 1345 Green Pheasant Lane, Bayavla, IL 60510, 630-879-5061

Quest Learning Systems, Len Cormier, 409 Claremont Crescent, Dakville, ON, L6J 6J9, Canada, 905-338-1832, 905-338-0076

Quo Vadis, Patricia A. Hopkinson, Lakeside #26 Whiteface Inn Rd., Lake Placid, NY 12946, 518-523-4736

R.J. Graham & Associates, Robert Graham, PO Box 2537, Mendocino, CA 95460, 707-937-5732

R.V. Moffat, Inc., Richard Moffat, 580 Front St., Suite #B305, Issaquah, WA 98027, 206-391-7587

Randal B. Lorance, 9553 East Calby Circle, Englewood, CO 80111, 303-689-0836, 303-713-0727

RA's Management, Jang Ra, 2310 Loren Circle, Anchorage, AK 99516, 907-786-1862, 907-786-1079

Ravien Associates, Peter J. Warren, RR #2 Box 4547, Camorn, ME 04843, 207-236-4539, 207-236-4160

Raymond C. Sutor, 28025 Camino Santo Domingo, San Juan Capistrano, CA 92675, 714-248-3192

Renaissance Educational Services, Paula Martin, 120 Amwell Rd., Flemington, NJ 08822, 908-806-3974, 908-806-3984

Revay & Associates Ltd., Steve Revay, 7015 MacLeod Trail SW, Suite 715, Calgary, AB, T2H 2K6, Canada, 403-259-5056, 403-252-0237

RGB Technologies, Didier Urli, 133, rue Julien Rehel, Off 217, Rimouski, QU, G5L 9B1, Canada, 418-721-2423, 418-791-2427

Rhodes Consulting Services, Inc., John Rhodes, 2326 Lake Park Dr., Longmont, CO 80503, 303-684-6632, 303-684-0205

Richard E. Larew, 510 Larch Lane, Iowa City, IA 52245, 319-341-8361

Ritter Construction Management, Ted Ritter, 2964 W. 8th Ave., Vancouver, BC, Canada, 604-732-7520, 604-732-7575

RJS International, Robert Symonds, 6200 Eubank NE, Suite 1217, Albuquerque, NM 87111, 505-332-9245, 505-332-9345

RMC-Project Management, Rita Mulcahy, 5228 Logan Ave. South, Minneapolis, MN 55419, 612-929-7539

Robert J. Thompson Consulting, Bob Thompson, 61 Gran Via, Alamo, CA 94507, 800-688-8149, 510-820-8526

Robert Yourzak & Associates, Inc., Robert J. Yourzak, 7320 Gallagher Dr., Suite 325, Minneapolis, MN 55435, 612-831-2235

Robert-Andrew Assoc., Jonathan Japka, One Martin Ave., Cherry Hill, NJ 08002, 609-662-1290, 609-662-8540

Robles di Management, Marcelo Robles, Via Cadorna 32/5, Vimergate, 20059, Italy, 39-39-667982

Roger G. Gilbert, 1041 MacIntosh Dr., Rochester, NY 14626, 716-225-2714, 716-225-9214

Rowland Project Management, Lawrence Rowland, PO Box 10631, Honolulu, HI 96816, 808-735-9938, 808-735-6553

Ruggles & Associates Inc., William S. Ruggles, 2-10 Saddle River Rd., Fair Lawn, NJ 07410-4811, 201-794-6119

Russona Consulting Corp., Russ McDowell, 26 Turret Court, Kanata, ON, K2L 2L1, Canada, 613-836-6182, 613-836-1552

Rust and Associates, Inc., Linda Rust, 35 Pleasant Lake East Road, St. Paul, MN, 612-415-1214

Ruswyn Associates Inc., Russ Chapman, 297 Poyntz Ave., N. York, ON, M2N 1J8, Canada, 416-512-0191, 416-512-0329

RWS Consulting, Ward Smith, 210 Hunterage Private, Ottawa, ON, K1V 2I3, Canada, 613-526-1221

Ryman Technical Services, Inc., Douglas D. Ryman, 2477 Marshland Rd., Apalachin, NY 13732, 607-625-4258

Sanderling Consulting Inc., Larry E. Baker, 496-B Sunnyoaks Ave., Campbell, CA 95008, 408-374-0263, 408-374-0264

Saperstein Consulting, Paul Saperstein, 4474 East Mercer Way, Mercer Island, WA 98040, 206-232-6373, 206-232-3735

Schema Konsult, Inc., Jose A. Palac, 7F JMT Corporate Condominium ADB Ave., Pasis City, 1600, Philippines, 631-1691-97, 0632-632-0740

School of Industrial Engineering, Adedeji B. Badiru, University of Oklahoma, Norman, OK 73019, 405-325-4359, 405-325-7555

School of the Built Environment, Coventry University, Joseph A. Wright, Priory St., Coventry, CV1 5FB, United Kingdom, 44-1203-838485

Scitor Corporation, Fred Ansick, 333 Middlefield Rd., Menlo Park, CA 94025, 415-462-4211, 415-462-4275

Seager & Associates, William V. Seager, 8227 Everwood Court, Memphis, TN 38138, 901-758-2179

SFG Technologies, Vincent R. Willett, Jr., 990 Hammond Dr., Atlanta, GA 30328, 770-804-9699, 770-395-0305

Shuler Consulting, Ben F. Shuler, 524 Spaulding Lake Dr., Greenville, SC 29615, 864-281-1334, 864-234-7671

Simmons College, Alice Sapienza, 300 The Fenway, Boston, MA 02115-5898, 617-521-2374, 617-521-3046

Simpson & Associates, Bill Simpson, PO Box 21854, Greensboro, NC 27420, 910-685-0715

Singer & Associates, Inc., Jean Singer, 401 Sherry Way, Cherry Hill, NJ 08034, 609-795-3894, 609-428-1428

SJC Associates, Steven Cohn, 31 Adams Dr., Belle Mead, NJ 08502, 908-281-9755

Skofteland Management, Inc., Pete Skofteland, 20641 Hazelnut Court, Germantown, MD 20874, 301-540-6084, 301-540-5298

Software Analysis Corporation, Gerri Lynn Martin, 890 E. Higgins Rd., Suite 300, Schaumburg, IL 60173, 847-619-6464, 847-619-8164

Sol Kutner Associates, Inc., Sol Kutner, 1160 Industrial Rd., Suite 2, San Carlos, CA 94070, 415-593-2001, 415-593-0927

Sound Project Mgmt. Ltd., Anders Thisner, 2750 60th Ave. SE, Mercer Island, WA 98040, 206-232-4231, 206-232-7293

Spigai Associates, Inc., Dr. Joseph J. Spigai, 1506 Vivian Court, Silver Spring, MD 20902-3536, 301-649-4583

SPM—Consultant, Dipl. Ing. Manfred Saynisch, Dueppeler-Stlr-79, Munich, 87929, Germany, 49-89-93-930951, 49-89-93-930952

SPM Consult, Manfred Saynisch, Dueppeler-STR-79, Munich, 87929, Germany, 49-89-93-93-09-51, 49-89-93-93-09-52

SPM Group Inc., Bryan Vermander, 3266 Yonge St., Suite 2022, Toronto, ON, M5M 1S7, Canada, 416-485-1584, 416-481-4903

SRM Solucoes EM Sistemas S/C Ltd., Eng. Samuel Rocha De Mello, R. Doma Igmacia Uchoa, 353, Sao Paulo, 04110-021, Brazil, 55-011-575-0551, 55-011-573-2312

Stan Wolfe Associates, Stan Wolfe, 1785 Dalton Place, San Jose, CA 95124, 408-264-1932, 408-264-5934

Stanley E. Portny & Associates, Donna A. Portny, 44 Dorison Dr., Short Hills, NJ 07078, 201-376-8887, 201-912-8386

Sterling Planning Group, Thomas C. Belanger, 37 Heywood Rd., Sterling, MA 01564, 508-422-6611, 508-422-7282

Stevens Institute of Technology, Aaron J. Shenhar, Institute Professor of Management, Hoboken, NJ 07030, 201-216-8024, 201-216-8355

Stewart Technologies, Inc., John S. Phelan, 3708 N. Sheffield, Suite 408, Chicago, IL 60613, 773-244-3684, 773-244-3685

STI Inc., Donald A. Poirier, 6724 Perimeter Loop Rd., Suite 201, Dublin, OH 43017, 614-440-9232, 614-793-0067

Stout Consulting, Pen Stout, 1829 N. 52nd St., Seattle, WA 98103, 206-547-6065, 206-547-3711

Strategic Expertise, Peter Goldsbury, 20 Hastings Parade, Devonport, Auckland, New Zealand, 09-445-4454

Strategic Management Group Inc., James A. Brodo, 3624 Market St., University Science Center, Philadelphia, PA 19104, 215-387-4000, 215-387-3653

Strategic Resources, Inc., Lori Lindholm, 7700 Leesburg Pike, Suite 108, Falls Church, VA 22043, 703-749-3040, 703-749-3046

Strategy & Process Experts, Margery Mayer, 951 Laurel St. #550, San Carlos, CA 94070, 415-591-4255, 415-631-8663

The STR Company SA/NV, Steven Ryckelbusch, Messem 9, Brugge, B-8200, Belgium, 32-50-31-9859, 32-50-31-9219

STS, Roland Saurer, Pl. St. Francois 5, Lausanne, 1003, Switzerland, 41-21-351-86-86, 41-21-351-86-83

STS Associates, Inc., Richard Ordowich, 5 Tomlyn Dr., Princeton, NJ 08540, 609-497-0757, 609-497-4787

Sukumar Consulting Company, George Sukumar, PO Box 15830, Long Beach, CA 90815, 562-497-1886, 562-497-1967

Sumner Alpert, 15833 Castlewoods Dr., Sherman Oaks, CA 91403, 818-788-1707, 818-981-7387

Sun Mountain Mgmt. Corp., Arlyn D. Solberg, 3232 N. Hamline Ave., St. Paul, MN 55112, 612-636-9739

Susan A. Peterson, 7411 Keisha Terrace, San Diego, CA 92126-6093, 619-549-0592

Symantix, William C. Brennan, 24 Channing St., New London, CT 06320, 860-442-9212, 860-443-2223

Symbol Technologies, Rick Kelly, One Symbol Plaza, MS A-42, Holtsville, NY 11742, 800-927-9626 ext. 3745

Synergetics, Jim Paul, PO Box 4137, Las Crues, NM 88003, 505-532-1440

Synerproject, Inc., Dr. Brian Petersen, 4131 72nd St. North, St. Petersburg, FL 33709, 800-847-2851, 613-830-5277

SynPro Systems, Inc., Roger Voight, 9025 E. Kenyon Ave. #60, Denver, CO 80237, 303-889-5979, 303-889-5969

System Partners, Inc., Marianne Clauw, 1070 Leigh Mill Rd., Great Falls, VA 22066, 703-757-6591, 703-757-0236

Systematic Management Services Inc., Tom Jeskie, 90 Tempura Dr., Oak Ridge, TN 37830, 423-481-0036, 423-481-0038

Systemation, Heather Ramsey, 2101 S. Clermont St., Denver, CO 80222, 800-747-9783, 303-756-2211

Systemes D'Integration Kyber, Inc., Michael A. Andronov, 2278 B Moduguo, St. Laurent, QU, H4R 1W6, Canada, 514-232-5645, 514-334-2688

Systems Engineering Int'l Inc., Wilbur Armstrong, PO Box 2087, Winter Park, FL 32790, 407-894-5521, 407-894-1308

Systems Management International, Gene D. Carlow, PO Box 580, Fulton, TX 78358, 512-790-5585

Systems Management Services, Michael D. Taylor, PO Box 416, Mount Hermon, CA 95041-0416, 408-335-1902

Sysware Consultants Ltd., Charles Chinnaiyah, PO Box 634, Wellington, New Zealand, 64-4-499-7878, 64-4-499-7177

Tarabin Enterprises Ltd., Richard J. Dyer, Box 30736 Lower Hutt, New Zealand, 64-4-586-6303, 64-4-586-1447

TASC, Dale Kelly, 30801 Barrington Ave., Suite 100, Madison Heights, MI 48071, 810-585-0700, 810-585-2628

TBC, Technopole De Chateau-Gomert, Europarc BlC, Marseille, 13013, France, 33-4-90-05-50-11, 33-4-91-61-25-67

TCH, Greg Winter, 9801 Old Winery Place, Sacramento, CA 95827, 800-308-2679, 916-369-1099

TEC-Con, Inc., Stephen C. Ford, 5188 Buckeye Grove, Columbus, OH 43214, 614-848-4201, 614-848-4380

Tech Knowledge, Inc., Mickey McRoberts, 1000 Shelard Pkwy., Suite 360, Minneapolis, MN 55426, 888-TEAMTKI, 612-513-9681

Techman Consultants AB, Berta Andersson, Sandkullsv 17, Spansa, SE-16257, Sweden, 46-8-369-102, 46-8-761-656

Technology & Business Solutions, Dr. Russ Purvis, 770 Summer Oaks Court, Oviedo, FL 32765, 407-365-8007

Technology Associates, Kelvin Kirby, Timothy's Bridge Rd., Stratford-upon-Avon, Warwickshire, CV37 9NQ, England, 44-1789-297000, 44-1789-292191

TEEM Project Management Consulting, Mati Wertheim, 10/30 Recanati St., Tel Aviv, 69494, Israel, 972-3-6421970, 972-3-6416236

Temple-Inland, Inc., Aaron C. Yetter, 303 S. Temple Dr., Diboll, TX 75941, 409-829-7815, 409-829-7887

Templeton Enterprises, Robert E. Templeton, 12718 Old Oaks Dr., Houston, TX 77024, 713-464-5966, 713-464-5878

TeraQuest Metrics, Inc., Abby Eden, 12885 Research Blvd., Suite 207, Austin, TX 78750, 512-219-9152, 512-219-0587

Themedia Limited, David F. Weston, PO Box 10654, Wellington, New Zealand, 64-21-937866, 64-44-758797

Thomas Barron, Business & Engineering Consultant, 3351 Beech-wood Dr., Lafayette, CA 94549, 510-283-8121, 510-283-6746

Thomas W. Burns, Jr., 211 Cassati Rd., Berwyn, PA 19312, 610-644-8196, 610-725-8723

Thurlow Associates, Peter Thurlow, 367 Oak Ave., Randburg, 2194, South Africa, 27-11-787-6226, 27-11-787-6526

Tignosis, Theo Clarke, 98 Choumert Rd., London, SE15 4AX, United Kingdom, 44-171-358-1613

Time & Cost Managers, Frank B. Mitchell, PO Box 72528, Mari-etta, GA 30007, 404-713-0447

Time to Market Associates, Inc., Ray Hopper, PO Box 1070, Verdi, NV 89439, 702-345-1455

TMA—Technology Management Associates, Dr. Dundar F. Ko-caogli, 17187 SW Rivendell Dr., Portland, OR 97224, 503-620-1054

TMI Unit, University of Waikato, R.A. (Bob) Mills, PO Box 3105, Hamilton, New Zealand, 64-07-838-4593, 64-07-838-4578

Tomorrow's Enterprise, Paula Shafer, 220-K Stony Run Lane, Bal-timore, MD 21210, 410-366-6430

Totten Sims Hubicki Associates, John Campbell, 300 Water St., Whitby, ON, L1N 9J2, Canada, 905-668-9363, 905-668-0221

TPM Consultants, Pierre Parent, 1745 Trappist Lane, Gloucester, ON, Canada, 613-824-8118, 613-824-6886

Transformation Leadership, Michael Trimble, 1038 E. Bas-tanchury Rd. #282, Fullerton, CA 92835, 714-738-4836

Trauner Consulting Service, Tracy M. Doyle, 1500 Walnut St., Suite 800, Philadelphia, PA 19102, 215-546-0288, 215-546-0285

Trijwijn Atocrates Lush, Inc., Anthony N. Lush, 360 Thames St., 2 South, Newport, RI 02840, 401-847-8090, 401-847-8091

TWCA Pty Ltd., Tom Crow, 53 Walker St., North Sydney, Australia, 61-2-9900-6666, 61-2-9955-5602

TwinStar Consulting, Brad Malone, PO Box 286, Bellbrook, OH 45305, 937-640-2400

UNICADE Inc., Paresh S. Parekh, 1806-136th Place NE, Suite 4, Bellevue, WA 98005, 206-747-0353, 206-747-0316

Unisys Corporation, Bill Woofter, 307 N. Hurtsbourne Pkwy., Suite 120, Louisville, KY 40222, 502-339-2670, 502-339-2601

Universite Laval, Gilles R. D'Avignon, Business School, Sainte-Foy, QU, G1K 7P4, Canada, 418-656-2930, 418-656-2624

University of California, Prof. C. W. Ibbs, 213 McLaughlin Hall, Berkeley, CA 94720, 510-643-8067, 510-643-8919

University of Detroit Mercy, Prof. Vladan Jovanovic, 54501 Mound Rd., Shelby, MI 48316, 313-993-1237, 810-781-0230

University of Idaho, Paeviz F. Rad, 1776 Science Center Dr., Idaho Falls, ID 83403, 208-526-5541, 208-526-1442

University of Phoenix, Victoria Levin, 4605 East Elwood St., Phoenix, AZ 85040, 602-804-7665, 602-921-1044

University of San Diego, Dr. Charles Teplitz, School of Business, San Diego, CA 92110, 619-260-2258, 619-260-4891

University of San Diego, Katy Petersen, School of Business, San Diego, CA 92110, 619-260-2258, 619-260-4891

University of Southern Queensland, David Cowper, Faculty of Business, USQ, Toowoomba, 4350, Australia, 61-76-312419, 61-76-312945

University of St. Thomas, Emul Hall, 2696 Horseshoe Lane, Woodbury, MN 55125, 612-731-5127

University of Wisconsin–Madison, David Antonioni, 31186 Rainger Hall, 975 University Ave., Madison, WI 53706, 608-265-4004, 608-262-4617

U.S. Equal Employment Opportunity Commission, Garrett Coleman, 1801 L St., 4th Floor IRMS, Washington, DC 20507, 202-663-4432, 202-663-4451

Venture Projects, Terry L. Herrick, 411 Periwinkle Dr., Asheville, NC 28804, 704-658-0825, 704-658-0840

The Versatile Company, Eric Verzuh, 6227 50th Ave. NE, Seattle, WA 98115, 206-525-0970

Vision Consultants, Gordon H. Aronson, 15601 N. 50th St., Scottsdale, AZ 85254, 602-992-5438, 602-482-2712

W. Wawruck Project Management Consultant, Walter A. Wawruck, 16 W. 19th Ave., Vancouver, BC, V5Y 2BZ, Canada, 604-879-8752

Walter Robbins Bowman Associates, Walter Bowman, 1313 Pennsylvania Ave., Oakmont, PA 15139, 412-826-9451

Webber Management Services, Art Webber, 10 Leavey Court, North York, ON, M2H 1E6, Canada, 416-730-8928, 416-730-8882

Welcom Software Technology, Co., Betsy Smalley, 15995 N. Barkers Landing Rd., Suite 275, Houston, TX 77079, 281-558-0514, 281-584-7828

Wessels International, Don J. Wessels, 207 Cheswick Court, Nashville, TN 37215, 615-665-1602, 615-665-1783

Westhill University, Constancio Rodriguez, Montes Carpatos No. 940, Col. Lomas De Chapultepec, 11000, Mexico, 525-540-4005, 525-282-4446

Westney Consultants Int'l Inc., Richard Westney, 2435 Nantucket Dr., Houston, TX 77057, 281-469-6888, 281-469-7887

White River Training and Consulting, Dr. B. J. Bischoff, 107 N. Pennsylvania St., Suite 500, Indianapolis, IN 46204, 317-687-1850, 317-687-1942

William M. Hayden, Jr. Consultants, Inc., Bill Hayden, 11571 Sedgemoore Dr. East, Suite 1200, Jacksonville, FL 32223, 904-260-7700, 904-260-7701

Working Knowledge Group Limited, Nadine Wooller, PO Box 5406, Wellington, New Zealand, 64-4-499-2500, 64-4-499-2511

World Class Productivity Inc., Paul Bergman, 35 Hinda Lane, Thornhill, ON, L4J 6S2, Canada, 905-660-7184, 905-660-1247

Write Technology Limited, John Gale, PO Box 931, Wellington, New Zealand, 64-21-622700, 64-21-788700

X-Pert Projects, Michael De Abreu, St. Andrews Office Park, Meadowbrook Lane, Rivonia, 2055, South Africa, 02-711-709-7136, 02-711-709-7050

Yarra Associates Inc., Harry M. Stuart, PO Box 424, 1000 Stone Bridge Rd., Gwynedd, PA 19436, 800-769-2772, 215-540-0682

Zervigon International, Ltd., Carlos R. Zervigon, 938 Lafayette St. #307, New Orleans, LA 70113, 504-556-0762, 504-523-3680

ZSC Consultoria S/C Ltda, Zigmundo Cukierman, Rua Barata Ribeiro 283/1001, Rio De Janeiro, 22040-0000, Brazil, 55-21-257-0501, 55-21-235-6066

Index